The SOUND *of* LIFE'S
UNSPEAKABLE BEAUTY

The Sound of Life's Unspeakable Beauty

MARTIN SCHLESKE

Translated by Janet Gesme
With photographs by Donata Wenders

WILLIAM B. EERDMANS PUBLISHING COMPANY
GRAND RAPIDS, MICHIGAN

Wm. B. Eerdmans Publishing Co.
4035 Park East Court SE, Grand Rapids, Michigan 49546
www.eerdmans.com

Originally published in German as *Der Klang: Vom unerhörten Sinn des Lebens*.
© 2010 Kösel-Verlag, a division of Verlagsgruppe Random House GmbH,
München, Germany

Printed in the United States of America

26 25 24   4 5 6 7

ISBN 978-0-8028-7614-0

Library of Congress Cataloging-in-Publication Data

Names: Schleske, Martin, 1965- author. | Wenders, Donata, photographer
    (expression) | Gesme, Janet Leigh, 1971- translator.
Title: The sound of life's unspeakable beauty / Martin Schleske with photo-
    graphs by Donata Wenders ; translated by Janet Gesme.
Other titles: Klang. English
Description: Grand Rapids, Michigan : Wm. B. Eerdmans Publishing Co.,
    2020. | Includes bibliographical references and index. | Summary:
    "A luthier reveals the secrets of his profession and how each phase of hand-
    crafting a violin can point us toward our calling, our true selves, and the
    overwhelming power and gentleness of God's love"–Provided by publisher.
Identifiers: LCCN 2019047955 | ISBN 9780802876140 (hardcover)
Subjects: LCSH: Schleske, Martin, 1965- | Violin makers–Religious life. |
    Violin–Construction. | Violin–Religious aspects. | Christian life.
Classification: LCC ML424.S35 A3 2020 | DDC 787.2/19092–dc23
LC record available at https://lccn.loc.gov/2019047955

For Jonas and Lorenz

"Let all the trees of the forest sing for joy."
—PSALM 96:12 (NIV)

Contents

CONTENTS

Foreword

This is a beautiful book. This word "beauty," in the Japanese definition, requires sacrifice. The sacrifice of death to preserve honor or the natural process of decay is beatified. So when I say that this is a beautiful book, it is not to say that this book is full of the ornamental sentiment of beauty; no, this book is filled with deeply wrought words of wisdom echoing within the grains of carefully selected wood (or the "charisma" of the violin, as Martin Schleske notes), full of the time-tested sacrifice of serving artists and the honor given to what patient violinmaking requires.

A violinmaker not only produces an instrument that makes an extraordinary resonance that can stir the heart; rather, a true maker sacrifices the ego, so as to create an overlap with the life of the musician to whom the instrument belongs. Here, in *The Sound of Life's Unspeakable Beauty*, that process of surrendering is opened up, revealed to us as an offering, a gift that requires us to pay attention to its minute details. I could not read this book fast, or simply scan the paragraphs; the language would not allow me to. Instead, like the hundred-year-old fir wood that surrenders to a master's hand, the reader must invite the resonance behind the words, to discover an echo of one's own soul and let the words of this writing begin to seep into one's own journey.

I have a friend, an extraordinarily gifted thinker and musician, who recently has had his bouts with severe depression. He found solace in learning from scratch how to make a violin. I thought of him, and my prayers were uttered on behalf of him and many other friends who need to encounter the words written here. To mend is to make new, to recover that sense of our call to be stewards of creation and to journey into the New Creation.

The echo ringing from the deepest realm of the forests becomes the sound of a violin. Perhaps the Sound is not heard, but is captured best, paradoxically, in the silence. The wood grains of a violin capture such a history, and the resonance is felt, and then heard only if the one who plays it is a master as well. That sound, no doubt, catches the *musica universalis*, the music of the spheres, the song of angels that we have always heard, but we have learned to tune out. The signature of the wood has already captured that sound, and it is up to the masters to bring it out.

So the words of this beautiful book do not just describe, explain, or share information; these words are, in themselves, part of the Sound, and I can hear it from the first paragraph. Then, after, the words begin to overlap with music; I wanted to savor every paragraph, as if I, too, am a tuner listening to the timbre.

My father, a pioneer in acoustic research, at the end of his life could no longer hear well. And he complained that he could not "hear the timbre." He found himself frustrated, and he could not listen to his favorite Bach or Vivaldi.

Martin Schleske's writing speaks into the gap between what we know to be ideal and the reality we face every day. It is in the journey into the darkness, into what we may call "doubt," that we may very well find our final voice. In the well-known "answer" that God gives the grieving Job, to hear the question "Where were you when I laid the earth's foundation?" (Job 38:4) is to hear a song sung to all those who believe and struggle to believe. "Where were you?" That is not an "answer" or even an interrogation to me; that is what a Maker asks one who is entrusted to carry on the task of making and mending. I believe that to be a song: a song of lament, a song of loss, and a song of love and New Creation. This beautiful book echoes that song of God that all of us will face and hear one day. To be able to hear it now, to access it through this book, is a remarkable gift and a beautiful offering.

MAKOTO FUJIMURA

Translator's Note

I first came across Martin Schleske's book *Der Klang* on the day a debilitating car accident altered the course of my life. The changes that I was about to undergo were devastating, and yet *The Sound* somehow cast a beautiful, purposeful light on the whole situation. The poetic, life-giving prose walked me through one of the most difficult chapters in my own life.

I was so touched that I bought the book for my German-speaking friends and wanted to do so for my English-speaking friends as well. However, I could not find an English version! It became my mission to find a translator and a publisher. I knew I could not translate it myself—after all, this book is the work of a genius who thinks on a much higher level than I. But to find a publisher, I had to translate. Each publisher wanted to see a little more: one chapter, then three, then five, then the whole book. So I translated *Der Klang*, but not alone. I met with a writer (David Jacobsen), an architect (Don Stevens), a physicist (Bruce Emerson), a luthier (Edward Geesman), native speakers of German (Ulla Mundil, Brigitta Diener), and a translation expert (Steve Miller). These people, along with William Paul Young and my husband, Maestro Michael Gesme, helped me craft a book that went through many stages: exact, word-for-word translations; poetic renderings; and finally the version you hold in your hands. It is slimmed down from the original, omitting some information that is pertinent to German readers but less so for an English audience.

Martin Schleske accompanied each step of the process. The conversations we had were sometimes practical and sometimes charged with passionate emotion, but they were always filled with respect for each other and for God's mighty hand, working in our lives in the same way Martin's hands work on the violin: shaping us, shaping the project, holding us lovingly, pouring out creativity and new life. May you, too, be blessed and created anew as you read *The Sound of Life's Unspeakable Beauty*.

JANET GESME

Preface: Creating Metaphors for Life

"We have lost the ability to create metaphors for life. We have lost the ability to give shape to things, to recognize the events around us and in us, let alone to interpret them. In this way we have ceased being the likenesses of God, and our existence is unjustified. We are, in fact, dead. . . . We feed on knowledge which has long since decayed."

These are the words of painter Friedensreich Hundertwasser (1928–2000). He wrote them to accompany one of his graphics on display at the Kultfabrik in Munich.[1] I stood in front of that picture, electrified, and scribbled down the quotation in my notebook. His exhortation became a leitmotif for me in the years to come, and this book emerged out of it. *Creating metaphors for life*—Hundertwasser meant that the events within and around us long for interpretation. But how can we learn to interpret if we do not learn to truly listen and truly see?

When I am working on my instruments, remarkable moments happen, holy moments in my studio through which I understand differently and anew the inner and outer elements of my life. These experiences invite us to go beyond learned knowledge. Everyday moments of epiphany are bestowed on everyone. Our role is to simply learn to pay attention. It is remarkable how often the parables handed down to us from Jesus end with the words: "Consider carefully how you listen," and "Whoever has ears to hear, let him hear." This is the sort of knowledge Hundertwasser was writing about.

We cannot afford to feed on "knowledge which has long since decayed." Simple religious correctness cannot nourish our inner world. A truly relevant faith involves a loving search and a searching love. This love is not something that you command; it is something under whose command you put yourself. It is an emerging work, similar to a work of art, for here we find a creative power and holy presence out of which we can truly live.

When I, as a luthier, describe the development of a violin throughout this book, it is not only a guided tour through my workshop but also an inner journey into the world of faith. The knowledge of the wood's fibers and medullary rays, the search for acoustic colors, the fascination of luminous depth in the varnish along with the diversity of its resins, the beauty of the arch, involvement with passionate musicians—these all create a myriad of metaphors.

The philosopher-theologian Bonaventure (1221–1274) long ago understood what Hundertwasser was exploring. He said: "Humans have lost the ability to read the book, namely the world. Therefore, it was necessary to give them another book, enlightening them to understand the metaphorical nature of the world, which they could no longer read. This other book is the Holy Scriptures, which is full of parables about things written in the world."[2]

Although the order of this book follows a certain logic, it isn't essential to adhere to it. This is a collection of little books, so feel free to begin with the themes and sections that interest you most.

MARTIN SCHLESKE

01

The Singing Tree

The Heart's Search

You who seek God,
your hearts shall live.

—PSALM 69:32 (NKJV)

*T*HE OLD TIMERS KNEW how to find a "singer." Families rooted in the tradition of violinmaking tell of their fathers who stood daily at the rapids of mountain rivers, listening to the logs crash into each other as they floated through the torrents down into the valley. On colliding, some of the logs began to vibrate, to sing, to sound. In this way, the masters identified from among the many those special "singers" used in making their violins.

Hundreds of years ago, tiny seedlings searched for water in the thin soil of the mountain forests and, over the course of time, grew into stately trees. For the violinmaker, those tightly populated forests at high altitudes are a treasure. They force the green crowns to start very high up on the tall mountain spruces. And so the trees form proud, limb-free trunks that soar up over 150 feet. Their wood is superior to any other natural material for the acoustical resonating surface needed to make musical instruments.

This wood that grew slowly for more than two or three hundred years has nothing in common with the ordinary fir trees growing in the lowlands. Lowland firs shoot up quickly, so they have wide annual rings. The cells themselves have thick walls and short fibers, so they are not resilient. Their limbs start low on the trunks. In the mild climate, they grow their heavy, dark wood long into autumn, and the resulting high proportion of winter grain ruins the sound. The charisma of the violin—its sound—can find no substance here.

With the mountain giants, it's different. These firs cast off their lower branches in the course of their slow growth. In the dark mountain forests, they stretch their green crowns of branches upwards toward the light. Their lower branches die off because their needles no longer reach the light. Even though the poor soil and the harsh climate just below the timberline pose a severe challenge for the mountain spruces, this difficult climate is a blessing for the sound. This hardship of meager soil lends them great strength. In this substance lies the sound.

Windfall on a Mountainside

Anytime an instrument maker goes high into the mountains in search of these "singing trees," an unforgettable adventure ensues. How often have I knocked against individual trunks with the dull side of an axe, felt their resonance, and listened to their sound. The heart of the violinmaker comes to life when he searches, with all his senses attuned, for the wood for his own violins.

Many years ago—just after my apprenticeship at the famous violinmaking school in Mittenwald—I took off with a fellow violinmaker into the Bavarian Alps. It was a cold, cloudy, winter day. After many hours of strenuous mountain hiking, we left the marked trail and fought through knee-deep snow to find the place about which we had heard rumors. Finally, completely exhausted, we reached that high place and were shocked. A cliff at the timberline had been hit by a violent storm and countless enormous fir trees—some over three feet in diameter and 100 to 130 feet long—lay crisscrossed, uprooted and broken. It was a windfall on the steep mountainside. Just as we arrived, the cloud cover parted and sunlight fell on the whitish cross-sections of the split-open trunks, which lit up in front of us. The sheer quantity of the annual rings was overwhelming.

Andreas and I boxed each other euphorically on the shoulders: this growth, the regularity, the fine superiority of their years! We had rarely seen such high-quality tonewood, and never in such quantity. We carefully inspected everything and then set off for home, feeling like we were flying. We leapt down the mountain like young antelopes, hoping to get to the forest service office that same evening and secure our find. When we arrived—dirty, sweaty, and overjoyed—the district officer could not believe we had attempted such a climb at that time of year. But we knew other violinmakers had likely heard about this windfall, so we acted quickly. We were worried that our extraordinary find would be snatched away if we waited for the snow to melt.

The Ringing Bell

We secured permission to harvest the storm-ravaged trees. A few days later we returned with backpacks and provisions, but this time with a chainsaw and two cant hooks with which to maneuver the logs. Amid the enormous trunks, we felt like two aphids on a mountain of pick-up sticks. Naïve beginners, we were equipped with neither winches nor pulleys, but we were nonetheless determined to secure the best wood among the broken trunks. The work required vigilance and forethought, given the ever-present danger that the giant stack would begin to shift drastically and fling us out as if from a catapult. In retrospect I must say our plan was reckless and dangerous.

Next we needed to bring the freed sections to the logging road, which lay at least two hundred meters below. We didn't have the tools for this job. So, we lay on the ground on our backs and, with all the leg strength we could muster, braced ourselves against the sawed-off sections of trunks, pushing on them until they began to roll. They were supposed to tumble down the rocky mountainside and wedge themselves into a convenient crevasse. But although the first trunk segment weighed almost a quarter-ton, it proved to be too small. We stared in horror as it bounced twice, once over the crevasse for which we were aiming and then once more, before plunging into the valley below. (Luckily no one was hurt.) We realized we would have to cut larger segments that would wedge themselves in the crevasse. This plan worked, and the logs soon piled up between the two cliffs. From there we could roll them onto the logging road.

The way the logs fell into the crevasse proved to be a fascinating acoustical experience. We had cut up three trees into two-meter sections. As they rolled down the mountainside, they naturally bounced high, again and again, off great slabs of rock. The mighty tones released by this process resounded throughout the entire valley. To our surprise, there was an immense difference in timbres produced. With each bounce, the sections from one of the three trunks emitted a sound like a ringing bell. And the sounds lingered on, free, bright, and clear. The logs from the other two trunks produced a dull, wooden thud upon impact, but not the wood from this trunk—it was a singer! In that moment we understood what the luthiers of our fathers' generation meant when distinguishing logs as "singers" and "non-singers." As we rolled the logs across the logging road, this acoustical pattern repeated itself. Those from the singer hummed! Even as we rolled them along the gravel path, a full, resonant tone emerged. In comparison, the non-singers remained practically mute.

By the time we were finished, we had worked for a good twelve hours. We were dead tired and deliriously happy. The logs were deposited in a secure place and marked with our sign. Now they belonged to us. In two or three months, after the snow melted, we would haul our tremendous find down into the valley and from there, float it into a sawmill's collection area.

The Heart's Search

A violinmaker does not accidentally happen upon marvelous tonewood. Our search for treasured timber became a metaphor for the pursuit of something deeper and more meaningful. If the sound of a good violin requires traveling such difficult paths and putting in such arduous effort, how could the sound of our lives demand less? Did not God give us a longing heart so that we would search for him? This pursuit will change our lives from the ground up. In the Psalms it says: "You who seek God, your hearts shall live" (69:32 NKJV). This verse does not speak of finding but of seeking. The wood is to my violin as a searching and listening faith is to my life.

Authentic life is not a path through the lowlands where things grow quickly and are easy to find. No, life's trail leads through the rocky places, through adversities and impasses. The many ways of searching for God all have one thing in common: passionate longing. A spirit devoid of passion is a dangerous enemy of faith. Growing accustomed to what one already believes is a subtle form of unbelief. Life slows to a stop, powerless. An alert faith does not become accustomed either to God or to the world. The soul loses its hope by conforming, and the spirit is left with no questions.

Life becomes bland when one accepts everything and therefore reacts to nothing. Conforming, in biological terms "adaptation," is when the cells' response rate decreases until they stop reacting at all. Our set answers in spiritual matters, however calming, lead us to become lethargic. We no longer react authentically. The end result of adaptation is stagnation.

When we wonder whether good tonewood might be found on the wind-ravaged, mountainous regions of our world, we are often told to calm down. "Better wait here by the warm stove for the snow to melt!" Such advice assumes that harmony is the same as peace and that an untroubled mood is evidence of consistency. It lulls us to sleep and deprives us of real faith.

Some of our colleagues might have said: "We looked for good wood too but didn't have any luck up there. Sit here with us and don't spoil the good mood of those who have come to terms with reality!" Many supposedly mature people present their advice as "experience" in order to avoid facing the truth that hides behind it: resignation. Guard yourself from this kind of "experienced" person. They poison all hope. Nothing hinders our path more than the refusal to release our closely held disappointments. These are the shackles of the soul.

The command to keep searching is written deep in the human spirit. For me, it was a call to the tree line of the Bavarian Alps. Our questions, visions, and longings should turn us into people who seek, hope, and, love. And in order to behold life's gaze upon us and return it, we need to nurture a loving and searching spirit.

The Wisdom of the Seeker

We show what we believe not by what our mouths say but by what our hearts seek. Belief manifests itself not in ideological dogma but in how we spend our time and energy. Show me what you do, and I will tell you what you believe. If our search for meaning does not cost us anything, then we have not ventured out onto the path. When the embers of longing have grown cold in us, what was once our faith has become the cold ashes of religious doctrine. Sometimes a sense of God's presence withdraws from us so that we will continue questioning. This defines us as people who live in the light of Jesus's promise in the Sermon on the Mount: "Keep asking, and it will be given to you; keep searching, and you will find; keep knocking, and the door will be opened for you" (see Matthew 7:7). All the prophets speak of this searching spirit of faith![1]

Without passion and longing we would have said back in the lowlands: "Let's take this tree here. It won't really produce sound, but at least it is easily accessible, right here next to the path." But its only merit is that it causes us no trouble! To find God, we must frequently trouble ourselves. I must not replace the loving search with just formal religious words. What is that worth if your searching love has been lost?

Had we not been sure that we would find wonderful tonewood, we would not have mustered the strength to travel those hard paths through difficult circumstances. The search for God and the search for tonewood have much in common. We cannot count on finding something precious by the side of an easy road.

A basic rule in empirical physics pertains to the inner life as well: "The task defines the tool." To measure temperature, you don't use a stopwatch but a thermometer. But what instrument will take the measure of God? The prophet Jeremiah provides a clue: "When you search for me, you will find me; if you seek me with all your heart" (29:13). What can this mean but that God wishes to be found by the seeker? A receptive attitude, when lived out, finds expression in searching, asking, exploring, questioning, and prayer. This is how the heartfelt inner person comes alive. For me, our discovery of the tonewood in the Bavarian Alps has become a powerful, personal parable.

Psalm 69:32 says, "You who seek God, your hearts shall live" (NKJV). Life is found in the seeking, for it is a holy and persistent unease that causes us to awaken and experience life. There is no place for apathy, because the search is fixed on an empowering vision, a calling fed by longing. Sadly, our lives often swing from the immature ease of settled indifference to the immature unease of being driven by circumstance. In the wise words of Chuang-tzu (300 BC): "You go, and do not know what drives you. You rest, and do not know what is carrying you."[2]

As in our search for the singing tree, we have to choose to overcome apathy. These days we think spirituality means, above all, that our hearts find peace. It is actually the reverse: if my life is worth something to me, then I will get moving, understanding that my existence is a pilgrimage, a life of searching and listening. And so I will break camp, ask, search, and begin the journey.

Purposeful Poverty

Our lives do not run along fixed tracks. We move through a jungle of options and must constantly decide what we will do or leave undone. In the mountain spruce we encounter a special kind of wisdom. In accordance with its nature, it develops a green crown of branches. By stretching these branches toward the light, it allows life-giving limbs to grow. Only by exposure to light are needles formed; only so do they become a source of strength for the tree. This is true for all living things: whatever pulls away from the light dies and becomes a burden on the organism. In its natural wisdom the mountain spruce casts aside dead, withered branches that remain in the dark, because there is no life in them. But right there, at the very place where the dead material has been cast aside, the material for the treasured sound is to be found. This is the tonewood, rich in years, limb-free, long-fibered, and workable: out of this wood a violin will be made.

A resonant life demands wisdom and courage. We must discern which things are dead and separate ourselves from them. An honest heart recognizes the dead limbs that are robbing us of strength and self-worth. For the tree, this wisdom is self-evident, but the myriad of options granted by our freedom makes our journey much more complex. *Nothing* in our life is self-evident. We must learn to stretch ourselves up toward the light in every area of life, through every branch, twig, and shoot of our existence. This is why Jesus says:

"I am the light of the world. Whoever follows me will never walk in darkness but will have the light of life" (John 8:12).

The mountain spruce teaches us to cast off whatever is dead: things that are not right, internal intrigues that hide from the light, the retreat to dark places devoid of honesty, truth, righteousness, forgiveness, mercy, and reconciliation. A resonant, sounding life has learned to sacrifice what is dead and unjust. "Not sinning" has, in fact, something to do with sacrifice, with sacrificing some options. The only way to derive meaning from sin is not to do it, even though you could.

Those who seek the light of God must make many decisions that seem to limit them or make them poorer. This is the kind of poverty Jesus praises above all else, when he says in the Sermon on the Mount: "Blessed are the poor in spirit, for theirs is the kingdom of heaven" (Matthew 5:3). The poverty of the spruce cultivates precious wood. The poverty of a person cultivates self-imposed limitations. But it is precisely through poverty that real substance emerges. A life limited by grace may indeed become slower, but surely it will also be more conscious, more concentrated, more passionate, and more sustainable. All power, everything we receive, arises out of this poverty before God, out of times of honest self-awareness and quiet in which we shed dead branches and are pruned.

Every authentic life must dig deep and search for its wellsprings. The rich run the danger of not finding these sources because they are never thirsty; they will not search and will not find. In the Gospel of Luke, we find not only Jesus's blessings but also his warnings: "Woe to you who are rich, for you have received your consolation. Woe to you who are full now, for you will be hungry" (6:24-25a). They have already received their consolation, for they searched in the wrong places! The "woe" is not a decree of judgment but a cry of pain, a holy sorrow, for the rich have satisfied themselves in a way that hinders them from searching with their whole hearts. They injure themselves and the world entrusted to them because they no longer know what it means to be persistent in hope, to listen and to search.

The poor before God know how to be still and receive the gifts of grace. The poor whom Jesus blesses are aware of a void that only God can fill. In their thirst, they head out on their search. By becoming seekers they become rich recipients. Here an unusual truth comes into play. Instead of the normal differentiation between "active" and "passive" faith, there is a third way: the way of receptiveness. One might call it *the Law of Grace*, which says: you are powerless to create the essential things, you can only receive them. But you can make yourself receptive.

Our search for the singing tree speaks of that kind of receptiveness. It is necessary to become poor for the sake of our calling. Making ourselves poor means not wanting everything. It means to purposefully pass by certain things. In this poverty we gain the strength to cast aside things that will never produce true sound, to prune off our deadwood. We gain strength to live toward something not yet visible. This strength is also called hope, and it is well illustrated in an old story:

> Three men were working on a construction site. Each one had a shovel with which he was digging in the ground. The first seemed listless and tired. Someone asked him: "What are you doing?" He replied, "I'm digging a hole." The second seemed happier. Someone asked him, as well, "What are you doing?" He answered: "We are laying the foundation for a big wall!" The third was also digging away. He worked tirelessly and, defying exhaustion, was full of joy and strength of mind. Again, the question: "What are you doing?" He answered: "We are building a cathedral!"

Our search for the "singing tree" is like that. Like the first man we could have answered: "We are climbing a mountain," but as it got colder, dirtier, and rougher, we would have given up. With the second man we might have said: "We are looking for wood." But being like the third man, we were drawn on by the beauty of the tonewood that we already heard in our mind's ear, and the sound of our future violins in all their purity, flexibility, sweetness, and luminous strength. This longing gave us wings. Our violins had long been living inside us, in a life dedicated to the sound. For our vision to become incarnate we needed good wood, and so we had the strength to bear our troubles. Everything we do depends on which inner search gives our vision wings. The moment when we found the wood was sublime, almost magical: the clouds parted, the sun cast its beams on the hillside, and we were awed by the wood in its crosscut sections.

The "tree of calling" to which we turn goes through a kind of death: it will be struck down or broken by the wind. It sees the abyss and the raging stream. Floating down into the valley, it will be taken out of the water and brought into the master's workshop, baptized into a new life. The tree submits to the formative strength of the master and is there shaped into a sound of which it knew nothing when it was in the forest. One psalm says: "Let all the trees of the forest sing for joy" (Psalm 96:12 NIV). To live in this formative power of God is to be made "holy"—whole and unique.

What dies in this space is not our created nature or goodness, but rather our immaturity and chaos: our lovelessness, hopelessness, godlessness, and lack of joy and peace. As a master luthier makes the tree sing, so does the Master work in us. With the poverty that our inner life requires, we are meant to cast off anything that damages our calling, whether riches, fallacies, or an overflow of options. A person who cannot take on the poverty blessed by Jesus risks harming his soul and losing purpose.

~

Not all trouble works against us, and what is easy is not always a blessing. In the rich earth and mild climates of the lowlands, trees grow strong and fast. So it is with the material and spiritual abundance that we take to be blessings: we grow fast and fat but become unsuitable for sound. Very few regions in the Alps fulfill the conditions needed for the production of good tonewood. The instrument is given its sound not only by the altitude, the incline, the wind, and the overall climate, but also by the kind of ground in which the tree grows. Tonewood grows in meager soil, where it has learned to hold on through daily adversities and challenges. Reverberating cells grow there and produce the resilience lacking in fast-growing wood. It is like a person with a dulled heart, who, in the thick walls of his abundance, has not learned to listen to the Spirit of God because he has never known a longing for God! How different is the testimony of the prophet Isaiah: "My soul yearns for you in the night; in the morning my spirit longs for you" (26:9 NIV).

The singing trees, like our calling, will be granted a new, second life. They will sing. The Master will form them in his hand. New life is a quality of eternity that can dawn upon us today amid our hardships and challenges. Our calling will be tested, just as good sound grows out of testing. The beginning of the process is the whisper of the trunk that symbolizes a searching heart. Here, the bell-like tone of a "singer" is born.

02

The Tree's Wisdom

The Beginning of Spiritual Strength

Look at the trees and learn a lesson.

—LUKE 21:29 / MARK 13:28
(ADAPTED)

VIOLINMAKER ACQUIRES a strong intuition about the structure of wood. You develop an eye for the course of the annual rings, the regularity, luster, density, and quantity of its winter growth. I am always captivated by the flames in the wood's design and the clear course of the medullary rays.[1] The smell of fresh-cut wood awakens strong emotions in me. My passion for wood is intensely personal, but also practical: good tonewood will produce instruments with which I, as a luthier, can feed my family. I simply cannot describe the making of a violin without first looking to the tree, so before describing how a violin is crafted, I would like to look at what nature has crafted.

Many great cultures of the world attribute a strong symbolic power to the tree. From the beginning, wood was necessary for human life. As building material for our huts, tree wood provided us with a safe dwelling space and served as our fuel. Burning wood provided protection from wild animals, served for food preparation, and gave us warmth. Without the tree, humans would not have been able to survive amid the adversities and dangers of the natural world. Perhaps this is why humans are so strongly emotionally connected to trees.

In addition, our cultural and emotional life, our joy, sorrow, passion, dance, and consciousness, are intertwined closely with the tree. Wood provided instruments for the art of music and so gave life to the human soul. The genealogy in the book of Genesis shows how early the need for art and sound anchored itself into human consciousness. There we find Jubal, the father of all those who play the harp and flute (4:21), and Tubal-Cain, an instructor of every craftsman in bronze and iron (4:22) listed in the eighth generation—the forefathers of all musicians and craftsmen.

Even so, there is a deeper, more compelling reason to look more closely at the tree. Jesus said, "Look at the trees and learn a lesson" (see Matthew 24:32/Mark 13:28/Luke 21:29). So also Hermann Hesse testified: "Trees have always been for me the most powerful of preachers. . . . Trees are a sanctuary. He who knows how to speak with them and who listens to them will experience truth. They do not preach doctrine and formulas; unencumbered by minutiae, they preach the primordial law of life."[2]

The Bristlecone Pine

Among all the types of trees, the bristlecone pine especially appeals to me. Not because it would serve as good tonewood, nor because it is mentioned in Scripture, but because of its maturity, growth, and antiquity. Some of these pines are the oldest living things on our planet, with approximately eighteen living examples that are over 4,000 years old. The oldest of these were germinating as the Egyptian pyramids were being built. During ancient Israel's heyday under King David they were already 1,500 years old—and they are still growing today.

Surprisingly, the oldest representatives of this species live under the harshest conditions imaginable. They are located at an altitude of more than 9,000 feet above sea level on the east side of the Sierra Nevada in the White Hills of California, one of the driest regions on Earth. They grow in a most adverse climate, with hardly any rain, facing strong, extremely cold winds. They need very few needles and only a little living bark to survive. The oldest have an annual growth of just a few tenths of a millimeter and reach only about sixty feet tall. However, they continue to grow and produce seeds from which seedlings spring up, their quiet strength preparing them for thousands of years to come.

The oldest living bristlecone pine, named Methuselah, is 4,850 years old. Its exact location is kept secret by the US Forest Service due to the danger of vandalism. It owes its name to the patriarch Methuselah, mentioned in Genesis 5:21 and Luke 3:37, the oldest person recorded in the Bible.

These life giants continue to grow even into the fifth millennium of their lives. It is not difficult to hear what these trees have to say to us: that which has ceased to grow is headed inevitably toward decay and will soon die. The trunk may stand for some time, but strong winds or fungal infestation will weaken it internally, until it collapses under its own weight.

Likewise, as long as a person is alive inside, he will continue to grow, even through adversities, crises, and weakness. Paul spoke of this in his second letter to the Corinthians, when he said: "Therefore we do not lose heart. Though outwardly we are wasting away, yet inwardly we are being renewed day by day" (4:16 NIV). The person who knows nothing of this inward renewal will eventually weaken and collapse under destructive thoughts or troublesome winds. We did not choose the soil and location of our life's climate, and we all experience tremendous growing pain throughout our lives. Those who, like the bristlecone pine, hold out through wind, drought, and adversity and keep up their inner growth are worthy of the same wonder and honor due to these life giants.

The Cry for Water

How did the tree start out? In the beginning there was a seedling. The tree's seeds contain just enough nutrients to sustain life for a couple of days—at most, a couple of weeks. Without growth, the seedling will inevitably die. But what sets this growth in motion? The absorption of water through the seed's shell.

The believer is like a seedling. There is a life inside of us that thirsts for something more. It is the soul's thirst, as the psalmist says: "As the deer pants for streams of water, so my soul pants for you, my God" (Psalm 42:1 NIV). There is no life without growth, and there is no growth without water. Therefore, it is important to ask ourselves if we truly know the Living Water that ignites and satisfies the soul. In the Bible, water represents the recognition and presence of God. It is strange, but those who come to know this water also have a thirst for God growing inside of them. Whoever does not know the cry for God has not yet had their faith called into life. For wherever a person's faith is alive, a sincere thirst for God is developing, an unquenchable longing.

Only that which is not alive does not know thirst. A lifeless faith can be no more than the dried-up belief in claims that can be neither proved nor refuted. However, the faith spoken of in the gospels is an intimate fellowship with God. This faith will not stay alive without taking in water. But what is the water of faith? The Gospel of John says, "On the last and greatest day of the festival, Jesus stood up and said in a loud voice, 'Let anyone who is thirsty come to me and drink. Whoever believes in me, as Scripture has said, rivers of living water will flow from within them.'" John then adds to this: "By this he meant the Spirit, whom those who believed in him were later to receive" (7:37–39 NIV). Those who do not know this thirst for the water of the Holy Spirit are like a seed that is still closed up in itself.

Life's Ground

First, the seedling secures itself by sending fine roots downwards. Through its tiny root hairs, it can take in as much water as it needs, while the ground gives it security, something to hold on to. We see what Jesus means when he points us to the trees to learn a lesson. Unlike many of us today, the tree does not search inside itself for the living water or support. Roots symbolize the wisdom of not trying to be self-sufficient. We cannot merely have a proud trunk, heavily laden with branches, and a magnificent cloak of leaves; we must also make an effort to search for a world that will support us within.

As life can be sustained only if and when it "goes outside of itself," so only the faith prepared to go outside of itself and connect with other people will take hold and grow. This is a decision of humility. Fulbert Steffensky writes,

> How old must we be in order to recognize that preoccupation with ourselves, self-actualization, does not yield a basis for living? An old virtue must be relearned: humility. It is the realistic confession that we, in and of ourselves, do not provide our own compelling agenda for life. . . . I do not need to be isolated in a greenhouse so that I can find my own truth. I need brothers and sisters and fathers and mothers and teachers and books and theories and stories; with

them I must negotiate what truth is and what truth demands. . . . Growing up and becoming old confirms the fact that we do not have much on our own with which to nourish ourselves. The hope that we can generate out of ourselves is too small. The courage that we can muster on our own is not enough. The dreams of our own hearts are too trite and temporary. We are beggars. We cannot nourish, comfort, and encourage ourselves all on our own.[3]

Faith requires the surrender of our prideful reserve. The person who sorts out matters of faith, doubts, and hopes all alone is like a seed that stays closed inside itself. There are two reasons for this: self-centeredness and fear. A seed must die in order to live and become a tree. Its roots are expressions of faith in a promise, and because of this promise it surrenders its strength to fulfill the law living inside of itself. Pride and fear keep us from the active surrender we need; they close us off. As Jesus described it: "But when the sun came up, [the plants] were scorched, and they withered because they had no root" (Matthew 13:6 NIV).

Opposites That Create Life

Now that the seedling has pushed its roots into the ground, the life within it begins to emerge. The leaves are the next to unfold. Here is another lesson about communal life, one that seems to contradict common sense. Roots not only nourish the tree but need nourishment from the leaves as well. That is the two-way system found in all wooden trunks: in the wood's vascular tissue, water and mineral nutrients climb up out of the roots. A sugar solution in turn travels from the top, into the outer layer of the bast fibers, and back down to the roots.

This process describes the secret of a truly Spirit-filled community. If the roots were to keep the water all to themselves without passing it on, that would be the death of the leaves; by the same token, if the leaves were to keep the light all to themselves and not pass it on, the result would be the death of the roots. To take but not to give is a form of suicide. When the leaves allow the roots to die, or the roots the leaves, they are killing themselves.

The gifts found in the roots and the leaves could not be more opposite. The one bores down deep in the earth, the other stretches out toward the light, but both remain true to their character. To be true to oneself does not mean to be true only to one's *gift*, however, but also to the *task* associated with that gift: the roots are searching in the depths for water, and the leaves are opening up to the light.

Water and light are vivid biblical images for the presence of the Holy One. Just as roots and leaves experience strength differently, so people experience God's presence in various ways: they will hear his claim upon their existence differently and will care for others in diverse ways. They will treasure different things and be overwhelmed by different challenges. But what connects them is the dichotomy of living from each other and for each other. Roots and leaves each exist wholly in their own element while each allows the other its uniqueness. Neither tries to be everything all alone. They resist the pride of being only givers or receivers. In their diversity, they do not merely *tolerate living next to each other*; rather, they consciously *live for each other*. They understand that diversity is not simply an aesthetic luxury but is vital for life itself.

Respect for others manifests itself by refusing to demand or expect another to be like us; rather, it recognizes what others already have and are. The organism of the tree teaches us that, for the sake of the whole, love must manifest itself in diverse ways. Particular gifts and callings would dry up or rot away if the different parts of the tree were forced to copy each other. The leaf, if it tried to be a root, would not gain an understanding of how a root lives in the ground; it would dissolve into the earth and decay. Likewise a root, if it stretched up into the air like a leaf, would not gain an understanding of leaves; it would only dry out and die. True community is not dependent on our *understanding* each other, but on our *trusting* each other.

Trust can be painfully disappointed, but it is essential for our life together. Jesus said: "If anyone forces you to go one mile, go with them two miles" (Matthew 5:41 NIV). It is by experiencing the detours of disappointments that we learn not to give up on each other. That is the profound understanding at the heart of a Spirit-filled life. It means others live and love by faith in a way I myself do not understand. Leaves and roots cannot comprehend each other, but they are still there for one another. That is their secret.

Our modern society claims to have achieved so much in terms of "self-actualization": our consciousness of personal freedoms and individual gifts, our cultivated experience of self, our freedom from outdated conventions and burdensome traditions. Perhaps this has led us to swallow the naïve misconception that self-actualization is our primary calling. If we look at the world honestly, however, with its incongruities, injustices, and brokenness, we realize, all too starkly, that the world we face is not friendly and service-oriented. It is not waiting to help us actualize ourselves. In the Bible, a person's identity and calling have more to do with the formation of the communities and relationships in which we live. The more fervently we search for our own meaning, the more decisively we will lose it; the path will go dark in front of the one seeking only individual wholeness and autonomous encounters with God. To consider only oneself is to be like a leaf that breaks away from the tree and—as it happily floats downward—philosophizes about its calling. Faith is, above all, the calling to be a friend of God and of your neighbor.

Roots and leaves don't waste time trying to tell each other, "Light is not damp!" "Water is not bright!" Rather, they bear fruit by serving their communal life. The tree gives shade to a scorched world and offers birds a place to build their nest. We live amid this movement of mutual recognition and respect. The New Testament calls for a respect that binds congregations together above cultural and political boundaries (2 Corinthians 8:14). We devote ourselves to Christ in others not for the sake of an abstract concept but for the sake of this tree that Jesus calls the kingdom of God.

The Photosynthesis of the Spirit

Every leaf of a tree is a workshop in which invisible light is transformed into vital energy. Biologists call this process photosynthesis. In this process energy from sunlight transforms carbon dioxide gas, which is invisible in the atmosphere, into a solid state of carbohydrates. The sun's energy is processed and becomes "incarnate" in life. Light and spirit have long been linked with each other,[4] so we can well say (especially with our focus on trees) that something like a photosynthesis of the spirit occurs when God's presence fills us. It is a holy process by which the light of God is transformed in us into vital life. The Spirit of God is like an inner prophet and teacher. He does not simply come over us, nor is he merely in us. His first question is always, "Am I welcome?" God heeds our heartfelt "yes." He is the one who suffers with us, who advocates for us, who loves through us. He will not force himself upon those who shut themselves up in their own darkness. Nothing, however, invites the Spirit in more fully than the call of our heart: "Come, Holy Spirit, help me to do God's will!" Those who pray in this way will witness their life unfolding, like a tree whose leaves unfold and stretch up toward the light.

A New Spring

Look at the tree in the springtime. The branches of the aged tree were as barren as death; the leaves had long since withered and fallen away. But then it becomes warm and without knowing what is happening . . .

Just as deciduous trees need warmth in springtime to unfold their strength, new strength unfolds in us in the warm climate of active faith. After the cold of winter, every spring seems like a miracle to me. None of us knows how many springs we have left, but we shouldn't miss a single one. In the springtime I make a point of walking into the forest behind my workshop every day to look at the buds on the chestnut trees. Such sensual vitality! This emerging life asks me: You want proof of God? Then open your eyes, your nose, your ears! This is not proof in the logical sense. Of course not! Nevertheless, here is proof that my soul is alive. If we cannot perceive this proof, if we are incapable of being amazed, then we have lost our soul. And if our soul is dead, how can we be convinced of anything? If faith is a sanctuary, then our amazement is its outer courts.

I do not delude myself with yearning for a "second spring." I have already lived through my youth. And yet I know that there is a springtime of the inner life. Whoever wants to experience the inner spring must be prepared to end the ice age of unbelief and consider the possibility that seemingly dead branches hold life in them if we will only expose them to the climate of faith.

There is a luminous strength creating something new in us. Perhaps it is for this reason alone that the earth's axis is tilted and thereby gives us the seasons, so that spring can show our hopelessness that life and beauty can miraculously emerge out of all that seems barren and dead. And we, too, have a part to play. The bursting forth of the buds should inspire us to take co-ownership of the strength and the inner climate of our lives.

~

My wife, Claudia, witnessed the last years of Ilse, a woman in her nineties. In spite of her advanced age, Ilse became a spiritual mentor for Claudia. Amid her fragility and pain she retained a fresh, faithful hope and strength; a youthful light played in her eyes and an enthusiasm in her voice. When my wife told her about the problems I faced in starting up my workshop, Ilse offered just the right words: uplifting, strong, and clear. Her words often drifted into prayer on their own. We had the impression that despite her fragility, she was so near to God she didn't seem to notice a difference between a prayer of blessing while talking with you and words of wisdom welling up in the midst of prayer. Her doctors and nurses, like us, often became oblivious of time and space while lingering at her bedside. They were not really needed there but, like us, they seemed to sense something rare through and beyond the frailty of this woman. She was a saint to us in her nearness to God. Physically she grew weaker and weaker, and yet she retained immense inner strength until the end. In her we witnessed the truth of Psalm 92:

> The righteous shall flourish like a palm tree,
> [And] shall grow like a cedar in Lebanon.
> Those who are planted in the house of the Lord
> Shall flourish in the courts of our God.
> They shall still bear fruit in old age;
> They shall be fresh and flourishing,
> To declare that the Lord is upright.
>
> (Psalm 92:12–15a NKJV)

03

The Design

The Harmony of Opposites

He has made everything beautiful in its time. He has also set eternity in the human heart.

—ECCLESIASTES 3:11 (NIV)

*T*HE WOOD THAT I USE spends many years in the special climate of my workshop before being turned into an instrument. Mountain spruce is required for the violin's front and bass bar; maple for the ribs, back, and scroll; ebony for the fingerboard and pegs; willow or spruce for the linings and blocks. For the purfling, I often use walnut or sycamore. Black ebony is traditionally used for the nut and the saddle, but for my concert instruments I carve these out of the cream-colored horns of Ankole longhorn cattle, a material frequently used in Africa to make jewelry. The white nuts and saddles made from these horns are prettier than the black ones, but they also have a fabulously hard, though not brittle, surface that can bear the strings' weight and strength. They give my violins their unique visual "signature."

Some special pieces of wood used for the front of my violins came from trees felled long ago. They were stored for decades in the workshop of an old luthier dynasty in Bern. I heard about them from a customer who one day mentioned that the old master was intending to give up his workshop. Without waiting a day, I got in my car and drove there. The old master's great-grandfather had also been a violinmaker. The wood from his shop, now in my shop, had been felled in 1884 in Davos, Switzerland. The passing of many years has given this old wood a golden texture and a unique tone. For my work, these pieces are the special-sounding "gold nuggets."

It isn't strictly necessary to work with well-aged wood, but it is thrilling. To be sure, some of my best violins come from newer wood. But the difference between the two emerges clearly when you are working with the wood. Old wood has a blunt, dry surface as you cut off shavings, whereas young wood has an oily sheen. You have to be more careful when working with old wood, but it is worth it, because it offers an especially mature, velvety sound.

Before the work begins, you have to recognize the pattern in the wood, with its form and proportions. The outline of the violin will emerge, and with it, a new metaphor.

In his book about the history of beauty, Umberto Eco describes a moment around the sixth century BC when beauty was conceptualized as proportion and harmony. These principles were recognized in the order of numbers and in the harmony of music, but also in the human body, in sacred buildings, and in the cosmos: "For the early Pythagoreans . . . harmony consisted in the opposition between odd and even, finite and infinite, unity and multiplicity, right and left, male and female, straight and curved, and so on."[1]

We grasp the harmony of opposites not by eliminating one of the two elements but rather by holding them together in constant tension. The ancients recognized such purposeful oppositions in the visual realm as symmetry. In Greek art, symmetry was always vital; it became the criterion of beauty, the defining characteristic of the classic.

In this chapter I hope to unfold a basic aspect of the beauty of the violin that can help us better understand the beauty of our own existence. This standard of beauty can also inspire us to see basic truths of the Bible in a new light, for the Bible overflows with harmonious tensions that illuminate the profound beauty in something or someone, in an experience or a piece of wisdom. Tuning into these harmonious oppositions doesn't aid just our intellectual but also our moral development. Ultimately, it deepens our love for God.

Beauty and Disrupting the Pattern

What is beauty, really? As a young luthier I was driven by this question above all others. I had just finished my training and was constantly designing my own models. During this process, I kept on asking myself: what makes a violin a violin? Which laws must I follow to build a truly beautiful instrument? What secrets underlie the perfect sound? It was clear to me then—this was thirty-two years ago—that these questions could never be answered if I just copied existing templates and held to sizing requirements without understanding the fundamental ideas on which an instrument is based.

It became clear to me that I could not simply follow a standardized process if I wanted to achieve an extraordinary result. And so I set out to forget everything I had learned up until then. This was quite naïve! Still, I forced myself to abandon as much of my assumed knowledge as possible in order to explore the fundamentals that lay beneath the whole. I knew that only by taking my own path to success would I finally understand why the violin is what it is. Only then would creative power and freedom open up for me.

My first attempts were anything but gratifying. I constructed a pattern for a violin but found myself following measurements that I had learned but could not explain. In effect I was a serial copycat. The underlying criterion of beauty was not clear to me. Then I found out about an exhibition at the Würzburg Residence celebrating Balthasar Neumann's three hundredth birthday.[2]

I drove there hoping to gain insight into the famous Baroque architect's intellectual world. His structures are testaments to a great aesthetic strength. Such beauty is inexplicable without a convincing foundational idea. To my great delight, the exhibit planners displayed some of his original architectural sketches. I stood for at least half a day staring at one of the larger-than-life construction plans, searching feverishly for the tiny holes pricked by the point of the architect's compass, for lines that he had traced out, and for any other clues to his design principles. I knew that, with some luck, I could dive into the aesthetic world of a whole epoch. Perhaps searching here for the foundation of beauty would help me, since violin craftsmanship had blossomed during this same era.

During those long hours at the exhibition I was asking: What ideas did the guiding lines follow? How did such tension-packed and yet well-balanced forms develop? Did Balthasar Neumann's ovals follow a mathematical function? If so, then from observing the beginning of the line you would be able to predict what happens at the end. Or were the lines based on simple, yet tremendously skillful free-hand drawings that bent here and there until they somehow fit together? Or were they spline curves, such as were used for centuries in building boat frames? What is the secret to good form?

And so I stood with my notebook in front of the enormous parchment, copying lines, points, and axes, until I finally recognized an intriguing concept. It is as simple as it is convincing. The ovals depict neither a simple mathematical function (like an ellipse) nor random freeform. Instead, they take shape by means of purposefully intertwined segments of circles. The foundation forms a rectangle, whose borders, extended out, determine the breaking points from one circle segment to another. (A sketch depicting this basic concept step by step can be found at the end of this chapter).

With this discovery I hit the jackpot, and what was revealed to me at that moment has stayed with me ever since. In terms of aesthetic power, Neumann's concept is worlds ahead of the conventional curves generated by computer-aided design (CAD): one is bored to death by a curve generated by a spline function. What will happen at the end is already clear from the beginning. There are no surprises. The result is an ordinary curve, trite and predictable. Neumann's idea is quite different: here the eye is caught off-guard by two familiar patterns cutting in on each other. The two circles could not be more boring *in and of themselves*. And yet that's the trick. Our eye is possessed of an irrepressible urge to recognize patterns. This is the job assigned to a network consisting of billions of cells. As a result, the eye begins to catch hold of the line and is on the verge of turning away, because it understands the idea. But at that very moment it stumbles. Suddenly the expected pattern is broken. Another radius breaks in with no advance warning, and the eye is forced to discard the familiar pattern. There is a rupture; the predicted must succumb to reality. The transition points of the oval's radii trigger an optical crisis. Neither slope nor curve of the radii holds steady. The path simply continues, but on a completely different track.

It is not necessary to completely understand this illustration, just this one decisive factor: beauty calls for constant alteration between familiarity and surprise. The circle's curves, if taken alone, are the epitome of familiarity. They represent perfect consistency. But the tangent points between the circles are the epitome of crisis. They come unannounced.

Familiarity and *surprise*: two elements of a remarkable dialectic seize each other here. They form a harmonious contradiction because in them opposites are united into a whole. In this form one cannot and may not exist without the other. You can easily imagine what would happen if one of the two opposites were missing: Without familiarity in the pattern, surprise degenerates into being *purely random*. With no surprise in the pattern, familiarity degenerates into *boredom*. If the harmony of the opposites is impaired, two deep pits, or abysses open up:

> › The abyss of randomness: *allowing* no claims to be made. Anything is possible. Nothing plausible can be found, there is no pattern to be followed. By offering nothing recognizable, randomness asks too much of us.
> › The abyss of boredom: *requiring* no claims to be made. Everything is explained in and of itself. It is a pattern closed within itself. Boredom asks too little of us, because everything can be understood from the very start.

As I went back to my little shop, I immediately began applying this new knowledge to violinmaking. I quickly found out that Stradivarius's patterns follow similar laws. Here, too, the curves follow an interplay of radii and not—as would be easier—a function increasing the curve or a self-contained contour. Apparently, the great Italian masters also understood the aesthetic interplay between familiarity and visual breaks, and they infused their works with this concept of beauty.

The Allure of Music

The attraction created by building and breaking patterns is not limited to the violin's lovely appearance. The interplay between familiarity and surprise occurs in musical compositions as well. Familiar melodies, rhythms, and harmonious sound structures are intentionally "broken" time and again. The break announces that something unexpected is happening.

Mozart played masterfully with this concept. Some of his motifs are so self-explanatory that you can begin to hum along even if you do not know the piece. But just when it all seems so familiar, every-thing changes. That is what keeps us listening to music. It is a mix of regular, orderly patterns alternating with surprise and suspense.[3] While listening to music, it doesn't take long at all for us to develop an inner "listening forecast."[4] The excitement lies in our uncertainty of whether our expectations will be fulfilled. With any music, if the measure of familiarity is too high, we take the piece to be aestheti-cally trite, unappealing, and crude. We feel *insulted* because we are not challenged. But if there is too little familiarity, we feel that we have been handed over to a random series of events. We feel *humili-ated* because we are over-taxed.

Take, for example, the resolution of a seventh chord. It relentlessly plays upon our internal tension and is resolved only when our musi-cal expectation is fulfilled. As a young person, I once took the liberty of having a little fun with my violin teacher, Attila Balogh, using this concept. He had been a viola soloist with the Berlin Philharmonic in his youth but was forced to give it up due to an accident that injured his left hand. From that point on he taught simple violin students like myself at a rural Swabian music school. Surely the deep, passionate musical understanding with which he taught me during my formative years was the fundamental reason for my later becoming a violinmaker.

At this time, we were occupied with J. S. Bach's A Minor Con-certo. Attila had worked out the appropriate phrasing of the violin part in the previous hour and had played much of it for me. He em-phasized (a bit too much for my youthful taste) the necessity of the musical tension and the corresponding resolution of the piece's last chord. During the lesson, he sat with closed eyes, smiling in concen-tration, and sometimes happily, sometimes less so, listened to my playing. But at the end of the first movement, I simply left off the last note! After a horrified moment, Attila jumped up and roared toward me full of Hungarian passion and yanked the violin out of my hand. He was not prepared to be denied the resolution of the tension that should have occurred naturally in that last note.

Of course, it is not only about the last note. Music continuously creates emotional promises, and our consciousness as listeners expe-riences a constant interplay between expectations and fulfillment. One can truthfully say that the music plays us.

The Strong Instrument

It is not just the one who listens, but above all the violinist herself who constantly experiences the founding principles of harmonious opposites: the instrument's tone colors must be familiar to her. She must be capable of finding her voice in the violin, and yet the violin must be a living opponent, challenging and inspiring her. Familiarity helps form the tone, but with *only* familiarity, nothing is demanded of the violinist tonally and her playing will not come alive. Some notes, whose harmonic components find their corresponding frequencies in the instrument's strong resonances, can be downright ugly if poorly approached. On the other hand, notes can truly form only with the aid of strong resonances. Only there can they be enriched with color, liveliness, strength. It is easy and effortless to play a violin without resonance—but also banal.

The various parts of the violin, most notably the body, respond to notes being played with a stronger or weaker vibration response. Because it disturbs uniform vibrations, the instrument's vibration response creates a crisis for the string. The stronger (and therefore more alluring) the response produced by the violin's body, the more severe the impact on the vibrating string—those vibrations are disturbed. The instrument's sound would not be problematic without this feedback, and yet it would be mundane.[5] In the realm of the violin's distinctive sound profile, the musician can "knead and form" the sound. She can feel the instrument's resistance, its strength; it becomes a worthy living counterpart. Simply put: one cannot simultaneously search for life and reject crises. Banality and liveliness, like conformity and development, are mutually exclusive.

The resonance profile of a strong violin confronts the violinist with a two-fold, almost contradictory challenge: it is necessary to *enliven* some notes while *taming* others. That applies to all the tones that lie on strong resonances. When the effort to tame those notes is successful, something unbelievably appealing unfolds: the instrument's strengths start to interplay with its tone colors. It is different for notes whose harmonic components find no resonance in the violin's body. Those have to be *enlivened*. This happens when the bow stroke or vibrato is adjusted to let their overtones lean on the side flanks of strong resonances. A good violinist does all of this intuitively. She does not need to think about it as she plays because she feels the response, the liveliness, and the contrariness of the tones under her fingers.

A good violin will never capitulate to the violinist—the two are equals. It is her second teacher and will teach her how to form the sound and make it sing. A good instrument requires the musician to discover the sound. Something mundane is obvious: it cannot be "discovered," and we do not long for it. An ordinary violin can be put to use, but its sound will never come alive. One need not tame or conquer it because it has no strong resonances. The interplay between familiarity and surprise, closeness and resistance, can be obtained only with a good violin. The same principle found in Balthasar Neumann's structure is fulfilled in good sound. There is no inspiration in mere familiarity and, likewise, no communication in the totally foreign.

~

Our question of what makes something beautiful has not been answered exhaustively. Yet, clearly, the unfolding of an alluring power, charm, or strength is not merely random. That which has grace, what takes your breath away, an image or experience that you carry with you for years is not arbitrary. There is a basis for beauty. Those who seek access to the rule of beauty or vitality must enter that rule and follow its laws. You don't *have* to be interested in the profound laws of beauty, at least not if you're content with turning the successful outcome of your life over to chance. We decide for ourselves if we are the consumers or the artists of our own existence. The consumer does not need to understand. The artist, however, must have a deep certainty concerning which laws allow or forbid him to pursue and express what he seeks and wants.

We find this fundamental principle of beauty again in the laws of relationships. When successful, they too will encompass familiarity and surprise, expectancy and fulfillment. Within our relationships we can experience a mundane cycle in which crises disturb our sense of togetherness. And if the disruption is too great, we separate.

But what's true for a violin's resonance is also true here: development and uniformity, the lively and the banal, are mutually exclusive. To search for development in our life together while rejecting surprises is like putting a square peg in a round hole. Existence with no crisis, an instrument with no resonance, and a mere circle have this in common: they lack development. One response is to give up on an underdeveloped relationship rather than work on it. But this is to insult our potential to learn, discover, communicate, form, grow and mature.

In a *banal* relationship we seek nothing more intently than our own peace and are therefore incapable of understanding crises and meeting them as opportunities. Beauty's second abyss is randomness. There is nothing to discern in a *random* relationship. It is like a string that, because of an overly strong resonance, can no longer find a state of stable vibration. Cellists call these infamous sounds "wolf notes" thanks to their flickering, howling tones. A "wolf" extracts excess energy from the string's vibrations. Because of the body's strong resonance, the vibrating string cannot deliver the amount of energy being extracted from it and the vibration collapses in on itself. Only a few notes do this, but it is a real problem.

Our relationships and friendships can be burdened by such "wolf notes" when our detached nature (that is, an excess of randomness) drains our partner of all her energy. Such a relationship, lacking dependability, cannot have any beauty because a friendship or a marriage needs both. If my wife were only *familiar* to me, our relationship would be stale; if she were only *surprising*, then being together would get too complicated. A vibrant relationship craves this interplay: it is important that we remain trustworthy and *familiar*, and yet not lose sight of our imagination in order to *surprise* each other. Yet again it comes back to the founding principles of beauty.

In the floor plan of Balthasar Neumann's structure, I uncovered the principle of changing patterns. In the years that followed, I applied these foundational ideas to all areas of my life, first for the violin's pattern and sound, then to my relationships with others, but doubtless most intensely to my faith. More and more I got the impression that the beauty of harmonious opposites runs through all the great themes of Scripture.

Crisis and Revelation

I can no longer separate faith in God and a resonant life; they blend into each other. Through loving the one, you experience the other. This is more than a metaphor. You recognize the same truths and see the same things in both.

Through the harmony of opposites, I understand the life of Jesus in an exceptional, new light. What do the pattern and the disruption of the pattern look like here? It is the concept of trust and crisis. What Jesus embodies could not be more contradictory. Instead of the great messianic prototype that Jesus's disciples and many contemporaries had expected, his entry into the holy city ended in a catastrophe. Instead of working a miracle, the hero is nailed to a cross. The pattern of established messianic thinking is contradicted with unsurpassed brutality.

There are only two types of truly existential surprises in human life: one is *crisis* and the other is *revelation*. At these moments it becomes crystal clear that ideas about harmonious opposites have nothing to do with a saccharine glorification of life. If I am to follow the spirit of the floor plan of Neumann's cathedral, then the point where I'm deflected from the familiarity of the circle is nothing other than the crisis of the cross.

Our set pattern is here unsettled. If Jesus's life were all godly splendor, then I would give this hero a place in a legend but not in my own life, for he would have little to do with me. A simple circle, easy to figure out. An instrument with no resonance, whose vibrations are undisturbed. Nothing to animate, nothing to tame. The cross makes it clear that it is not messianic transfiguration that touches my heart. The glorified splendor of heaven is in one sphere, whereas the inglorious degradation of my own world is right here. If we are to see more than half the picture, then something *must* be shaken up.

"But we had hoped . . ."—these are the disappointed words of the two disciples on their way from Jerusalem to a village called Emmaus (Luke 24:21). It was three days after Jesus had been crucified. Their faith in a messianic hero who would free people from the adversities of their lives has been shattered. The clichéd hope for a messianic liberator has been transformed into deep disappointment. The pattern has devolved into an existential crisis.

"But we had hoped . . ."—it was a hope for the predictable godlike pattern. Familiar and trite. When Jesus entered Jerusalem a few days earlier, hailed by expectant, palm-waving crowds, everything was still on track, staying true to the simple, unbroken pattern. "God's glory is dawning! All who oppose his power will be ashamed! We will be on the side of the victor!"

The background music for this power fantasy can be heard in the disciples' words in the Gospel of Luke: "Lord, do you want us to command fire to come down from heaven and consume them?" (9:54). At that moment, Jesus turned and rebuked the disciples, because he knew that the relationship between heaven and earth is more complex. The disciples' clichéd faith inevitably breaks on the cross. How their worldview is threatened as their ears ring with the hammer strikes nailing Jesus to the cross!

Trust and the Cross

In the life of Christ, we find two age-old polar opposites of human existence: the inhumane *crisis of the cross* and the superhuman *authoritative power of trust*. Through both the cross and trust the floor plan is more clearly visible.

The Bible is full of the turning points of crisis and revelation. These are phenomenal moments experienced by various people: the ladder to heaven, the burning bush, the covenant on Mt. Sinai, among others.[6] Each of these moments is paradoxical: the extraordinary always targets the ordinary, surprise aims at the familiar, crisis at stability. How can this be understood?

The objective here is not for us to cry out: "Look how surprising and extraordinary God is!" Rather, the opposite: "You can trust God in the ordinariness of your life. He has shown himself to you for the sake of familiarity and trust." The paradox of revelation lies in the tension between the extraordinary and the ordinary, surprise and familiarity, a single moment and sustainability, crisis and stability. These contradictory aspects are purposely set against each other. Without them our lives can hardly have strength and beauty. Revelatory moments cannot create stability if I do not understand their message. That is what we mean by "lessons learned from experience." The experiences are surprising; the lessons provide stability. Each crisis shows us that we cannot subdue life, not in the least. The revelation itself is critical: what has existed up to now is called into question. A true revelation turns into a decisive turning point. It will transform life. And our false notions about God and ourselves will turn and flee.

~

Just as the radius leaves its familiar track at the breaking point, the catastrophe of the cross reveals an abrupt deflection. The church fathers called this point a *tropaion*. The word comes from the ancient Greek concept of *trope: to turn* or *to escape*. This was the word for the sign marking the point on the battlefield where the enemy had turned around and fled. It was usually a wooden stake on which the weapons or armor of the defeated were tied.

In this sense, the crucifixion is a living *tropaion*. The weapons of the evil one are tied to it, the utter scorn and hate that drove the nails into the body of the righteous One. But it is also the place where the enemy turned tail and fled the battlefield. No one could have imagined love of such supreme power as when Jesus said, "Father, forgive them; for they know not what they do" (Luke 23:34 RSV).

The first *tropaion* is said to have been erected by the Greeks after their victory in the battle of Marathon in 490 BC. It looks like a "military scarecrow" with a human appearance composed of helmet, shield, sword, lance, and the enemies' outer garments. In this way, the picture of the bleeding Christ has become a *tropaion* in our world: disfigured and mocked in human form, made like a scarecrow in scorn and hate.

A powerful statement is found here. It tells not of the Messiah's splendor, not the success of the strong, but rather of the faith of the outcast, the hope of the oppressed, the faithfulness of the called, the love of the reviled. There is no chance of making up a success story with this statement. Rather, a faith that takes this seriously contains salvation. After all, our world's motto, "I am, if I am successful," is an unbearable sellout. When such a statement dresses up in religi-

osity it is a sacrilegious belittling of God. A religion in which success
and blessing are perfectly congruent has nothing to tell the world,
because that religion says what the world itself is already saying.

The people stand under the cross ridiculing the dying person.
They remain true to their simple pattern and call for a strong god:
fulfill our pattern, for we want to believe! In the words of the Gospel
of Mark, "'Save yourself, and come down from the cross!' . . . 'He saved
others; he cannot save himself. Let the Christ, the King of Israel, come
down from the cross now, so that we may see and believe.' Those who
were crucified with him also taunted him" (Mark 15:30–32).

In Jesus's trust and the *tropaion* of the cross lies a powerful contradiction. His life shows nothing of the trite piety of an unbroken
circle, nor any denial of crisis—but likewise, no randomness of form,
which, when confronted by crisis, cannot inspire trust. Jesus brings
both the power of life and the power of death into effect: the power
to dare to trust and not allow oneself to be broken by crisis. In Jesus,
I see the *whole* picture, not a belittling half-truth. No simple pattern.
No cheap faith and no cheap doubt, but rather trust in what is stable
and the courage to embrace turning points.

Jesus is arrested, tried, whipped, and broken, but he does not
sing out, "Your love is so beautiful!" He rather cries, "My God, my
God, why have you forsaken me?" This is the great deflection point.
Jesus cries out with millions of others, and because his life was the
epitome of trust, he suffers an infinite pain in his abandonment. God
was not numb to anything in Jesus's life, but now in God's silence,
everything vulnerable in him is wounded. Jesus's outcry on the cross
comes from the beginning of Psalm 22. It is shallow to think that he
was merely quoting those words. In fact, he was pierced through by
them and would fully experience them until the end.

That cry from the psalms was written hundreds of years earlier
as a song for Israel:

My God, my God, why have you forsaken me? O my God, I cry
out by day, but you do not answer me. I am scorned by men and
despised by the people. All who see me mock me; they hurl insults,
shaking their heads: He trusts in the Lord, let the Lord rescue him,
since he delights in him.

I am poured out like water, and all my bones are out of joint. My heart has turned to wax; it has melted away within me. My strength is dried up like a potsherd, and my tongue sticks to the roof of my mouth; You lay me in the dust of death. Dogs have surrounded me; a band of evil men has encircled me; they have pierced my hands and my feet. They divide my garments among them and cast lots for my clothing. (from Psalm 22)

They had cast lots for his clothing at the beginning, and then they pierced his hands and feet. The mocking followed: "Come down from the cross and we will believe!" Then came the answer to his cry: "When some of those standing near heard this, they said, 'Listen, he's calling Elijah.' Someone ran, filled a sponge with wine vinegar, put it on a stick, and offered it to Jesus to drink. 'Now leave him alone. Let's see if Elijah comes to take him down,' he said. With a loud cry, Jesus breathed his last. The curtain of the temple was torn in two from top to bottom. And when the centurion, who stood there in front of Jesus, saw how he died, he said, 'Surely this man was the Son of God!'" (Mark 15:35-39 NIV).

The disciples ran away; at Jesus's arrest their precious pattern was broken and they had to forsake everything that had made sense for them up to that point. Their faith in the hero-god shatters. "All of them deserted him and fled" (Mark 14:50). This deflection point slays every hope. On resurrection day, the transformation occurs. Death, I am poison to you! Where is your sting? Where is your victory? Mortality is swallowed up by life. A new pattern emerges.

The first two deflection points—the disciples' faith breaking and Jesus breaking on the cross—are completely of this world. The following deflection points, Easter and Pentecost, are not of this world. Easter is a baptism in the assurance: "He lives!" But Pentecost plunges the disciples yet again into something new: the outpouring of the Holy Spirit! According to Orthodox Christian texts, the whole world received the baptism of light on Pentecost.[7]

Four deflection points have thus been revealed to us, and they allow a new pattern to develop. It is like heaven giving two simple answers to the world's outcry. Crisis and revelation speak clearly: if you want to be a strong person, then you must be *not only* of this world.[8] Faith in Jesus will never entail a contemplative retreat into an inner world but will defy every crisis to its face. It is only when we see that crisis and familiarity build the whole picture *together* that we learn to affirm that which life entrusts to and expects of us. The completed pattern says: Have courage! Have faith! That is the profound authority that will change you and present you to the world as a changed person.

The Confidence of the Beloved

The supreme pattern of Jesus's life is not made manifest in new wisdom or a new morality—what he offered had long been present.[9] Instead, his life shows us how this knowledge can be put into practice. The "lesson" to be learned from Jesus's life is in his complete trust, which made it clear how much a person who relies on God can achieve. What was Jesus's theology? Trust alone. As the Colombian author Nicolás Gómez Dávila puts it: "So great is the distance between God and human intelligence that only a childlike theology is not childish."[10]

Both the cross and the trust in Jesus's life are of primordial dimensions. Together they create the whole pattern. Jesus called God "Abba," an endearing term for *father*, like the word *papa*. The term resonates with deeply intimate familiarity, love, and nearness. It has no hint of formality and stiffness. It expresses a deep love for God.

I am convinced that exploratory knowledge about God can find its source only in a childlike trust. It was the root of Jesus's appeal. Being true to Jesus is to ask: Is my life filled with trust? Am I capable of trusting more deeply, more completely? We do not need to worry about the deflection points. Trust is the one gift that can bring our existence close to heaven and strengthen us to live a new pattern.

I would like to tell a story about my own children that taught me about this kind of trust. Lorenz was seven years old at the time, and he knew quite well that my work breaks are sacred—a cappuccino, the newspaper, and finally a little peace. My son saw me sitting there. He pushed in under my newspaper, crawled up on my lap, and said, "OK, make some room here!" He shoved the paper away, took my arm and laid it on his stomach, leaned back and put his head on my shoulder. I had to chuckle. Lorenz knew that he was being cheeky by interrupting my break, and he awaited my response of feigned shock.

The nature of his trust became a metaphor for me. Lorenz was looking for closeness. He knew this was not the right moment, but he also knew that I liked his self-assured approach. He who knows he is loved does not come as a beggar. He walks upright and self-assured. He also does not come only when he has something to show off. He can reveal his needs because he knows he is loved. When we have the confidence of the beloved, we need not be ashamed. When we are loved, we do not need to prove anything to each other. Who we truly are only manifests itself in love.

I remember another instance, an experience my wife had as a young student teacher at a special school for children with learning disabilities. She began the class every day with a prayer. At the end of this little devotional time, the children could present prayer requests for themselves. In the class was a nine-year-old girl who had multiple, inoperable brain tumors. She was almost blind as a result. Yet her childlike trust moved both of us. If my wife had a cold or something was going on with a fellow student, you could be sure that Karin would use the prayer time to pray unpretentiously and faithfully for them.

One morning Karin prayed for something unusual. She was relatively unathletic and hated gym class, so she prayed: "Dear God, please let gym class be cancelled today!" The wise and gentle teacher's answer was of course: "Karin, I don't think that the good Lord can answer this prayer. As you know, we have PE today, and when we are done with our prayer time, we will head over there." When the class went to the gym that afternoon, workers came unannounced to begin a welding project. PE had to be cancelled. Of course, the story made its way around the school and moved the teachers to amused amazement. Karin, standing nearby, gave my wife a happily defiant nod and said, "And next week I'll pray it again!" She became a great example for us in that respect. Both elements were in her life, a burden and a strength, and *neither* could be explained.

⌒

What pain we inflict on our souls when, as adults, we get accustomed to replacing our lost trust with hurts and disappointment!

We present ourselves as sophisticated, enlightened, reasonable, and free of delusions because we have lost what is essential: the ability, in spite of adversities, to entrust ourselves to the Love from which we come, out of which we live, and back to which, in all our brokenness but also fruitfulness, we will give ourselves in the end. The summary of all I have learned from my children is that *children take it for granted that they are loved!* In their child-like trust, they serve as a role model for us. The truth of Jesus prompts our deep healing. As he himself says: "Unless you change and become like children, you will never enter the kingdom of heaven" (Matthew 18:3).

Trust and crisis often come side by side. Indeed the whole Bible is evidence of this truth. As in the floor plan of Balthasar Neumann's Basilica (see p. 59), the deflection point causes the contour to follow a different track and curve. When we emerge from the deflection point, in spite of grief and disappointment, our lives take on new depth and meaning.

Word Pairs

Harmonious opposites always create a *double word pair.* So far we've considered one such—*familiarity and surprise*, with their negative reflection *boredom and randomness.* We aim to live in the first pair and avoid the second; we see what beauty requires of us and what puts us in a precarious state. We have each been entrusted to ourselves, and with God's mindset, we can see our soul as a friend and say: "Look, my friend, you are beautiful!" (see Song of Solomon 4:1). But this requires work and understanding.

We are sent out on a path, a human path. In this I see a loving act of God, as it appears in the most important command of Judaism: "Love the Lord your God with all your heart, and with all your soul, and with all your might" (Deuteronomy 6:5; Matthew 22:37-38). With *all* your soul. What is it that makes for the soul's beauty; how can we better understand the inner workings of our soul's strength?[11]

In the next chapter ("Tone Colors"), I will discuss certain other harmonious opposites, but first let's look at some foundational concepts about the beauty of opposites.

The Ugliness of the Solitary Good

The word pair *passion and serenity* establishes an essential contradiction for our inner lives.

Imagine a person who pursues his convictions with great passion. He recognizes his calling in them. He dedicates himself to whatever his calling demands with tireless devotion. The tasks that come with this calling touch and move him; they uncover a *creative restlessness* in him. He puts his time and thoughts, his gifts and strengths into this pursuit. For him, this commitment is living faith. He well recognizes King David's words to his son Solomon about building the great temple in Jerusalem: "Now begin the work, and the Lord be with you" (1 Chronicles 22:16).

On the other side we see the person with great *serenity*. He also has convictions and recognizes his calling. He does not have a heart that fights, but one that waits expectantly. There is a *faithful peace* in him, for he knows that the essential things in life cannot be produced but rather received. His heart understands the expectant gaze toward heaven. He knows what it means to wait. Even in troubles and need he seeks to be quiet before God. How many times has he found that the important things come about without him struggling! He recognizes the solace of his calling. He has experienced that "the Lord will fight for you, and you have only to keep still" (Exodus 14:14).

The passionate and the serene can be two different kinds of people. They can also be two different strengths of our own inner life. For the two to form harmonious opposites the *one* good thing respects the *other* opposing good thing and understands it as a blessing. That is the essence of unity that lives within all harmonious opposites.

Alongside word pairs, we are reminded by Martin Buber, in his famous work *I and Thou*, of *primary words*, words that are spoken out of one's whole being and that involve personal participation: "When a primary word is spoken, the speaker enters the word and takes his stand in it."[12] Primary words create space and seek a living manifestation in us. The question then becomes, what breadth or narrowness will they find there? The breadth of the *communal good*? Or a solitary good that makes our space and substance small and tight?

The glorification of the *solitary good* results in a lifeless, spiritually narrow-minded state because the solitary good is not capable of unity. The solitary passion that knows nothing of serenity is not passion, but *fanaticism.* The solitary serenity that knows nothing of passion is not serenity, but *indifference.*

Indifferent people risk nothing. They never venture something important or valuable. They would never come up with the idea of investing in something beyond the state of their own interests. They are content with everything as long as it does not affect them. They regard themselves above all else. They are prisoners to themselves.

Fanatics risk everything and everyone. They wear themselves out over matters and are never satisfied. They are possessed by an idea and blind to anything and everyone that are not part of it. They see the injustices that, in their eyes, should be rectified, and believe that everything depends on their own efforts. They, too, only regard themselves in the end. They, too, are their own prisoners.

Fanaticism and indifference create a word pair of their own. But they are the fallen reflection of passion and serenity. Each exaggerates itself. That is the essence of fallen opposites. Opposites that do not preserve unity signify alienation. Harmonious opposites are different: they are oriented toward each other. Their relationship invariably consists of giving esteem and honor to the Non-Me. Their essence is consistent with the order of love.

Space to Live in the Opposites

We could come up with countless examples of harmonious opposites and their fallen reflections. This is not a matter of mere words, however, but of their power that works in us. The fallen reflection follows a similar pattern. They try to justify themselves by belittling or judging the corresponding good:

› To the fanatic, *serenity* is indifference; to the indifferent, *passion* is fanaticism.
› To stingy people, *generosity* is an addiction to wastefulness; to the wasteful, *thrift* signifies stinginess.

> To the legalist, *freedom* is arbitrariness; for the uncommitted, *loyalty* means legalism[13] (in terms of religious compulsion, compare with Chapter 5).
> The self-seeking despise *commitment* to a close community as sect-like; in a sect-like community the *character* of a mature person looks suspicious and selfishly individualistic.

What traps us in a fallen condition is our own *self-righteousness*: the glorification of the *solitary* (usually *our own*) *good.* The immature person lives by his own self-righteousness in unredeemed strength. He glorifies his one-dimensional nature. He makes himself the norm and declares that this spiritual handicap should be highly sought after.

Life in harmonious opposites is different. In it, the person carries within himself the ability to change patterns. Changes in pattern are an essential component of beauty, as is apparent in Balthasar Neumann's cathedrals, Mozart's symphonies, and Stradivarius's violins. In the end, pattern changing is a sign of inner maturity. A person who can unfurl the restlessness of passion and yet always come back to rest in serenity is able to move his soul between patterns. In this way, harmonious opposites challenge us to spiritual vitality.

The Mistake of the Golden Mean

Every person has predispositions and influences that leave him with weak "spiritual muscles" in certain areas. Just as our arm can only move because flexor and extensor muscles are set against each other, so our spiritual life has inner freedom and mobility when opposites serve each other. And as with the arm, only when one muscle releases can the other muscle work. Otherwise we cramp up and cannot move. The muscles work in a harmonious interplay in *opposition* against each other, and yet only in that way can they work with each other.

The principle of harmonious opposites is, therefore, not a "golden mean." To choose a golden mean between flexor and extensor muscles in the arm would result in both muscles tensing a bit so that neither would be stronger than the other. The arm would remain in a straight position, unmoving. The concept of harmonious opposites teaches that spiritual mobility comes about only when one of these strengths releases at the right time.

To put it in terms of a landscape, living in harmonious opposites is not a "balancing act," a sharply crowned highway where a steep drop-off threatens on the right and the left. A better picture is of two mountain peaks with a wide expanse stretching out between them. That gives spiritual room for living. There is no ridge of solitary good but, rather, a space with corresponding opposite strengths that bless us. When spiritual pitfalls present themselves, it means that the relationship to the necessary opposite has been lost. I understand the "hardening of one's heart" to mean that a person, in his own self-righteousness, refuses to leave the place where he has fallen. He denies himself the room for living that is available for the sake of his maturation.

To love God *with all your soul* is to pay attention to the powers that work in *pairs*, for they expand our spiritual living space. To hold only to one or the other—*only* passion or *only* serenity—is to love the Lord with *half of your soul.* It is the same with all the other harmonious opposites, whether loyalty and freedom, love and reverence. In the midst of life's challenges, the solitary good will turn negative. It does not hold up, but collapses. When that occurs, spiritual mobility is *unnecessary*, but unfortunately, it is also *impossible.*

Spiritual Revival

When our inner life is trapped by one-sidedness and the liberating pattern change cannot be made, how can we acquire the missing good? Two concepts can help: *sincere respect* and the *power of words.*

Sincere Respect

We have emphasized that a negative fall is not caused by a positive trait becoming too strong or distinct, as if fanaticism is merely "extreme passion" or indifference merely "extreme serenity." It is not that simple and would imply that we should change everything into a lukewarm mediocrity where nothing is allowed to be strong, marked, distinct, or outstanding. Spiritual strength does not make things happen in safe mediocrity with a good dose of consensus; rather, "for everything there is a season" (Ecclesiastes 3:1) and for everything there is a measure. This is how inner space and spiritual power develop.

The apostle Paul says: "Rejoice with those who rejoice, weep with those who weep" (Romans 12:15). In other words, live in *both* and participate in *both* at the appropriate time. Life is not about a quiet state, a "happy medium" free of vibrations, where there is neither laughing nor crying, no song of praise and no song of sorrow, no doubt and no hope, neither good jokes nor powerful prayer, but everything is just lying somewhere in between. That would be a pathetic goal for our inner self. Instead of experiencing an interplay of energies, life would be stifled and finally robbed of any soul whatsoever.

If the soul is suffering because it is stuck in a fallen state, then the cure is not *stifling* but *enlivening*. In the example above, to be a bit less fanatical or a bit less indifferent would be to stifle. To enliven is to come to the place where *both* strengths are potent and can share with each other. How can that happen?

Our spiritual strengths are enlivened when we see and respect *the other* good (the *weakened* good) in ourselves. The secret is to take ownership more and more of the good that is missing or wounded in us by meeting it with respect. Like the respect between the roots and leaves I mentioned in the previous chapter, this has a creative and healing power.

We are called to nurture ourselves, to sanctify our lives, by respecting what is weak in us and thereby strengthening the weak places. By the same token, we will not allow what is strong in us to become more and more solitary by being self-satisfied. Instead, we lead that strength to humility. In other words: if our strengths can be humbled, what is weak in us will be strengthened. Without this humility, every strength becomes a weakness and every gift a sin. What Paul said to the Philippians is valid, not just for reconciling people within a community, but also, less obviously, for reconciliation inside one's holy spiritual world: "In humility value others above yourselves" (2:3 NIV).

The Power of the Word

When we get used to voicing that which we consider good and praise-worthy, we experience a profound power transforming us. For *words* steer our process of *becoming*. Here we find the secret of blessing and cursing. From recent studies we know that the speech area in the brain has a strong influence on other areas of the brain as well. The letter of James expresses the power of the "tongue" with two images: "Take ships as an example. Although they are so large and are driven by strong winds, they are steered by a very small rudder wherever the pilot wants to go. Likewise, the tongue is a small part of the body, but it makes great boasts. Consider what a great forest is set on fire by a small spark" (James 3:4-5 NIV).

The words we speak convey not only information; they carry within them a creative power. Through our words we take part in an activated strength. As the earliest history says: "and God said, 'Let there be light'" and it happened (Genesis 1). Humans have had some of this power "loaned" to us. We are made in God's image: by speaking, by articulating "action" words, we witness an interior and exterior effect. Therefore, the beginning of every change starts with our owning it through *respecting* it and *emphasizing* it with our words. That is how the word became light and immersed the world in meaning and, subsequently, into reality. So, pay attention to your words—most important, what you say about yourself. Our words may be used for or against ourselves—for good or for evil. This very truth is laid powerfully on our hearts by the wisdom found in Proverbs: "The tongue has the power of life and death" (18:21 NIV).

The connection of sincere respect and the spoken word may also capture some aspects of our spiritual revival. The Torah's saying, "Be holy!" is written in the active voice. This means you participate in making your soul come alive; you have co-ownership of your inner beauty! Every person is given to himself or herself; we are entrusted to ourselves. God will not replace that which he asks of us and entrusts to us with himself.

The Beautiful and the Ugly

We also discover these thoughts concerning the harmony of opposites hidden in the ancient Chinese teachings on wisdom as expressed in *The Beautiful and the Ugly* (300 BC):

> When Chuang-tzu came to the state of Sung, he spent a night in a hostel. The innkeeper had two wives, one beautiful and one ugly. He honored the ugly one; he disdained the beautiful one. Chuang-tzu asked the innkeeper's servant why this was so. He answered, "The beautiful one knows about her beauty, and we do not see her beauty. The ugly one knows about her ugliness, and we do not see her ugliness."[14]

After all that has been said, it is not hard to understand this story. It tells us: if you are a passionate person, then know that serenity is beauty; but if you are a serene person, then know that passion is beauty. If you love your freedom, consider loyalty as beauty, but if you are a loyal person, consider freedom as beauty. If you give yourself spiritually to the "we" of a community, then know that your "me" is beauty. If your "me" asserts itself over commitment to a communal life, then know that the "we" is beauty.

In this way we behold our soul's opposing strengths. We strengthen our weaknesses through respect. We take ownership more and more through respecting the good that is missing or wounded within us.

FLOOR PLAN FOR THE BASILICA OF THE FOURTEEN HOLY HELPERS

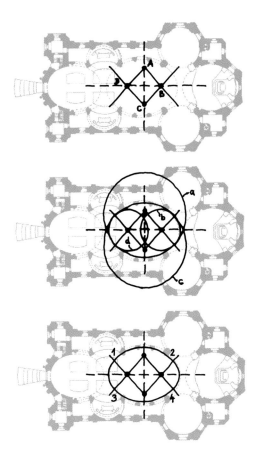

Balthasar Neumann's sketches for building the Basilica of the Fourteen Holy Helpers show the following:

- The basis of the oval is made by a square (corners A, B, C, D), whose edges are lengthened to the right and left.
- The four corners of the square are also the midpoints of four circles (a, b, c, d).
- These circles create four circle segments, out of which the oval is eventually pieced together. With this, the four deflecting points arise (1, 2, 3, 4). At these points, the oval's outline holds steady, but its curve breaks form.

04

Tone Colors

Beauty's Vulnerability

How beautiful you are, my love!

—SONG OF SOLOMON 4:1

*J*UST AS THE OUTER BEAUTY of the violin, like Balthasar Neumann's basilica, follows the concept of the harmony of opposites, so does the allure of the sound. From intensive work on the tone colors of my instruments I have learned that they have much to teach us.

The Teacher

In the years after I received my degree as a violinmaker, my mentor, the acoustician Helmut A. Müller, opened an important door for me by offering me a position as a violinmaker in his company. For about forty years, he had driven to my violinmaking school in Mittenwald to teach the fundamentals of physics to the students there. Only after my apprenticeship did I witness him in his own domain, the Advisory Bureau for Sound Technology in Munich, and understand what he was in "real life": a world-renowned expert in the field of room acoustics. The acoustical concepts and planning of numerous famous European concert halls can be traced back to his pen.

An international symposium for musical acoustics was scheduled to take place in Mittenwald, and he planned to do research in preparation. So as a brand-new luthier in his company, I was allowed to set up a little violin workshop between the architects' offices and the climate-controlled rooms for the mainframe computers. The tremendous possibilities of vibration physics were my first opening into a new world. I could finally follow up on the basic questions that had haunted me during my luthier training. How does good sound originate? What is the acoustical difference between a good violin and a bad one? What influence does the varnish have? Which tone colors are affected by gradations in the thickness? What do the wood's medullary rays do for the violin's capacity to transfer sound? At school I had continually pestered Mr. Müller with these questions, in class and after hours. When, to my great surprise and joy, he offered me a position at his institute, he gave me the chance to pursue these questions myself.

While my violin teacher, Attila Balogh, played a significant part in my decision to become a violinmaker, Mr. Müller, as my mentor, set the course for the way I practice my profession. When I started my studies at Mittenwald, I had just finished the tenth grade. In retrospect, my experiences in school to that point had been a long series of answers to questions I never asked. What interested me never came up in school. My repeated inappropriate comments in class, which teachers took note of in my seventh-grade file, brought me to the verge of temporary expulsion from the public school in Marbach am Neckar. Luckily, just then my family moved to a new city, so I could begin anew with good intentions in Beilstein, just twenty minutes north of Marbach. Admittedly, I started out there, too, by being called repeatedly to the principal's office, but over time that cleared up.

After tenth grade, I had the minimum schooling required to enter a technical college, so I was able to start my studies at the violinmaking institute in Mittenwald. Each year, out of hundreds of local and international applicants, only twelve were chosen. Now the old question and answer game was suddenly reversed. The more violinmaking took hold of me, the more I was moved by questions no one was answering. This was simply because no one had yet found the answers. I remember how one of my teachers lost his temper and gave me, as a first-year student, an unmistakable "answer." I had asked, once again, why we were to undertake a certain thickness gradation one way and not another, when suddenly he hit the workbench with the palm of his hand. The loud crack was followed by dead silence in the workshop filled with around twenty other beginning violinmaking students. Then he yelled that if I wanted to do everything differently, I should pack my little bag and go. In short, it was a blessing for me to finally be able to pursue these unanswered questions at my mentor's physics institute. Exploring sound had taken hold of me and refused to let go.

Curiously, Helmut A. Müller, who considered teaching a hobby and had never studied pedagogy, was the best teacher I ever had. To this day I cannot think of a better mentor. I had the feeling he did not want to teach as much as help students with the learning process. He provided stimuli, and students felt alert and animated. As a student, you got the feeling you were discovering things yourself in that very moment. Müller taught by serving, and this resulted in his undeniable authority. Perhaps his wisdom also came from knowing how limited our knowledge truly is. He himself continued to be a humble seeker and researcher, a learner.

The truly good teacher does not want to *teach*, but to *learn*. A teacher who truly wants to learn is successful with students because his attitude is contagious. Müller always encouraged us to question things and to be amazed. Together we would work toward solutions, and nothing was more satisfying than real questions being answered in an "aha" moment. To be completely mentally present was very rewarding. He had nothing to do with the patronizing, humorless, domineering style of teaching that makes it crystal clear how superior the teacher is to the students. I remember Müller once saying that the teacher needs to be only one hour ahead of the student in preparation; that should suffice.

During Friday afternoon symposium discussions with physicists and engineers, conversations that completely overwhelmed me, I witnessed his brilliance from a completely different angle—as a scientist. He always presented his answers at the questioner's level. I once talked to him about how he successfully explained things to simple violin-making students like us in ways we could understand. He smiled sheepishly and said, "I believe that if you cannot express something *simply*, then you really don't understand it thoroughly yourself." Apparently, we forced him to thoroughly understand things.

As one of the preeminently gifted acousticians of his time, Müller continually reminded student luthiers that understanding physics alone was not enough. The ear, he emphasized, plays the decisive role. "You must learn to listen closely and accurately. You must acquire an intuition for the sound and document exactly what you do when making an instrument." With his emphasis on the empirical, he undoubtedly pointed us in the right direction. No top-down academic approach will hit the mark, as if these problems could be solved by simple formulas. When you are in the thick of the work, the violin being built in your hands is not just a technical object but something that appeals to the senses and to the human soul. It is absolutely necessary to trust yourself in the task.

The possibilities at Müller's company were overwhelming. I learned about modal analysis, an empirical method that originated in aviation and space-travel technology and began using it on the violin's design. Back then, no one had ever done that. Now, for the first time, we could *see* how the violin vibrates: the bulging breath in the deepest eigenfrequencies; the body's strong torsion in the middle registers; the extensive motion of the plates in the main resonances with broad, displaced areas around the bass bar; all the little vibrating islands in the higher frequencies in which the violin's front and back divide into numerous membrane-like areas, oscillating against each other. To see the vibrations forming in their diversity and brilliancy was like a revelation: we were discerning what had previously been hidden. Finally, the origins of sound were visible. We presented the results at the International Symposium on Musical Acoustics in 1989.

The longer I worked on modal analysis, the clearer it became that, while I had indeed gotten intriguing empirical outcomes, I did not yet truly understand the theoretical background. Therefore, Müller told me that I should go back to school and get my GED so that I could start studying physics as soon as possible. I did just that. During those years I was allowed to keep a key to his business, despite not being steadily employed there. I used my little but unique "research workshop" to take technical measurements. I could come and go as I pleased and continue researching to my heart's content. After graduation, I secured an internship as a violinmaker, then took the master's exam, and finally had my own master studio with an acoustical laboratory.

Acoustic Space

I would now like to share the secret of the violin's tone colors, because they serve as a magnificent metaphor for the "tone colors" of the human soul.

Eigenvibrations are the acoustic essence of a violin. They shape all the tones we hear. Over the years I have heard fabulous violins played in concert halls, instruments that I already know from the intimate acoustic space of my studio. One violin that I found especially impressive is a 1721 Stradivarius. It sounds calm and composed, has a clear tone, yet fills the concert hall with all its spaciousness. It has a passionate tone but is never harsh. The sound can become as dark as a musty cellar, yet remain recognizable. This violin can hiss and snarl without sounding vulgar. Its sweetness in the higher registers is somehow sensuous without being trite. In all this you can hear that it does not speak with just one voice. Different sound patterns are at work in it simultaneously.

These contradictions make the sound's allure; they create acoustic space. A fascinating sound always emerges out of ambiguity. Without ambiguity, the sound would be trite and one-dimensional. Through these inflections the tone colors first acquire the life and charm that makes them so human. For me, the malleability of the sound is the most important feature of a truly good violin. It lets you move through the sound. There is an ambiguity between warmth and brilliance in the tone color: the warmth is not muffled, and the brilliance is not harsh, because warmth and brilliance maintain an auditory relationship in every tone. They build tonal harmonious opposites.

The same thing is true for dynamics. With a truly good violin you can modulate the dynamics to create a piano that takes your breath away in its tenderness, yet can unleash a roaring, snarling fortissimo that cannot be resisted. These ranges create a space. It is the result of reconciled contradictions. How small and lifeless, how artificial and unrealistic are spaces free of contradictions!

The sound of a good violin is an example of harmonious opposites. On the one side is warmth, dynamics, spaciousness, "guts"; on the other side, brilliance, radiant strength, focus, and clarity. Without the second, the sound would be dull and flat, without the first, it would be penetrating and sharp. As the pitfalls to the right and left show themselves, we understand more fully the wide tonal space opened up by a good sound.

A great sound is not a cowardly mixture of everything. It is not a little warmth and a little brilliance, a little bit of this and a little bit of that. It resounds with the *whole* of both elements! Only in the space of harmonious opposites can sound and beauty expand. This is a basic truth that has been poured out into the audible world. It is what is shown in the floor plan of Balthasar Neumann's cathedral: it is the harmony of opposites.

Resonances

A good violin has at least eighty resonances in its playing range. Each one radiates a unique directional effect and frequency so that we can hear the instrument's tone. Through vibrato in the violinist's left hand emerges an "acoustical fire." The hand's quick oscillatory movements modulate the way in which the string's harmonics excite the resonances of the instrument's body. That animated resonance contributes to the perceived tone color. Without resonances, the instrument would have no personality.

If we envision what resonance really is, we find that it comes from a continual interplay between two forms of energy; during each vibration-cycle the energy changes twice, back and forth between potential and kinetic energy. It is this interplay of strengths and energies that brings out the vibration and with it, the radiation of sound. Potential energy is like the energy of a spring under tension; kinetic energy is the energy of movement. Tension and movement are necessary opposites oriented toward each other. If there were no interplay between them, no sound could be heard.

Spiritual life is also defined by inner strengths. Tension and motion, expectancy and fulfillment, hope and action—what we associate with these word pairs resembles the potential energy and the kinetic energy of resonance. Just as diverse resonances form a violin's resonance profile, giving it tone color and charisma, so does the power of "spiritual resonances" define a person's character. They affect the "tone color" that we project. The pairs of strengths throw their own light on our inmost being and the calling of our human existence.

Here are seven "resonances of spiritual life" we encounter in Scripture:

> grace and works
> powerless and powerful
> allowing and forming
> hearing and doing
> "you are" and "you should"
> truth and kindness
> complete and preliminary

There are countless other "resonances" to be discovered. After all, the violin has over eighty of its own! For the sake of time, I will not attempt to show them as a detailed painting, but instead offer them as seven little rugged "wood cuts."

Grace and Works

The interaction of grace and works draws me deeper into faith. One can picture these strengths as the two hands of the body. They match up as mirror images, which is why they are able to work together. Grace and works lose their purity if they do not serve each other. One hand washes the other. The pitfalls that open when a person loses one or the other of these strengths are clear: the *dreamer* glorifies grace, but avoids painstaking work, having an "outward form of godliness" (2 Timothy 3:5). The *driven* see all the work but have lost their connection with grace and hence suffer from "the rod of their oppressor" (Isaiah 9:4).

The power of faith remains rooted in the tension between the *promise* (grace) and the *challenge* (works). Thus, faith is like love: things grow and maintain their attraction when we live in the interaction between grace and works. It means that we recognize the promise, yet still buckle down to do what is required of us. Everything that has meaning in our lives vibrates in this way. Grace will never offer itself as a substitute for the work of love necessary in every relationship. For in work we sense the substance of our lives, just as in grace we receive our life's strength. One would not exist without the other.

In a mature life, grace and works consistently form a resonance; the tension between them has its foundation in God. As the old saying goes, he is the Creator who gives and "the Commanding One"[1] who makes demands.

When we succumb to the temptation to eliminate the tensions that make our inner life grow, we inevitably trivialize our existence. It is the necessary tensions that allow our love to mature. How mundane would our work be if it consisted only of being driven, and how trite would our faith be if we took grace to simply mean that God loves us and leaves us just the way we are! We should always welcome contradictions. God's grace and human works are like the wave-particle duality in natural light. There lies in both a contradiction that we cannot understand, and yet it is clear that only through a healthy interaction between grace and works can human life be enlightened.

Powerless and Powerful

The same applies to the profound inner unity between being spiritually powerless and spiritually powerful. Jesus described this interplay perfectly when he said: "The Son can do nothing on his own, but only what he sees the Father doing; for whatever the Father does, the Son does likewise" (John 5:19). In this statement Jesus is both powerless—the Son can do nothing on his own—and powerful: "what the Father does, the Son does likewise."

Jesus's authority cannot stand without this powerlessness. It precedes his power and grounds all his actions. We can do a lot "without God," a terrifying amount, but in so doing will confirm our lack of sufficient power and our limited authority.

In spirit-filled powerlessness lies great humility. In it, we do not misappropriate that to which we do not have access—the things that can come about only through grace. When we lose awareness of grace, life begins to grind us down and we succumb to tunnel vision: we go from arrogant self-confidence to sudden resignation. But in spiritual powerlessness there is no sigh of resignation, only a sigh that fixes the heart's gaze above: "Then looking up to heaven, he sighed" (Mark 7:34). Things begin happening precisely through the sigh of the heart that knows God; that which is otherwise closed opens up. The apostle Paul describes the work of the Holy Spirit the same way when, in the letter to the Romans, he writes, "That very Spirit intercedes with sighs too deep for words" (8:26).

Jesus teaches his disciples to pray expectantly. He does not, however, teach them to "pray themselves out" of their troubled times; instead he counsels them to truly look at their situation and ask what they might learn from it. He does not say: "You who are weary and burdened, pray more!" But rather: "Come to me, . . . take my yoke upon you, and learn from me" (Matthew 11:28–29).

There is a powerful lie that wants to persuade the believer: "Why learn? After all, there are spiritual gifts! Why suffer? There are miracles! Why endure hardships? After all, God is here!" In times of crisis, the hideousness of these lies whisper in our hearts, "You're having a rough time? What? Did you sin? You weren't healed? Was your faith too small? You feel downtrodden and lousy? Has God withdrawn from you?"

If you think that being blessed means not having troubles, your faith will likely end up shipwrecked. I will falter if I do not know how to have fellowship with God in my powerlessness and bear it as a necessity of my calling. Emptiness and receptiveness are integral parts of love. So often we are full of our own will and actions! But Jesus says: "Abide in me as I abide in you. Just as the branch cannot bear fruit by itself unless it abides in the vine, neither can you unless you abide in me" (John 15:4).

The secret of Jesus's authority was his fervent dependence on God: "In the morning, while it was still very dark, he got up and went out to a deserted place, and there he prayed" (Mark 1:35). Jesus, like us, is dependent on listening and asking. He needs to be alone to have time and space for this dependency to express itself. His strength also wears out like that of a "normal" person. He does not shine supernaturally from within the circle of his disciples. If it had been so, it would not have been necessary for Judas to betray him with a kiss (Mark 14:44). If Jesus had been an illuminated super-human, then it would have been enough to say: "Follow that glowing apparition; that's him!"

Power and powerlessness create resonance. This interplay dies when we either give in to resignation or fall victim to overestimating our own power. I try to understand times of difficulty as invitations to walk on Jesus's path and identify with him in his powerlessness.

That way I give the Holy Spirit time and space, opening my empty hands to heaven like a sigh: Let my faith be a tool in your hands.

Recently I asked a conductor friend of mine how it is that some conductors have authority when they stand in front of the orchestra and others don't. (Musicians often talk about this in my workshop.) He said he didn't know the reason, but he confided that, before starting a piece, he pauses for a moment on the podium. It seems like he is gathering his thoughts in this moment, but he is doing something else. In the silence, he is blessing the orchestra. In his prayer, he blesses the musicians. Only then does he lift the baton.

One could certainly apply this attitude to many areas: How many teachers pray for and bless their students in the morning silence before entering the school? The secret to true authority lies in the heart that blesses.

Allowing and Forming

Another resonance of spiritual life is the coupled strengths of "allowing and forming." The evolving violin longs for these opposing strengths. I can best explain it by describing how I cut the f-holes.

Every violinmaker has a certain picture in mind of how the violin will develop. The outline and the placement of the f-holes in the arched front have a special effect on the expression the violin will have. Every time I cut the f-holes, I have the sensation that I am creating a being, because at that moment the face of the violin appears. Knife in my right hand, the front of the violin in my left, I cut broad slits with the razor-sharp blade—if possible without stopping so as not to lose the line's momentum. In paper-thin slivers, the transition from a mere shaft of wood occurs. Character emerges. The handwriting is recognizable. But this is no fabrication. The pre-imagined form and the imperfection of the manual craft intertwine rather naturally.

The eye perceives the developing line. The hand corrects the momentum. I search for coherence in the evolving being and work toward aesthetic satisfaction. A moment later the eye is surprised by one of the developing lines, hesitates—and knows that it is good. It is important to let something develop under your hand, even if it deviates from your original idea: "Yes, that's it! It is different from what I wanted, but good . . ." I accept it.

"I actually wanted to cut the shafts a bit thinner on the bottom. But this bold curve is not bad. It's got something . . ."

Toward the end, the moments of just sitting and observing become longer. You hold back more and more. It goes on this way, a continual interplay between allowing and forming. This, I believe, is a typical characteristic of beauty: it is *allowed*, and it is *wanted*. The process is neither slavishly forced nor randomly left to its own devices.

For me, art is all about this tension between allowing and forming. In this way our world renders itself as an overwhelming work of art. God's will is able to accept humankind, and human will is able to accept God's grace. Both take a little step back, giving each other space in faith. It is a mutual acceptance and formation. "*You in me and I in you.*" Faith is the call to appreciate this art.

Antonio Stradivarius's typical round, flowing f-hole shafts transform effortlessly before your eyes. They radiate serenity and gracefulness. Giuseppe Guarneri del Gesù's violin faces are completely different. They are cut differently and have a different temperament; they follow a different ideal. They are mavericks with a dark, passionate beauty. They are rarely symmetrical. The corners are abrupt without disrupting the flow. There is a fascinating attraction in this as well.

But in a fallen state, what happens to *allowing* and *forming*? *Aimlessness* has no awe; everything is left to itself. *Compulsion* offers no love; everything is enslaved.

Aimlessness is not able to follow any vision. A lot may happen, but nothing is formed. The result is ugly. No character, no handwriting. Arbitrary and aimless. The "little brain," the cerebellum, is enough. The supposedly spiritual adage of "letting go" is a shoddy alibi for not really wanting something. In the end, such a person must say, "I only happened, I didn't live. Because I did not live for anything, I avoided life." Living without desire is not a sign of enlightened devotion. Letting go of everything, including your calling, is to throw the baby out with the bathwater.

Compulsion, on the other hand, is not able to deal with unplanned events. It can't change directions or allow disruptions. A compulsive person is intent on implementing what he has "got in his head." He is helplessly at the mercy of an inner dictator, be it religious or neurotic, and "can't do otherwise." Religious compulsion is the corset that replaces the backbone of religious identity.

A compulsive person—or a compulsive community—tries to live life by means of undisrupted construction, as if their existence has been designed on a drafting table. If the natural world with its imperfections is not good enough for the drafting table, then perhaps the artificial world build by our religious rulebook will do. Then nothing will endanger our own thoughts, commitments, and plans. The compulsive community survives by converting freedom into enslavement. Disturbances are perceived as threats against which we must protect ourselves because they push the system off its carefully arranged balance point. Such a spiritual attitude lacks courage and openness. It is not aware of the promise or the possibility that a disruption can actually be a holy prompting. You can seldom find a more effective test for a community than its ability to let itself be disturbed.

A truly wise person leaves plenty of room in life for disruptions, allowing things to go awry. A person of faith knows that it is precisely in the unexpected that good things can emerge. Great wisdom may be gained through adversities—or at least through surprises.

If we do not have the courage to be surprised or bothered, sometimes even to the point of breaking down, then we are not living up to our potential. We cannot be faint-hearted and follow the way of grace. We justify our lack of courage by making stability our top priority, but how much dust collects on the truth when we do not allow anything in our lives to be touched! As Max Frisch says: "What is tradition? I thought it meant tackling the problems of one's own day with the same courage one's forefathers brought to bear on theirs. Everything else is imitation, mummification."[2]

$\sim$

The Gospels tell wonderful stories about moments in which disruptions became proclamations. One of my favorites is the story of the healing of the paralytic (Mark 2). Jesus was preaching. Mark does not consider the details of that sermon to be worth mentioning, because the real lesson came by means of an interruption. Four men lowered their paralyzed friend on ropes down through the roof to Jesus's feet, because getting through the crowd was impossible. For this act of faith, the roof of the house was temporarily damaged, Jesus's sermon was interrupted, and the petty, pious way of thinking of those present was snubbed. The *actual* disruption, however—the spiritual and physical paralysis of a human being—was overcome. In order to overcome evil, Jesus accepted interruptions and irritations—at times even provoked them. This all serves to overcome the *true* disruptions. Genius! It is the power of a faith that can listen and act, accept and form.

Hearing and Doing

The fourth resonance comes from the interplay between *hearing* and *doing*. At the end of the Sermon on the Mount, Jesus tells a parable about a wise man who built his house on a rock. A downpour, flood, and wind came one after another. They beat against the house, but it did not collapse, unlike the house of the foolish man, which was built on the sand. The house of the wise man was grounded on the rock. The wise man, Jesus says, is the one "who hears these words of mine and acts on them" (Matthew 7:24). Hearing and doing!

The great Jewish teacher, Hillel (70 BC – AD 10), said something similar a few years earlier: "He whose wisdom is greater than his deeds is like a tree whose branches are many but whose roots are few; the wind comes and uproots it, and overturns it."[3]

Hearing and doing form a powerful set of spiritual strengths. As in any resonance, one strength begets the other. The pitfall of hearing that does not result in action is *intellectualism*. The pitfall of action that does not feel the need to listen is *pragmatism*.

Pragmatism belittles our understanding. It turns everything into a formula because it has no love. This attitude is the surest way never to acquire a listening heart. The utilitarian mind-set of a pragmatist cannot hear anything without reflexively asking: What's in it for me? Such a heart-attitude devalues faith's loving search and searching love. Great scientific achievements have often been made by those who have a curious love for researching. A person who measures everything by its immediate effect trivializes God and the world: he has neither a heart for research nor the tools to become someone who listens to God. Continually dealing with this kind of person is exhausting.

The opposite attitude, *intellectualism*, belittles the act of doing by reducing faith to an inspiring system of thought. In this state, one is not moved to act but only to ask: Is it a beautiful concept? Does it excite me? This is a shallow attitude, for according to Jesus and Hillel, that which gives a person support and maturity is not wisdom, but deeds.

Intellectualism and pragmatism are fallen virtues. Our true calling lies in the harmony of *hearing and doing*—and then in the proper time. Often, we must understand something *now* that will only bear fruit *later*. The time of hearing may not be the time of harvest but the moment when something is being sown. A demanding pragmatic attitude that constantly asks, "What does that do for me?" pulls and tugs on the plant as if to make it grow faster or produce fruit sooner. We need a greater respect for God and God's timing to withstand the danger of asking only about the immediate usefulness of things and allowing nothing to ripen and mature.

So also hearing requires us to act at the appropriate time. Jesus did not allow himself to be pressured into moving prematurely. He waited and observed and, at the right moment, acted in the right way (John 7:6). In Jesus's life there is no knowledge for the sake of knowing. No hint of intellectualism. He is able to recognize God's will simply because *he desires to do it*.

A *spiritual restlessness* will warn us when we overload ourselves to the point of burnout without accomplishing anything. The pendulum's swing between duty-bound drivenness and addictive relaxation can only come to rest in us when we know that we are connected to a holy will.

"You Are" and "You Should"

We are called to grow deeper in the mystery of God's love by understanding *who we are*, and not only *what we should do*. Love assures us of who we are. If you don't believe in your God-given identity, you will be caught in the trap of trying to prove yourself. No amount of "doing" can replace what is missing in the person who rejects God's assurance and therefore does not know who he or she is.

If the star that gives our lives meaning and assurance is dead, then it forms a "black hole" in the soul from which no light can escape. Being driven by troubles, duties, fears, and the need to prove ourselves is a gaping pit that swallows up everything but is never satisfied. It is the restless lack of peace in a person who, outwardly, has power and possibilities but inwardly is completely powerless—void of strength and self-worth. We are dumb enough to believe that things would be better if we did more, tried harder, offering up whatever the chasm of dissatisfaction in us desires. That hunger will only grow. We are feeding the greedy fat cells of our insatiable emptiness. Only the loved person can have peace. Everything else is an illusion!

At the beginning of his *Confessions*, St. Augustine (AD 354–430) wrote in prayer: "Our heart is restless until it rests in you."[4] Once I counted more than forty unique "you are" phrases in the New Testament: "You are the children of God"; "heirs of the promise"; "a royal priesthood"; "the salt of the earth"; "the light of the world"; and many more. These are phrases of dignity. They tell us that we are not all those things because of what we do, but rather because of how God made us. This involves not just a moral conversion but, much deeper and earlier, a conversion of our identity.

The founding father of the Taizé movement, Brother Roger, transformed the words of Augustine to emphasize our willpower: "My heart finds no rest until it can lay down in you, Christ, what was keeping it far from you."[5] Here he addresses the human will, the "you should."

A mature life cannot be spared from the interaction between *being* and *doing*. We must live in this conflict because in it there is an active power. Our *being* must cross the ocean of *should*, and our *should* must drop anchor in the assurance of *being*. If we lose one of the two, then we risk shipwreck or eternal stagnation. If we do not know who we are, we lack inner weight, the weight in the ship's keel that prevents it from capsizing. But if we do not know what we should do, we have not yet raised the sail. There will be no departure, no travels.

If everything is *should*, we will capsize in the storms of demands. It is the shipwreck of self-degradation that says: "I am nothing because I don't do what I should do!"

If life consists only of *being*, then we stagnate in *complacency*, claiming: "I don't need to do anything, because what I am is enough!"

Neither is true. Resonance emerges only through an interaction between two strengths. Demands and assurances must both work potently in our lives. The Bible warns of self-degradation and complacency in equal measure.

Truth and Kindness

"For your lovingkindness is before my eyes, and I have walked in your truth" (Psalm 26:3 NKJV). Here we discover a resonance between two powerful forces. This tone rings out: Don't walk in the truth without having God's kindness front and center! For without kindness, your truth will be deadly hard and sharp. Where kindness is missing, truth becomes a nightmare. It becomes a lie against a grace-filled, merciful, and patient God.

It is wretched and restrictive to impose upon the world only one's own version of the truth. Every fanatic believes that he is fighting for God or something higher when he "fights for the truth." This is a lie. When kindness is lost, he loses that which he is fighting for. Indeed, the shameful conditions that we so often see in a broken world can only find healing and mercy through kindness. The fanatic does not have kindness in mind but focuses on what is wrong—and often justifiably so! And yet, without kindness, his truth becomes an idol. God is truth, but the truth is not God. The fanatic believes that he has the truth at his command, but he forgets that God is not at our disposal!

Truth and kindness are both vitally important. Truth protects kindness from *arbitrariness*; kindness protects truth from *lovelessness*. Both peaks and both pitfalls were captured by St. Augustine in his saying, "Hate the sin but love the sinner." Whoever loves kindness loves the sinner.

Refusal to orient ourselves to any form of truth is like soft wood that lacks resilience and so produces only a dull sound. We need moral resilience! It cannot be procured by kindness, but only by the truth.

Our sensitivity to truthfulness, unfortunately, seems to be finely tuned only when it has to do with someone else, not ourselves. If we sense that someone else is in the wrong, we can suddenly expend vast amounts of energy in turmoil and outrage. We think that we are disgusted by the injustice, but we are honing our own indignation for self-righteous pleasure. The apostle Paul reminds us: "In passing judgment on another you condemn yourself" (Romans 2:1).

Intuitively we sense that kindness without truth is not kind, and truth without kindness is not true. We know that ideological truths cannot be proved, and, thank God, the church has lost its inviolable power to dictate what truth is. But our intuition still drives us to an honest, active search for truth (for *Logos*, for meaning), and gives shape to this truth. Our lives should reflect the inexpressible. This is what it is to be human!

As in violinmaking, truth and kindness should create a resonance. The sound of our human life needs this resonance. The whimsical justification of our sins has a *dullness* to it; it is wood that is too soft or has been carved too thin. It has no inner vibration resilience! But when our heartlessness leads us to judge the sinner, the sound is *sharp*. A violinmaker can avoid a dull sound only by preserving *brilliance* in the warmth of the sound; conversely one can only avoid a piercing sound by retaining *warmth* in the brilliance of the sound. Truth told at the cost of kindness is like a harsh, vulgar sound. Kindness overvalued at the cost of the truth sounds anemic and dull.

Geri Keller, an inspiring mentor of our time, says: "Only the pure are capable of accepting sinners in such a way that they no longer see the sin in them, but rather know them to be created by their loving Creator, true children of their eternal Father. For this reason, sinners flocked to Jesus. He was pure! Because we are still so stained and burdened with sin, we see the sin in others, instead of seeing God's creation."[6]

Complete and Preliminary

The last pairing of strengths shows that even the greatest of words cannot stand alone. What could be more perfect than the concept of *being complete*? What polar opposite is needed for it to harmonize with? What might it possibly depend on? Actually, completion also needs a strong partner, because taken alone it would degenerate into perfectionism. The perfectionist is not ready to respect the preliminary as a necessity of our existence. Without passing through a preliminary stage, nothing and no one would have the right to develop. Perfectionists take the life out of everything they touch and do not allow it to mature. They do not give things time but live in their bullheadedness without the strength of hope.

In one parable Jesus talks about a grapevine, saying that everything that has grown up within a relationship with God gives rise to something eternal (John 15:8-16). This brings the complete and the preliminary together. They form a healthy word pair. Their fallen counterparts are *perfectionism* and *half-heartedness*.

Through friendship with talented musicians, I have witnessed the severe challenges that perfectionism creates. Perhaps it is because you cannot retrieve or iron out a sound once it has left the instrument. Everything that happens in a concert is unique and instantaneous. It is pure presence in an undivided Now.

Once a singer told me, "I used to think that I had to be perfect first, and then I could go on stage and sing. That put me under unbelievable pressure. Today I can accept my preliminary nature and observe my own growth." One of her friends who was an oboist added, "Being unsatisfied was important when I was studying because it helped me make progress. But perfectionism leads to burnout. You cannot grow in fear."

No one wants to endorse musical indifference or average technique, and yet to become a truly whole musician requires something altogether different. I am convinced that this path ultimately is an opening that leads to God. I cannot think of any great musicians who are not convinced that they serve a truth greater than themselves in music.

A pianist friend once told me about a concert that he had given. "After the Mozart concerto," he said, "a woman I did not know came up to me seeming very moved. 'May I ask you something?' she said. 'The way you play—I have the impression that you are a believer.'" She had experienced something of God in the sounds themselves, not due to any words, for there were none. Perhaps she felt what the music meant to this musician. He once told me that for him, every note is praise to God.

It is not the music but what carries the music that makes you complete. Jesus says: "Unless a grain of wheat falls into the earth and dies, it remains just a single grain; but if it dies, it bears much fruit" (John 12:24). Herein lies a secret key to being both complete and pre-liminary. The grain of wheat is preliminary; after all, it is not even a sprout, let alone a full-grown ear of wheat. But this preliminary state does not take away the importance of the seed or the meaning it carries. What a person does here and now is no less important and no less real than life in the future world. As preliminary as our work may be, like a grain of wheat, it contains everything inside. And it comes to life through commitment, devotion.

Devotion is a characteristic of eternal life. Devotion is heaven's truth; it is what Jesus lived out completely on earth. It was through his commitment that who Jesus was became visible, and devotion was the power behind everything he accomplished.[7] A person who is capable of such commitment amid their preliminary stage is already carrying the life-trait of the future world, bringing eternity into our world today.

During a long, quiet car ride, our older son Jonas—who was four at the time—suddenly said from the back seat: "Mama, now I know why we don't know exactly what heaven is like! If we knew how beautiful it is there, no one would want to live here anymore!" We were amazed. He had voiced something of crucial importance.

Despite our provisional nature, we are meant to live *today*. We should not destroy our lives longing for a completion that rejects this world; rather we fulfill our present calling through troubles and disappointments. These are the labor pains of the future world.

We will always be "in the making." Even our passing away is another step in our development. The parable about the grain of wheat tells us: Your life is not a dying—not a process of living toward death. If it were so, then we would have to experience everything within the little seed-sized brevity of our lives—perfect everything, perpetuate ourselves. We would live in the terrible, continual comparison between the pathetic *is* and the relentless *should*, between the used-up life and the life that remains to be lived. Do we really know exactly what our *should* is? Do we know the time and strength, the circumstances and possibilities, that remain to us? Would we be a single seed obstinately trying to be its own fulfillment?

The nearness to God in which we can live today reveals another freedom. We do not live to die; rather we die to live. Death is not our last commitment, but each and every day commitment steadily awakens what is slumbering to life, giving us a sense of meaning and the experience of joy. That is the freedom of being preliminary: not everything has to happen here, and not everything has to come to fulfillment. We do not have to be the final product because we aren't. Life, in all of its preliminary nature, marks the beginning of completion. It is as precious as the dying seed. Of course, there is pain in Jesus's words as well. Because he says that if the seed does not "fall into the earth, it remains just a single grain." If it remains single and alone, and therefore lives *for itself*, then it misses life. As the oboist said, "You cannot grow in fear." Perfectionism promotes fears rather than overcoming them. Instead, let us cherish the assurance that the right thing will be given to us at the right time.

$\sim$

If I could speak one thing into the heart of the musician, it would be this: You are not an artist of perfection. When every tone must be flawless, the music becomes tedious and cowardly. Perfectionism steals your personality. The pressure on your shoulders can be removed only when you understand your calling: you comfort hearts, you touch hearts, you bless hearts! In your music you make heaven's language audible so that we can bear this world and love it despite all adversities. It lifts our hearts. As a musician, you must understand the meaning of your calling. You are not a performer of your abilities, but a servant with permission to bless people. Do not allow your fears to rob you of this authoritative power. If you don't take a chance and forgive your own mistakes, you will lose the power and promise of your calling. You are not led onto the stage to show what you can do but because God wants to speak through the voice of your sound. God knows the needs and circumstances of the people listening to you and knows how to bless them. And so you are called to be an instrument.

The pressure of perfectionism will vanish from our souls only when we are no longer slaves to our talent. The slave says: "I recognize myself when I do something well." And the slave's self-image must constantly be fed by applause. If this opiate is not trickling down into his soul, he loses self-confidence and falls into the spiritual coma of a person who feels worthless.

The self-assurance of the beloved is nourished by a different strength. What he does, he does because he is called. This calling lies far above and beyond any irreverent self-assurance. He has been entrusted with talent, but he does not need it to validate his own worth. The beloved lives out of the strength of him to whom he owes everything. Such a life is surrounded by the power of God's love. If we do not know that our lives have been entrusted to us, that we are called, that we are limited, then we will continually have to affirm, define, and enlarge ourselves through talent—otherwise we won't feel anything. Woe to the slave who never learns to aim for something other than himself! Woe to a life that has made itself the goal; it starves to death on its own substance. It has never learned to receive, never learned to be a child of God, never learned to be loved by this holy will and allow itself to be called. In such a life talent cannibalizes its own existence. Be a servant, or otherwise your talent will make you a slave!

Only the beloved understands what is essential. He knows: "I haven't reached the goal, but I am called in the whole of my preliminary state." That is the life of the servant. A holy reminder covers such a life: "Do not let the tyranny of your talent ruin your calling. It is only if you stay a servant that you will not become a slave. A servant of one's calling has authority; a slave of talent has only himself." This is the resonance sounding in the complete and the preliminary: it is a beautiful sound.

∼

The word pairs I have explored in this chapter are not intellectual exercises; they describe diverse strengths that are manifest in our spiritual attitudes and give shape to life. Like the modal analysis of a violin's vibrations, they reveal our calling and show us the fibers, the wood grain, of our souls. Just as the resonance profile gives an instrument tone color, these various strengths give sound to human life.

05

The Arching
and the Wood's Grain

Belief as Reverence and Mercy

See, I have engraved you
on the palms of my hands.

—ISAIAH 49:16 (NIV)

$\mathcal{M}$OST OF THE TOOLS that I work with on a daily basis I have made myself. My workbench is wider, shorter, and heavier than usual. I built it during my internship out of an old oak railroad tie that had supported a sawmill crane for a good sixty years. The workbench stands in the middle of my shop. I carved out the frame's wood joints and the cuttings for the bench hooks by hand. A locksmith came and made the threaded steel rods for bracing.

Most of my tools you cannot buy in a store. As students, we carved the handles of our Japanese multi-pleated steel knives ourselves so that they would fit well in the hand. Some of my friends and I had chiseling irons forged in the Stubaital, an Alpine valley in Austria.

An old local master shaped the handles with a lathe from a sketch I drew. At the front end, they have an extra knob because there are three distinct hand positions for guiding them. Each of my iron gouges has a different curve. In order to spot them more quickly when they are lying side by side on the workbench, I made each handle of a different kind of wood: boxwood, pear tree wood, ebony, jacaranda, rosewood, bubinga. We put a lot of effort and care into the production of our tools. To enhance the weight of my knives with their different cutting widths, I bound the wooden handles with soldered brass alloy inlays. The increased weight helps the knife work smoothly in the hand. If I am able to work long into my old age, all the hours that I will have worked with my 18-millimeter knife in my right hand will add up to about two years.

Familiarity with the Wood

I have not really written yet about how the violin grows in the maker's hands. I have described the search for the singing tree, the tree's life, the guiding lines of the pattern, and just now the inner vision of tone colors. Now everything is prepared for the most beautiful work to begin: carving out the arching! This is the curved shape of the violin's front and back, and it gives the instrument its tonal signature. In this more than any other stage of the work, you become one with the wood and responsive to its demands.

The wedges for the front, which spent many years stored in my workshop, are joined together with bone glue. The young sapwood that is found in the outer part of the trunk is positioned in the center of the front, and the heartwood that was the center of the trunk becomes the outer edge. I attach it firmly with the clamps to the aforementioned workbench. The cutting iron with its broad edge lies next to it. The little arching chisels are ready. The polished, curved scrapers are sharp, and I have kept the cutting edges keen. I flesh the arching out of the wedge-shaped wood—at first in long, coarsely drawn thrusts. The longer I work, the finer the maneuvers become. In the beginning they must be large to give the arch its character. Each thrust into the wood has its own hissing or ripping sound. If I am working with the fissure (that is, with the wood's grain), I hear a lighter tone and the iron runs smoothly. If I am working against the grain, the sound is harsh and ripping; the iron vibrates and lies uneasy in the hand. So, feeling and listening to the grain from the very first thrust, I start to understand the wood. To disregard the wood's grain would be to spoil the sound of the violin. The arch could still be beautiful to the eye, but if it does not do justice to the grain of the wood, then it is not the work of a master.

The Luthier's Secret

Of course, I won't reveal the secret completely, but it has to do with serving the wood in the right way. You have to know how to justify the wood.

A few years ago, three violins of the great Italian master Antonio Stradivarius happened to be in my workshop. It was an amazing stroke of luck that they arrived at almost the same time so that I could spend some very special days studying their handwriting. All three were crafted during the golden age of violinmaking, at the beginning of the eighteenth century. Their tone is velvety and deep. To play on such a violin is like a prayer cast into sound. In them two things come together that otherwise seldom do: gentleness and great strength. It is as if a cloud of sound envelops you, and a free, fulfilling, fearless playing unfolds. You play differently on such a violin. Indeed, sometimes it is as if you were "being played." It can be difficult for me to find time to work on such days. I can't stop playing these violins, savoring the hours they spend in my shop.

These three violins are unmistakably the work of the same maker. Their sound is intense and multifaceted in its colors. They are not loud to the ear and yet, even played softly, they have a carrying capacity that can fill an entire concert hall. Even in their varnish it is as if you can see through the wood's tracheid into another realm.

Although they share the same handwriting, each instrument is made in its own way. One is not a copy of the other. Their wood is different, and so the wisdom of the master gave each of them a different allocation of strengths. The plate thickness and arching follow a uniform thought; the wood, however, required a different measure in each case according to its density and elasticity. Even the outline did not rigidly follow a predetermined template. All this tells one thing above all else: Stradivarius was true to his signature and yet did not deny the wood the differences that it desired from him.

Perfectionism or Wholeness?

Each tree has an absolutely unique character both because of its adverse climate and its particular life within the community of the grove. It would be cheap, even profane, to force your own preconception on the wood. The art is to see what the fibers require. Someone fixated on the "ideal" or "right" shape only follows his own laws. A true artist knows the laws of acoustics, and yet sees something more: he first honors what is crooked and what has "become" in the fibers, knowing that these must not be cut in the wrong places. Inner wisdom, knowledge of the wood and its needs, come first, not a blind, predetermined "form." The perfectionist is content with fulfilling the law; the artist fulfills the sound.

In the book of Romans, the apostle Paul describes a similar process. Here, the "wood grain" of human existence follows the same wisdom revealed in the three Stradivarius violins.

> We know that all things work together for good for those who love God, who are called according to his purpose. For those whom he foreknew he also predestined to be conformed to the image of his Son, in order that he might be the firstborn within a large family. And those whom he predestined he also called; and those whom he called he also justified; and those whom he justified he also glorified. (Romans 8:28–30)

We can understand this passage from working on the violin's arch. This wood was diligently searched for and carefully chosen (called). The maker knew from the start what he was looking for; he respects the texture of the wood and feels its character, its solidity and density, under his fingers. He studies the wood's idiosyncrasies: the grain and the direction of the medullary rays in the cross-cut section. He pays attention to the wood's patterns and recognizes its mirror and flaming. All these show him both the possibilities and limits of the wood. Each quirk and peculiarity will influence the sound it will bring forth. With tonewood, I take special care for the lustrous shine in the surface area of long fibers, as with the summer wood's high percentage of thin-walled cells and long strands. Wood that lacks luster is usually too hard. It is infinitely difficult to create a good sound with it. If, nevertheless, you are successful, the result is all the more worth it.

Every piece of wood in my studio is stored according to its density and acoustic speed. You can feel its resonance with your fingers.

The acoustic dampening and the relationship between acoustic speed and density become audible when you listen to the wedge-cut wood's unique tones. To do that, you must hold the wood by its acoustic center (the nodal point) and tap with one finger on its vibration antinodes. Each eigenvibration[1] has its own acoustic center, and every vibration antinode has its own pattern. If you hold it correctly, a bright sound will come forth. Through these tap tones the wood reveals itself and its experience.

The deepest eigentone[2] is formed by torsion vibration. The wood vibrates in a cross of nodal lines. The next eigentone is formed by a lengthwise vibration, as two nodal lines run directly across each other. Then we find the cross-bent vibration, etc. Each vibration has its own pattern that you must be familiar with if you want to hear the eigentones. These tap tones show me how I must work the wood in order to honor its peculiar history, its idiosyncrasies.

~

Violinmakers know that if the tree was exposed to wind over a long period of time or if it was bent by a slope or the pressure of snow on one side, then a problematic growth called "reaction wood" will have developed in the trunk. Our lives, too, are sometimes exposed to less than favorable influences. Something went wrong; we were under pressure too long or exposed to too many storms. We see our difficult wood grain; we feel the lopsidedness and injuries in our souls. Indeed, we also have something in us like the eigentones of the wood. Yet it is through the big and little ordeals of everyday life that we show our true colors. These trials tap on our life and make audible the course of our wood grain fibers, our inner structure.

If I, as a violinmaker, have enough love for the wood to labor with its fibers, determined to work with what it has already become, however difficult it may be, how much more so will God. God's loving wisdom knows what is necessary to build something unique and beautiful with our given texture, our fiber, and our sometimes-difficult histories. This is what the apostle Paul meant in our Romans passage by "called," "justified," and "glorified."

The wood does not get in the way of the instrument's sound; indeed, it is what makes the sound possible. I will only become a good violinmaker if I am willing to embrace and work with the "despites": *despite* this particular flaw, *despite* this tapering, *despite* this odd structure, *despite* this damage, I will give this wood its voice. I will set it free so that it can sing.

Diary Notes

I am working on a new violin pattern. It is wider in the lower bout and more open in the C-bout than all my previous instruments. With this new shape, I am in search of a particular tone—a full, lush-sounding G-string; an earthy, deep, rich sound; a warm mezzo-soprano. The new outline demands that I form the arch differently, as well. The possibilities will have to prove themselves within the work.

How should I carve the grain fibers out in a wider arching? How will the channeling of the periphery cross over into the convex, widely stretched-out bow of the chest area? I haven't settled into this pattern yet.

In the course of time the arching emerges under my hands. It has just one source: the hand is transforming something that is foreign to the eye. And so, the shape of the arch becomes more and more familiar in the process of the work. Nothing else can cause this, only its growing familiarity to the eye. That's what guides the arching plane. There is something exhilarating about the process. Sometimes it almost seems as if my eye is not controlling my hand but is merely observing what is happening in a quite bewilderingly self-evident way. In fact, there is no other work that is more fulfilling to me and to which I devote a higher level of attention, and yet at the same time, I have the sensation that I am actually not thinking, but things are happening of their own accord.

Suddenly, right here I feel a tapered area in the wood's grain. The arching plane vibrates between my fingers in a completely different way. I hear right away whether the blade is going with or against the fibers. The scraping noise becomes harsh. The wood is breaking down. The plane tells me: "You have to leave the idea of the arch you had in mind. It may not be pretty, but it is necessary." Everything that has happened to the wood now requires asymmetry. The arch's turning point must begin earlier than planned. It's all about feeling the fibers.

It is different with the medullary rays. In the tree these are the structural elements that run radially out from the inner pith to the cambium just beneath the bark. These are the conduits for the substances in the tree. In the violin they form the structural element that runs horizontally and are essential to give the instrument its side-to-side stiffness. If the ray's cell angles run even slightly out of the arching because the wood was incorrectly glued or the arch was poorly constructed due to ignorance or negligence, then a flexible bulge will develop in this area.[3] The violin's tone is then threatened and becomes weak or dull: weak if I let the wood remain thicker to make up for the missing stiffness, dull if I give the wood its traditional thickness at the cost of sufficient stiffness.

While working on the arching, I need to constantly heed both the wood's fibers and its medullary rays. There is this difference, however. You cannot see the course of fibers; you have to feel and hear it in the plane's vibrations. But you cannot feel the medullary rays, you must see them. When the light hits the wood at a certain angle, you can see how the rays reflect the light more strongly than do the longitudinal fibers. It is no wonder that the technical term for the markings created by the rays is "the mirror." Since the wood's cell structure shows up only in reflected light, the light in which you work is very important.

Evolution or Construction?

If the wood's fiber were mathematically definable lines, you could construct an ideal arch even before the work begins. The wood's fiber-course is not perfect or ideal, however. Therefore, the process of making a violin is not an act of construction. It is an act of creation.

What's the difference? In a construction, the material must fulfill the plan. The act of creating a violin is different. The violinmaker must respect the wood's *past*—what history does it bring? He must envision the wood's *future*—what can unfold? Grown wood grain cannot be made right by an uncompromising plan. In the act of creation, it is not only the wood that meets the needs of the maker, but the maker that meets the needs of the wood. The entire process of creation allows for promised possibilities to unfold, and in that everything depends on the respect, submission, goodness, and wisdom of the maker for his creation.

Whether you understand the world as creation or as evolution makes no difference from the artist's point of view: the work is always evolving. Opportunities unfold. The creation forms amid the beauty and the pain of development. It is not the idea of "Evolution" that robs faith of its breath but thinking that the world is a divine construction site. Herein lies the difference between a Plan and a Promise, between Ideal Form and Emerging Art, between Subordination and Dialogue, between Religious Legalism and Spirit-filled Faith. I would like to explore these differences further.

An Almighty Engineer subdues the material. "Faith in God" then means *capitulation* to God. Building violins has taught me something quite different. Creating involves both "what is given" and "what has already become." Faith means to trust in the indwelling wisdom of the Creator and the promised possibilities while still acknowledging, even embracing, the history of the wood that is now essential to the unfolding of its sound. The wood finds its own voice in being born again.

When I feel the course of fibers through its interaction with the plane, it is like I am in dialogue with the wood. Only amid the work does it become clear how the arching should be formed. The wood has its say in this co-creation.

Construction forces a predetermined ideal onto the material. Everything has to yield to that ideal; the grown fibers are ignored. This is the heart of legalism, where life is submerged in and subdued by unrelenting ideal conceptions. It is the curse of religion.

The "justification" of a human being in the passage from Romans means, first and foremost, that there is Wisdom at work that does *justice* to life. The real fibers of life are respected and given a voice in an act of love that embraces the imperfect and preliminary and sees its worth. Love sees all the beauty, joy, desire, and hope that are the possibilities of the soul, but it also sees all the weaknesses, disappointments, sadness, and pain, the soul's crooked fibers. Into all of this God's wisdom enters as in a dialogue in which we have our rightful say. Our life is not a construction.

When the fibers of our life come into contact with the Creator, the future develops in respect to the *past* and an interplay with what has *developed* emerges. This is ingenious. *Construction*, on the other hand, creates the future by coercion. This is too small; it is pitiful.

The Work of Art

Scripture reveals that God has much more the heart of an artist than of a grim construction planner. If the world were the work of a cosmic engineer, he would be in a constant state of discontent. We would all suffer from the constant nagging of a dogged designer whose plans just never work out like he intends or expects. Reality could never live up to his spotless, perfect plans. But there is a different wisdom at work in the artist. A true creator knows he not only has to shape but also endorse and allow. Wisdom allows things to evolve and unfold. In Scripture, God's wisdom is a spiritual force that explores everything, everywhere, penetrating the very depths of life.[4]

It is fascinating to view the whole world, ourselves included, as a composition, a painting or sculpture, an artistic masterpiece. Works of art can be both miraculously beautiful and sometimes odd and peculiar. We are works of art, not construction.

What moves me is the idea that God has the heart of an artist, who does not force reality into submission by bending and breaking and going against the grain. The thought of seeing every person, ourselves included, as a unique work of art in progress, an ever-changing and matchless expression of God, changes everything. In every encounter you suddenly see the odd, authentic, fascinating, sometimes enjoyable and sometimes devastating, often humorous but staggering interplay of what is created and what has become of it. What has the distinctive history of this person deposited within them, and what has grown out of it? What is now in the making?

Life is an expedition through a gallery of works in progress, and we are a part of it. We are invited to respect each other as living installations, representations, and forms of expression that long to be read, heard, and observed.

Seeing others as unique and original works of art has vast implications for our own ability to truly hear and see. An obstinacy that cannot think above or beyond its own imagination could instead yield to honest curiosity; we can learn to listen and dignify the unique sounds of others. This kind of "seeing" requires alertness and openness and challenges our assumptions: What is meeting me here? Whom do I see in front of me? What is being expressed? What is the message? What am I learning from this? What is developing in this situation?

~

A little while ago our family visited the Centre national d'art et de culture Georges Pompidou in Paris. Because of our different interests, my wife and I split up, each taking along one of our sons. My younger son and I found the modern sculpture wing to be intoxicating, riveting, and inspiring. For Lorenz, who was ten at the time, it turned into a time-consuming experience. Without any discussion, he sat down, took out his sketchbook, and began to observe and draw with the utmost concentration. But the lines on the first pages turned out to be neither sufficiently straight nor parallel, and he ripped the pages out in fury. In his mind, things were not as they should be. Lingering in one of the rooms for a long time, I finally felt the need to speak to his little (no, big!) artist's heart: "You are not an engineer right now! Yes, the lines would be perfect with a computer, but that would be construction. That's not what your sketches are about. Pay attention to what is evolving in your pictures! What is important is what you see 'in' it!"

Lorenz apparently understood, for his drawings became deeper and freer. Lost in time, he immersed himself in observing the sculptures and paintings, sketching them with great gravity and impressive endurance. Joy captured him in a new way. In the end, his pictures were unique and courageous.

Perhaps every concert, every performance, and every museum should be a kind of primary school for this type of worldview, teaching us the ABCs of perception: a love of truly seeing and hearing, the fascination of asking and discerning. How wonderful it would be to go out in the world and look at it as a magnificent work of art, a breathtaking expression of life. When we observe our world as a place of courageous creation, we gain a new love of life and will experience a new joy. Such love will overcome our dullness. Such fascination will grant us strength.

If we demand a perfectionistic ideal, we will not learn to see the real fibers of life. By true hearing and seeing, we will grow in compassion and courage, and they will free us from the perfectionism that robs us of grace; they will protect us from the arrogance of forcing things against life's grain.

The Godlessness of the Straight Line

"It is God who justifies" (Romans 8:33). When the violinmaker makes the wood sound, he *justifies* the wood (3:26). The unchanged life is like a piece of wood that does not trust the wisdom that is shaping its form; it is blind to the promise and has no clue about its potential sound. A person of this sort looks at nothing but his wood grain and thinks that it is either good or bad. Romans says of such people: "Being ignorant of the righteousness that comes from God, and seeking to establish their own, they have not submitted to God's righteousness" (10:3).

Those who resemble this type of wood don't know the wisdom that works with crooked fibers. They do not experience how wisdom takes shape right in the middle of questionable wood. They continue to believe that the wood justifies the violinmaker. Nonsense! What tragic faith!

The painter Friedensreich Hundertwasser once spoke of the "godlessness of the straight line,"[5] offering a perfect image for an obstinate and self-deluded notion. There is much that is not ideal. The appearance of my body, the fibers of my psyche, my fumbling about the course of life, the search for a path and successful relationships—where is the constructed line in all this? It has never been about a godless, straight wood grain. That is an illusion hostile to creation.

The particular time in which we live, the opportunities that we have, the circumstances that we experience—all of these taper our growth and twist our fibers. Wisdom defies the godlessness of our imaginary ideals, which hold powerful sway over our existence. The legalist wears himself out fighting against God and, if he were brave enough to admit it, is outraged that God is apparently unable to draw straight lines. Our demands for perfection turn us into self-righteous judges of the creativity of God and try to make ourselves God's tutor.

Righteousness

The wood in the violinmaker's hands is called to sound. Our "sound" as human beings is given a notable term in Scripture: it is the call to *righteousness*. This word may sound just one note in our everyday speech, but in Scripture it is an entire symphony! Endlessly rich in motifs, polyphonic in meaning, comprehensive in its claims and beauty—such is the righteousness to which every person is called.

Righteousness is the highest form of living recognized in Scripture. It encompasses both our relationships and our behavior, our heart and our deeds, the inner and outer aspect of our life.[6] The great Jewish scholar Maimonides (1138-1204) depicted righteousness as the virtue of self-improvement. For him, to live spiritually and to unfold his true individuality meant to be just and to walk the path toward his neighbor. The righteous bear the world, or as Rabbi Yohanan put it: "If there be but one righteous man, the world is granted its existence."[7] The Talmud goes so far as to say that the righteous one is able to create a world.[8] The opposite would also be true: where unrighteousness sets the tone, people are weighed down and life is brought to ruin.

$$\sim$$

One of the major prophetic themes of Scripture concerns the dissonance of human existence: that is, unrighteousness! It is worth noting that the most severe judgments of the prophets in the Hebrew Scriptures fall upon this spiritual attitude, which begins with the line, "We will build . . . !" (Isaiah 9:10). The book of Genesis discloses the inner pattern of this attitude in the old story of the tower of Babel: "Come, let us build ourselves a city, and a tower with its top in the heavens, and let us make a name for ourselves!" (Genesis 11:4). The prophet Isaiah, hearing echoes of this among the proud people of his own time, prophesied against them: "In pride and arrogance of heart they said, 'The bricks have fallen, but we will build with dressed stones'" (9:9-10).

The development of a tower is not growth. It is construction. How many towers are *not* built on the rock of righteousness, but on the quicksand of growth-addicted self-referential individuals or systems.

In many parables, Jesus describes the heart-disposition that corresponds with "the kingdom of God and his righteousness" (Matthew 6:33). Rarely does he refer to building. Instead, he speaks about growing, seeking, finding, and being entrusted with goods. He uses the growth of a seed to illustrate other traits: humility, thankfulness, consciousness, alertness, a feel for healthy relationships and the right timing. "Righteous" growth does not mean bigger or more glorious. It entails the growth of insight, of concentration, of wisdom—also the wisdom that leads us to be more just, conscious, and calm. The amount of a sound's fortissimo that we can bear is limited by our pain tolerance. But a pianissimo is unending; it has an inwardness and transparency of which the bombastic knows nothing. The threshold of hearing brushes up against a heavenly quiet, and within this tone's soft strength, an entire concert hall holds its breath.

The growth of the kingdom of God is something holy. It is growth into our full potential as humans. The noisy demands of our world are often a disruptive and thinly veiled imitation of the holy growth to which we are called. The strident external demand for perfect performance is driven by shame, greed, and fear. First we *want* to grow, then we *have* to grow! In crises we experience the unmasking of unrighteousness. If we then refuse to learn, change, and truly grow, but repeat the same mistakes, a "crisis" (in the Bible called a "plague") follows forthwith. Sadly, short-lived scares rarely awaken us; it often takes many plagues before we realize that we must change.

Unrighteousness painfully reveals the dynamic of idolatry: the things that promised to serve us instead rule over us. They lure us in and then imprison us. Therefore, we must be vigilant, discern true growth from false and speak out courageously against any fraudulent imitation of authentic righteousness.

A cancerous tumor is nothing but a growth, a sickly growth that will do nothing but expand. Cancer embodies a bitter, suffering symbol of our times: not all growth is healthy organic development. We are suffering from a cancerous, expansion-addicted system, and our commercial structures and stock markets are simply their metastases. We feed their monstrous existence through our fear and greed.

To read Scripture purely for personal salvation is to be religiously blind. Prophets consistently confront impersonal systems and powerful people, taking a stand against unrighteousness: "Their land is filled with silver and gold, and there is no end to their treasures; their land is filled with horses, and there is no end to their chariots. Their land is filled with idols; they bow down to the work of their hands, to what their own fingers have made. And so people are humbled, and everyone is brought low" (Isaiah 2:7-9a).

The prophets question not only the virtues of the individual, but the moral strength of the system and its institutions as well.[9] A prophetic understanding of life insists that justice lead our consciousness as a community. When does a society cease to be a community and break into a thousand splinters of self-centeredness? Without righteousness, politics loses its meaning and authority, and society its inner solidarity. Such fragmentation leaves everyone vulnerable. Politics becomes a form of prostitution: "Satisfy our needs! Create economic stability for our outer lives and peace for our inner lives!" But it is wrong to think that the meaning of life lies in being left in peace. We are called to hold tight to justice in outward "temperance" and inward "holiness." In righteousness we refine the intonation of our calling.

Self-centered individualism that works its power through greed and fear is a part of the wood grain that is within us. As the violinmaker is respectful in working with twisted wood even as he heeds the laws of acoustics, so the inner law of righteousness does not go against the grain but works with it, helping us fulfill our sound through its life-giving guidance.

Without righteousness, the individual squanders meaning and the community is bereft of its inner music. It is true that a completely righteous and just society is a utopia, but a *utopia-less* and unrighteous society would be barbaric.

~

Art is a teacher of righteousness. When righteousness is fulfilled, it is not something alien but truly your own in the deepest sense of the word. Like the carving and crafting of a truly good violin continuously and respectfully corresponds with the wood to the very end, so righteousness is something that works to bring about wholeness of the soul to every person, every people. Just as the violinmaker does not make cold judgments about the wood but works with it, so righteousness does not offer legalistic judgment but opens a path to life. Faith is not something artificial coming *to* our lives but the flow of life itself. As Isaiah says: "I have raised him up in righteousness, and I will direct all his ways" (45:13 NKJV). Also, "I am the Lord your God, who teaches you to profit, who leads you by the way you should go" (48:17 NKJV). Just as acoustical laws serve the developing sound of an instrument in process, so the goal of righteousness is the sound of a whole life. Wisdom directs the evolution.

The old Italian ideal of the violin's arch is based on the cycloid form.[10] It is visually lovely and acoustically ingenious! It is a consummate law. The great Italian violinmakers of the seventeenth and eighteenth centuries all took their orientation from it. We must not lose the acoustical ingenuity that is fulfilled through the law of good arching; for the sake of the sound it commands me. A good sound simply cannot be achieved while ignoring this law, so to try to do so would simply be folly.

This metaphor reveals the path of righteousness too. As the violinmaker fixes his gaze on the developing arch and looks for agreement between the work and the vision, so God's wisdom seeks to be in tune with our given grain and the call to wholeness, our true sound. A command then becomes a promise, and creative power for life is embedded in this practice. They say: Exercise what God has asked of you and you will understand who he is. Do what is commanded of you and you will discover your own identity. You will hear the voice of God most clearly when you are inwardly in tune with his heart.[11] That is why the issue of which god or idols we trust is of utmost importance.

We comprehend the beauty of righteousness through the way a work of art develops. In violinmaking we comprehend through a creative act: I transform that which is unfamiliar to me. This very act is the compulsion of God's wisdom in our world: the Holy Spirit enfolds and empowers what is estranged from him. It is the Holy Spirit's nature to transform whatever he touches, because he comes "to save, to heal, to teach, to admonish, to strengthen, to console, and to enlighten."[12]

Just as tools remove the roughness from the curves in order to complete their progression, so God's commandments remove our compulsive and illusory selfishness. They confront whatever makes us unable to move in true freedom. Saint Augustine said, "After he has by his gift justified us, the Spirit of God takes away from us the taste for sin."[13] The sin in the developing work is that which is *not harmonious*, anything that refuses to be transformed—as if the arch were to say to the master: "I don't want to you to know me!" It would be like the wood, instead of entrusting itself into my hands, deciding to drive splinters into my fingers. The sinner is the splintered person. For sin is not: "You have stifled growth, you are twisted, you are bad!" but rather: "You are withdrawing! You are missing your meaning! You are sticking up splinters. You don't want the righteousness and freedom to which I have called you. You have refused my offer to work closely with you and to fulfill your sound with real life."[14]

When the trust between the work and the creator has been disturbed, dissonance arises in our hearts and minds, our relationships, and our behavior. Do not only focus on what the commandment takes from us but also understand deeply what it is giving us. It catalyzes changes within us and forms us in wholeness and beauty.

Faith will lose its self-centeredness and become holy and mature only when we understand that a relationship with God will not first be *experienced* but *lived*. Faith should not be a passing feeling but the constant expression of a life *lived*. Incidental experiences of faith can be an enormous encouragement, but a heart that has known longings, love, and loss knows that these moments are an "accompaniment": they are kisses of grace along the way. If we join those who pursue experiences rather than the One who is the path on which we walk, our faith will burn out in the flames of an unholy compulsion for ever more experiences, fueled by our escapist need to flee to God so as to avoid the world.

If we seek a fulfilled life we must ask what will be fulfilled through us. That is perhaps the essence of happiness, much like with the violinmaker's care for the wood. This analogy reveals that life's unique, authentic sound will not bypass us, but will be fulfilled within the fibrous course of the human heart. That's how the arch becomes complete in the master's hands. As heaven's truth takes shape in us, the laws of acoustics are fulfilled, not broken (see Romans 8:4). When this occurs despite the fibers' twisted growth and weaknesses, we know that a true master is at work.

Jesus said of himself: You call me master, and you are right, for that is what I am! (John 13:13; Matthew 23:8). In these words, I recognize my appropriate place: I am the clay, not the potter. I am the wood, not the Maker. My life has found an inner master, an inner prophet, to which my ear inclines, for listening is an act of love.

In prayer, we speak into being that which should be awakened in us, allowing it to find its way into living expression. Longing itself writes these words on our hearts. There they will be read and explored; they will be transformed into something that we ourselves cannot express—something that touches heaven (Romans 8:26). It is good when we find the words to pray, and yet Saint Augustine's insight still applies: "Longing is always at prayer even though the tongue is silent."[15]

The Wrong Jury

What discourages us from seeking this nearness and inner guidance? What keeps us from answering God's wisdom with our trust? I remember the moment when I first received a beautiful seventeenth-century Amati into my workshop. Fascinated, I examined this treasure from every angle. It was a masterpiece, and yet not perfect. Across its top ran a dark knot, bold and striking. Nor were its corners cut symmetrically. The violin's overwhelming character came through in its handwriting, which revealed a mature understanding of beauty. My thought at the time was, "Definitely not flawless, but it really has something . . ."

Doesn't our lack of courage often come from our inability to come to terms with our relationships? How often do we criticize the obvious knots in the wood of others and thereby overlook the character of a wonderful signature? We see the crooked fibers in life, but we lack the kindness and joy that allow us to say, "Not perfect, but she really has something!" We might even be disgusted by the twisted growth that the pressures and experiences of everyday life have produced in a person, and we want her to change. But God says: "What's that to you? She will sound, too, in her own way!" (see John 21:22). We love others the way we love ourselves. No wonder we criticize ourselves because of our own "reaction wood," which has been formed out of our difficult life experiences.

As a violinmaker I will not throw away the wood that I hold in my hands. It is precisely that knot that shows Amati's true mastery. What immobilizes and crushes us are expectations: this person shouldn't be like she is. By contrast, compassion calls things into life. It forces nothing and yet, precisely because it does not force, it changes everything.

Compassion originates from the place where God's wisdom is enthroned in a love that surrounds people, creation, the life of the whole world. This is why the first question asked in Scripture is not, "What are you longing for?" It is, "Where are you?" (Genesis 3:9). The first question we ask ourselves should never be, "What do I want to change?" but "Where am I?" In my restless desire to change things, am I present with God in the world as it is?

If we live in the Spirit, we will not try to force matters. Rather, we know that "no one can receive anything except what has been given from heaven" (John 3:27). And, "What do you have that you did not receive?" (1 Corinthians 4:7). We will stop judging people for their oddness, or crooked fibers, but—understanding our own uniqueness—trust, discover, and respect what we see in them. We will pray that heaven would give others what is theirs. We will restrict the flow and strength of grace unless we see each other through the eyes of our heart. These are the eyes of compassion.

Jesus says: "Be merciful, just as your Father is merciful" (Luke 6:36). Therefore we should call out the good in our neighbor through love, just as God does. God calls our possibilities into life while dignifying what already is there. We are encouraged, "Be a *blessing*, and *protection* for each other." This is the shelter of mercy, creating true peace. We are allowed to have experiences and make mistakes. In the circle of those who respect us, there is no irredeemable failure, only learning together.

～

Thinking about compassion brings to mind violin competitions where judges usually give one score for craftsmanship and another for sound. The judges scoring the craftsmanship are violinmakers, while those scoring the sound are musicians. If you win a prize for craftsmanship while receiving no praise for the sound, it's clear that you satisfied the judges who think about what they see. But the more important score is the musicians'; they are paying attention to the instrument's essence, its sound. The violins that are entered in such competitions are usually hopelessly perfect. That is precisely why they so often have such a miserable, fainthearted sound—they are not allowed to have anything wrong with them.

The most important thing about a violin is its "handwriting." Sound and form come together to create a radiance that touches the human heart. That which is perfect leaves you cold. Just as a wondrous violin does not get its graceful expression through perfect form, a person is not beautiful for lack of mistakes or the absence of loss or failure. Rather, beauty comes from a transparent life. Why do we lack the courage to see our lives in this way? Scripture answers: because we subject ourselves to the wrong jury! (1 Corinthians 7:23). Too often, our lives seem molded to the rules of a formal competition where fear blots out the radiant handwriting.

When we tie our self-worth to a perfectionist ideal, we ignore reality. We serve the wrong jury. How the conscientious suffer from their self-inflicted demands rather than concerning themselves with the world for which they are created. How the aging person suffers from diminishing strength, the inability to complete tasks, the sense of how little time remains. The limitation of time then becomes an enemy, mocking the imaginary ideals which we take to be our true selves as they recede into the distance. Isn't it time instead to take our ideals and even ourselves off the pedestal and so entrust ourselves more deeply into God's hands? When we take ourselves and our ideals too seriously, we become overly sensitive, and the more sensitive we are, the more quickly we are hurt.

Noble ideals and forced expectations will knock the wind out of you. Of course, I have high standards, and my customers do too. But when fear comes into play, things tighten up. They cannot develop if they are not given *time* and *hope*, the two key ingredients for healthy growth.

There are many who constantly judge each life's supposed mistakes and weaknesses, but there is just one judge of sound—God's wisdom. As it is written: "The Lord does not see as mortals see; they look on the outward appearance, but the Lord looks on the heart" (1 Samuel 16:7).

Wisdom

Judaism recognized the formative power that gives us life and named it *Wisdom*. Wisdom sanctifies the things she touches and brings them to wholeness. As my plane and scraper give the violin's arch its shape, so too there is a deep and delicate feel for form in God's Wisdom that removes the estranged parts of our lives and instead shapes something familiar and trustworthy to God and to us. Wisdom is the potent, active power of God. By it the essential characteristics of eternity take form in us and also in the world entrusted to us: the tone colors of righteousness, the beauty of compassion, and the power of reconciliation. God does nothing in us without Wisdom, and through her God's familiarity with his work evolves.

Hebrew literature contains a prophetic declaration of love toward the creative power that is Wisdom, which can also be translated as an "artist" or "craftswoman":

> And now I understand everything, hidden or visible, for Wisdom, the designer of all things, has instructed me. For within her is a spirit intelligent, holy, unique, manifold, subtle, mobile, incisive, unsullied, lucid, invulnerable, benevolent, shrewd, irresistible, beneficent, friendly to human beings, steadfast, dependable, unperturbed, almighty, all-surveying, penetrating all intelligent, pure and most subtle spirits. For Wisdom is quicker to move than any motion; she is so pure, she pervades and permeates all things. She is a breath of the power of God, pure emanation of the glory of the Almighty; so nothing impure can find its way into her. For she is a reflection of the eternal light, untarnished mirror of God's active power, and image of his goodness. (The Book of Wisdom 7:21–26)[16]

The book of Proverbs says that God gave Wisdom's artistry a role in the creation of the world: "The Lord created me at the beginning of his work, the first of his acts of long ago. Ages ago I was set up, at the first, before the beginning of the earth" (Proverbs 8:22–23). Wisdom is visible as an artist and craftswoman in the process of becoming. She does not work with a template. She sees the wood's grain and seeks the sound. She says: Why do you bemoan your wood's grain and don't believe in the sound that has been promised to you? What is stopping you from believing and thereby permitting me to be at work in you? God's Wisdom is a formative power touching life.

~

My wife and I are distressed with the cookie-cutter school system our younger son has to endure. How much of his creative and self-motivated fiber, how much initiative is being cut in the process? Lorenz has his own little workbench in my workshop. Quite often, I have come to grasp intriguing concepts through his carefree ideas. He is familiar with all my tools. When he was eight years old, I could already let him handle my sharpest cutters because I saw that his hand position was correct. But the school's benchmarks and un-imaginative tests take up more and more of his time and energy. They are required to fulfill the law. Yet personalities cannot form this way; they are merely pressed into preexisting models. I believe we should strive to give young people the courage to believe in themselves, develop passion and not to lose their awe and amazement for their interests and the world around them.

It is a sign of poverty to strive to fulfill the demands of the legalistic measuring system and act as if all wood had the same characteristics. A measuring chart or a template disdains the natural wood and its development. Therefore, I always hold the violin's top more and more carefully between my hands during its development, lightly strike on its tap tones, and bend it gently on its torsion, on its long and crosswise stiffness, in order to feel how far I can go. The violin's growth must be accompanied by intelligent love. Laws, templates, and measuring charts are not sufficient for violinmaking.

Words of Life

I was recently in a small group with a friend who is a wonderful professional dancer. She shared that one sentence, above all, dominates her life: "That won't do!"

That one phrase hangs over everything, over her dancing, her character, her gifts, her finances, her style: "That won't do!" She hears it in her mind all the time. Listening to this, we were shocked, and we took the time not only to lovingly confront such an idea but also to ask God in the silence what and how we could pray. Clearly, such praying is not meant to replace action but to strengthen and accompany us on the path on which we are already walking.

We give words like "That won't do!" the right to impose their opinion on our life. The Good News instead calls out: stop trying to prove yourself to God and the world. You will be ruined by this line of argumentation! "It is God who justifies" (Romans 8:33). It's normal to wish everything were better than it is, to look at the fibers of your own life's course, the tapered and twisted growth, and say: "Everything in and around me should be better!" But this is a self-judging curse, leading you to a life of wanting and wishing but not of growing. You will cease taking joy in your development. Instead, believe in the holy power that has been put in your life. There is something in you that can grow and rise up even if you do not understand it. You have a secret, a life, a song of praise! How can you look at the fibers of your life and not believe in the sound promised to you? Pour your warm heart's blood into what you are! There is no heartbeat in a life that remains a *pipe dream*! Let your eyes see that growth comes all by itself. You have something to give and can place your faith in your calling, in the promise of your sound.

Move into your worth and rip up your self-accusations. The letter to the Romans asks,

> Who will bring any charge against God's elect? It is God who justifies. Who is to condemn? It is Christ Jesus, who died, yes, who was raised, who is at the right hand of God, who indeed intercedes for us. Who will separate us from the love of Christ? . . . In all these things we are more than conquerors through him who loved us. For I am convinced that neither death, nor life, nor angels, nor rulers, nor things present, nor things to come, nor powers, nor height, nor depth, nor anything else in all creation, will be able to separate us from the love of God in Christ Jesus our Lord. (Romans 8:33–39)

Within these words is something eternal, something healing, and a holy strength. Some words are poison while others have a healing power. Holy words have the power to form. They are holy work-tools that give our life its sound.

Which words do you let do their work and have their effect across your soul's fibers and rays? Words that devalue and harm us might not be compelling, but they are subtly persuasive. Scripture warns us not to allow ourselves to believe their curse. Show them the door. We are entrusted to be our own councilor and bouncer!

Your insufficiencies and losses are both tasks and gifts because they will teach you to be compassionate. If you were only brilliant, how could you be compassionate? There would be nothing else demanded of you than to take note of your brilliance. Compassion radiates from the heart of God and is worth more than any success or brilliance.

Any soul that has been weakened by self-degradation should know that it has a godly Comforter and Teacher. God does not mock but suffers with you: God's Spirit "helps us in our weakness" and "intercedes with sighs too deep for words" (Romans 8:26). There is one thing he will never say to those who trust him: "You are not good enough for me!" For that sentence contains death.

How quickly we explain who we are and what we are like without really knowing ourselves! Why do we not stay excited about our lives and about what God's touch can trigger? How often do we underestimate the not-yet-awakened in ourselves and others, the hidden, the promise? We allow judgment to be passed on the grain of our wood but have sadly forgotten to trust the One who dignifies our fibers, who brings us to sound. This is why our soul has lost its faith and comfort. Don't allow accusations to abort your soul. Let us have holy words be our midwife. We can be born into something new—but we must learn how to be a child again. While I write this, I hear inwardly a baby's cry, inaudible and yet terribly loud and clear. I actually believe that biblical truths are bringing new life into existence. Something new is being created in you, which will make you grow. So turn around and be a child before God! You have been given to yourself; learn to be good to yourself and protect what is inside. As one psalm says, "I have calmed and quieted myself, I am

like a weaned child with its mother; like a weaned child I am content"
(Psalm 131:2 NIV).

The Degrading Faith

There is such a thing as self-degrading faith. It drives us to lose who
we are and try to replace ourselves completely with God. In such a
faith, God is made into a stop-gap for a lack of self-respect.

There is a kind of piety that equates humility with having low
self-regard. That is a great mistake! Faith in God was never meant
to replace faith in ourselves. Humility does not lie in thinking little
of myself but in thinking enough of others to serve them. There is
an important difference. God does not value subservience but does
greatly value humility. This corresponds with God's essential nature. It is true that we do not have to be strong, for God's strength
is made powerful in the weak, but we should not believe that we
have to make ourselves weak or devalue ourselves in order to make
God strong.

The Holy Spirit makes us see our courage with our own eyes,
so that we can overcome the discouragement that comes from looking at our weak fibers and convincing ourselves we are too little, too
weak, too sick, too burdened, too guilty, too unsure, too broken, too
damaged, too limited, too worthless, too doubtful, and too hurt to
matter, or to change. It is important to oppose these religious feelings
of low self-worth with something strong and true. Don't underestimate the gentleness and power of the Holy Spirit. Trees and herbs
are soft when they sprout, but hard and dry when they die. God's
Spirit promotes a soft, young heart in us because he makes us *young
and brave* enough to trust God (Psalm 103). As the strings awaken
resonance in the violin, so God calls to our hearts.

> My friend, do not say, "How should someone like me lift others
> up, when I myself am so beaten down? How can someone like me
> strengthen people, when I myself am weak and insecure?" Do not
> repeat nor believe the sentence: "How can someone like me . . . ?"
> For I see your doubt, your sickness, how downtrodden you are. And

yet I have called you to rise up, to comfort and to strengthen. I will be with you. Do not believe that the strong, the healthy, and the secure can serve me better than you.

Seek my presence and trust me. My Spirit will rest upon you. In your weakness, he will do his work in you. You will comfort others with the same comfort that you have been given and will anoint with the same Spirit that rests on you. So, come to me, my weak and burdened, sick and insecure, beaten down and doubting friend. Be strengthened, rise up. Learn of me and take up your calling![17]

We return this love through the power of simple trust. It cannot be otherwise because love is *always* trusted. When we see our lives in this light, we will live differently. We should not imagine our calling as a chore but as a dance partner. It is not the one who makes everything better but *only the beloved* who actually offers a different life. As it says in the Scriptures, "In all these things we are more than conquerors through him who loved us" (Romans 8:37). God is not obstinate. It is important that we allow God's wisdom to lead our life, for love sees opportunities for development where others see only destruction, damage, and handicaps. Love perceives *what has come about* and lives in the hope of *what can come to be*. In these two dimensions of time we are created anew by a holy presence.

~

You can estrange yourself from your calling by religious fervor. This estrangement is called "legalism." Legalism is not an exaggerated love for the law but a lack of love for life. Hence, legalism is a degradation of life. The legalistic person is disappointed with himself and others, with life as it is. Therefore he makes his law a god to rule over his life. Legalism is the stone rolled in front of the grave of his deceased love for God.

In a quaint section of the Deutsche Museum in Munich, there are some odd musical instruments on display. You stand in front of what looks like a piano but see that it is played by a roll of paper with holes in it! Inside, paper rolls are mechanically unwinding, and the keys seem to move on their own. You push a button and the keys tinkle and repeat phrases from long ago. These automatic machines have no room for inspiration. They give the listener a false impression of a life that is in fact lacking. They are fake instruments, a terrible symbol of an estranged existence that performs rituals without filling them with life. A living instrument is capable of interpreting life. But for that, one must truly listen and truly see what is happening. Inspiration and interpretation, hearing and doing—this is the calling, to give life an "inner musicality."

Faith also can mutate into this sort of automated instrument. Preprogrammed. In such a phase, quietly listening might still save us if we only recognize the hypocrisy of habits that have no true inner life. Religious automatic instruments try to play their game with us. If this automation were the sad reality of the world, then it would merely be heaven's toy. And a boring one at that. Without inspiration and interpretation. Technically perfect, but lifeless. We would have no reason to complain, but also no reason to live.

Jesus addressed legalism with great severity. It was not the lax but the stick-straight pious people who could not stand him. They "went out and conspired against him, how to destroy him" (Matthew 12:14). Jesus was attacking a religious power that took the wrong approach to life. In it he saw an assault on humanity. Jesus did not oil the machinery of legalism but put the sound of God's kingdom in our hearts. We are true, living instruments touched by God, co-creators in making music.

The Law

The metaphor of the violin's curves and arches has been building inside of me ever since I carved my first violin at the age of seventeen. All along the sense has kept growing inside me that the wood taking shape in my hands resembles what is described in Romans 8:30! To quote it again: "And those whom he predestined he also called; and those whom he called he also justified; and those whom he justified he also glorified." That same verse had introduced me to Scripture at the age of thirteen, the moment when I first came to faith—against my father's formidable will.

The metaphor of the fiber course of our human existence scrutinizes every legalistic and compulsory version of faith. Is it appropriate to talk of faith in this way? Doesn't this mislead us into a romantic-religious infatuation until, in the end, only some ludicrous emotional state, a "Torah of inwardness," remains? Furthermore, is not Scripture *law* as well? Does it not contain hundreds of "measuring charts" and "templates" to show us how to live? Is this not precisely the essence of religion—to issue moral and religious laws that we must keep? Right here we must insert a big "but" into the metaphor of the violin's arching and wood grain, lest the parable not reach down to the depths where the perceived worth of our inner lives will be decided.

What, after all, is law? This term is found 430 times in the Old Testament and 191 times in the New. That frequency alone shows it to be of more than marginal importance. When the letter to the Romans says, "Christ is the end of the law" (10:4)—that is, the end of the *nomos*—is this an announcement of the beginning of autonomy? Does Christ free us from slavery under the yoke of the law in order to lead us to self-determination, into being a law of our own (*auto-nomos*)?

The term *law* awakens hesitation and aversion in people. We imagine it to be something judgmental, coercive, even despotic. It conjures up a religiosity filled with the demands of a strict god who crushes our freedom, who ties us up with rules and harsh commands. We fear that our hearts will degenerate into automatons—that we will be spinning pre-cut paper rolls without a trace of real inner life. That is the essence of legalism. However, all this has little to do with the law (the Torah) of Scripture.

It is important to set the Hebrew word *Torah* free from hard, misleading Western concepts and understand its original meaning. In the third century BC in Alexandria, when Jewish scribes began translating the Hebrew Bible into Greek, they used the Greek expression *nomos* to represent the Hebrew word *Torah*—in English, translated "law."[18] For the Greeks as well as the Hellenistic Jews of Alexandria, that translation was perfect because *nomos* had a lofty and celebratory tone that resonated with the respect belonging to *teaching*, *instruction*, and *guidance*.

The rabbi (teacher) sits down; the lesson is about to begin. We see this with Jesus as well. The disciples gather around him and are silent. The scene is formal and dignified. The rabbi's disciples listen, memorize his sayings, and at the appointed time begin to debate. They want to more precisely "sound out" these truths as well as explore doubts and questions, make the teachings more vivid, and convince each other through mutual exchange.

Since my early youth I have been familiar with these kinds of disputations.[19] They are not mere intellectual pursuits but more like a mirror through which you can see your own life. They don't mean to mold you according to preset instructions. Something much more comprehensive is going on, a spiritual deepening.

For Jesus, the Torah was teaching for life. It is also called *Torat Hayim* in Judaism: *The Law of Life.* Its content always concerns the art of living. Whoever does not listen, destroys art and holiness itself. Therefore, the most important confession of Judaism, as well as the highest commandment given by Jesus, starts with the word "Hear!" (Deuteronomy 6:4; Mark 12:29). The law received its meaning from God, to serve the people who kept it. But the legalistic person turns this around. He tries to give his life meaning by keeping the law and thereby to earn something from God.[20] That is not the heartbeat of a living law but the cardiac arrest caused by legalism. Legalism lives from self-righteousness or in the religious fear of weakened hearts.

Nothing attacks our ability to love more aggressively than legalism, because it drives us into narrow straits, to fear, and to obstinacy. But that is only *one* direction of danger. Lawlessness is an attack on life as well. Jesus spoke of it as a sign of "the end of the world," a time when *unrighteousness* will take the upper hand; with that the *love* of many will grow cold (Matthew 24:12). Jesus speaks of a person's *outer* and *inner* lawlessness, for the law of love is the command given to the heart which then expresses itself in the world.

To proclaim that the heart needs no law, that it is able to love deeply on its own, is both a true and an abysmal statement. It is true that the loving heart needs no law because it has found its law in that it loves. Augustine says just this with his provocatively true words: "Love and do what you will."[21] The one who loves needs no law.

And yet on the flip side we see that the one who fears the law of love shows that he does not love. Only the nonloving heart will declare that it needs no law in the sense of guidance or instruction. The law speaks of righteousness, and its fruit is peace (James 3:18). But the nonloving heart places self-righteousness first, self-satisfaction above peace, its own rights above reconciliation, etc. It is the creed of inner lawlessness that places the naturally given wood grain over the carving of wisdom. Inner lawlessness is cheap. The heart requires some opposition! It needs a rock on which to ground its strength. Without that, the moral restorative force of the human heart has no point of leverage. Strength cannot ground itself on nothing. That would be like the tall tales of the Baron Münchhausen, who grabbed hold of his own hair to pull himself out of the swamp. Magical autonomy! That is the claim of the law-denying heart.

The lie of lawlessness is propagated by a romanticized glamorization of the self-serving "me." Adding a pious and noble tone to the mix changes nothing. Without inner order, every search will become an addiction. To lose the law is to lose the heart's truth, and without that truth we will be destroyed internally by selfishness and externally by injustice. By contrast, the Psalms and prophets speak of the person, as well a whole people, who have the law of their God in their hearts (Psalm 37:31; Isaiah 51:7). Law and love are inner pillars of faith, harmonious opposites that manifest themselves externally in communal life. So also it is with their fallen counterpoints, legalism and lawlessness.

There is only one reason to say with Paul that "Christ is the end of the law." He is its end because he is its completion. He is the master of life and fulfills the law of love through our lives as well. Whether one piece of wood is "better" or "worse" than another is not the question. In violinmaking, it is only a matter of how I, as a master, can work with the wood to fulfill its sound. The complete text from Romans is this: "Christ is the end of the law so that there may be righteousness for everyone who believes" (Romans 10:4). The master violinmaker justifies the wood by taking care with respect to the fibers and fulfilling acoustical demands. True mastery is just this: "Christ in me" (Galatians 2:20; Romans 8:10). It is living together, abiding with a master.

The most "Spirit-filled" chapter of the Bible (Romans 8) is not concerned with exuberant voices but with fulfilling righteousness (8:4). Our metaphor of wood grain and arching leads not to *legalism*, which subjects everything to the template, nor to *lawlessness*, which supposedly frees people from the burden of commands. But if we are to be neither legalistic nor lawless, then what?

The Three Paths

Metaphorically, the dilemma posed by the natural-grown wood grain and the requirements of the arching allows three possible solutions. The first two are captured in one sentence of Jesus: "The gate is wide and the road is easy that leads to destruction" (Matthew 7:13). This wide, easy road can be either a religious path or one lacking religion. Neither leads to life. Of the third option Jesus says: "The gate is narrow and the road is hard that leads to life" (Matthew 7:14). What are these three paths?

The wide religious path is *legalism: "It is of utmost importance to see a perfect form emerge!"* To this a good violinmaker would respond, no! If you pay attention to the curve of the arch but not the wood fibers, then even the most beautiful of shapes will never acquire a beautiful and good sound. Wisdom asks: do you respect the crooked and twisted growth in your life and in the life of your neighbor? Or do you ignore reality and bend the truth to fit your template? The legalist's motto is, Bend it until it fits rather than see what has evolved and what is developing. Legalism makes us numb to the essential question, "What does God want to say to me through reality, the reality of what *I am*?" Life's fibers will not let themselves be bent out of shape. You have to respect them.

The second path, equally broad, is the non-religious path of *autonomy*. This path claims: *"Above all, let me follow my own fiber!"* To this a good violinmaker will respond, no! If you pay attention to your fibers but not to the rules of the arching, then even the greatest amount of care with the wood's grain will never lead to a beautiful and good sound. Here Wisdom asks, "Do you seek and respect the law of life? Or do you turn your twisted growth into law, as a person trying to *justify himself?*" "What is real is right" is the autonomous person's doctrine of justification, replacing the moral with the authentic. I am a law *unto myself: auto-nomos.*

The third and narrow path on which Jesus walks and to which he calls his disciples is one of *Spirit-filled faith.* This combines respect for God and compassion for others. Herein lies the vertical and the horizontal dimensions of our lives. The *arch* is the law that *commands* me. The *wood grain* symbolizes what has been *given to me.* These two will unite only when I recognize that God's wisdom is at work in me. In the process of building a violin, respect and compassion are somehow miraculously transformed into sound.

The meaning here is twofold: we have had enough of cheap autonomy! It is merely a glorification of *what has come about.* And enough of legalism, for it is only a glorification of *what is commanded.* Fibers and arching—the given and the commanded—are harmonious opposites that we must respect for the sake of our calling.

In the end, this path is an escape forward, flight into the arms of God. I do not fear what life requires of me, for what God demands he also makes possible. Heaven will never demand something that will overtax us. This escape forward puts faith in God's wisdom. When we are wood in God's hands, then morality can finally be authentic and the authentic can be moral.

Reverence

There is a Torah in violinmaking! The one who loves the laws of acoustics, understanding that they serve the violin's sound, has long since comprehended the difference between reverence and legalism. A good violinmaker must take the laws of the vibrating arch to heart. Intuition and knowledge will lead him to give the top of the violin the right measure of stiffness and mass. Then the resonances develop correctly and serve the tone color. I respect acoustical laws because they are the *teaching, instruction,* and *guidance* for good sound. Only someone indifferent to a good sound will set them aside. I do not respect the rules of acoustics for their own sake but for the sake of the sound I seek to create. So it is with the Torah. It is not there for itself but for the sound to which we are called: the *righteousness* that is the proper tuning of our lives (Romans 8:4).

A "sounding person" is not a slave but a servant. He serves God—not because he must and not because service is advantageous to him, but because it is his desire. Fear makes us small; reverence lifts us up. The life of slavery calculates usefulness; the life of service is generous. It is compassionate and therefore free because it gives itself without thinking about charging interest or repayment. The Spirit-filled life is reverence before the Creator who is Life, and it is merciful to all of creation longing for Life. Antigonos of Sokho (third century BC) said: "Do not be like slaves who serve their lord in order to receive a reward but be like the servant who serves his lord without considering payment; and may the reverence of being in God's presence be with you!"[22]

The reward that I receive by holding to these laws is not some kind of payment I strive for but life itself! Nehemiah's words about God's commandments echo here: "by the observance of which a person shall live" (Nehemiah 9:29). That is precisely what violinmaking teaches me: the reward for keeping the acoustical commandments is not a financial bonus but the sound of the violin itself! What more could I want? The audible sound is a metaphor for the well-lived life. And a good sound is a metaphor for righteousness. That's why God says in the book of Ezekiel that the one who "follows my statutes, and is careful to observe my ordinances, acting faithfully—such a one is righteous" (18:9).

The New Testament is not a softened version of the Old Testament. Grace is not like laundry softener! It is an active power, bringing what has been given (the fibers) to fruition in the way that has been commanded (the arch). In this way our sound is fulfilled. Just as a person cannot play fibers against arching in violinmaking, so you cannot call upon "New Testament grace," knowing nothing about God's commandments. That would make the profession of grace just a masquerade of autonomy.

In the tension between naturally grown wood grain and the right arch, what matters is that they fulfill each other! And this is the basic relationship between grace and commandments. A good sound unfolds only when the one brings the other to fruition and so fulfills the other's meaning. In this way Jesus says: "They who have my commandments and keep them are those who love me; and those who love me will be loved by my Father, and I will love them and reveal myself to them" (John 14:21).

The development of a good sound, which is the goal of all my work as a master violinmaker, is a sensory revelation of beauty and life. It is the same with the sound of our life. We need to develop a feel for the alluring power of Wisdom at work in us; we need to be overcome by love and the pressing power of grace that wants to create something beautiful through our lives.

Through the metaphor of arch and fiber I have tried to show that two principal truths sustain human life: *reverence* toward what is commanded and *compassion* toward what has been given. If reverence and compassion have no place in our life, the sound is ruined. A common, shrill, dull, nasal, ugly, and unfulfilled sound is its own punishment. As the apostle Paul says: "For you reap whatever you sow" (Galatians 6:7), and the prophet Habakkuk says: "You are sinning against yourself" (2:10 NASB). In this way we ruin life. But when we are led by Wisdom to reverence and mercy, a good sound will emerge: "Sow for yourselves righteousness; reap steadfast love!" (Hosea 10:12).

~

Previously I mentioned the historic quote from Antigonos found near the beginning of the Talmud. Antigonos of Sokho reportedly had two students, Zadok and Boethos. When they heard that there is no reward for keeping the commandments and no punishment for breaking them, they threw off the yoke of the Torah and gave themselves to life's pleasures, freely following the principle: "Let us eat, drink, and be merry, for tomorrow we die."[23] Apparently Antigonos overestimated the maturity of his pupils.[24] Scripture's tone colors are as diverse as the degrees of maturity of the human heart. The sound of Scripture does not patronize the immature and turn solely toward those who are enlightened. It sends a call to everyone to live a life of reverence and compassion. Scripture speaks to the immature rather simply in the concepts of sowing and reaping, rewards and punishment.[25] This is like saying to a violinmaker, "If you have no ears or love for the sound, then at least remember that you will have to sell that violin someday and live from the proceeds. Isn't that alone worth your efforts?" Perhaps this violinmaker will learn, through all his labors, to finally listen and one day find true fulfillment in the good sound.

06

To Be an Instrument

The Beauty of Our Calling

For if any are hearers of the word and
not doers, they are like those who look
at themselves in a mirror; for they look at
themselves and, on going away, immediately forget what they were like.

—JAMES 1:23-24

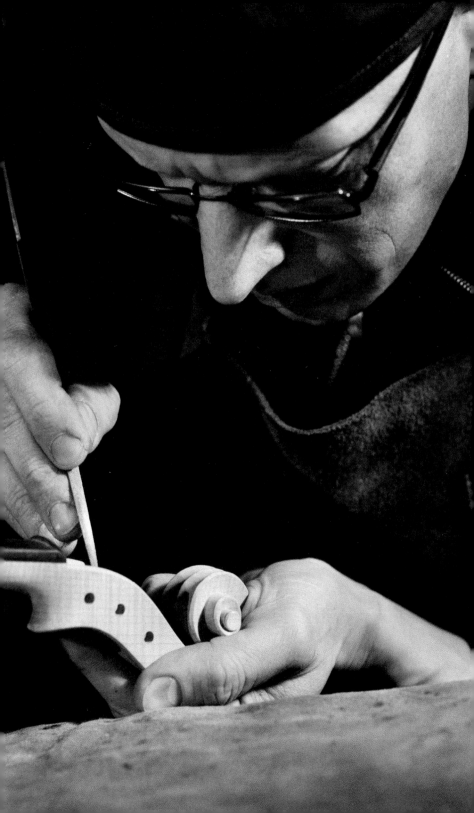

*Y*EARS AGO, I VISITED a renowned teacher at Munich's University of Music and Performing Arts to show him my newest cello. I had just finished it, working in the style of the eighteenth-century Venetian master, Domenico Montagnana. When I showed up, the professor was in the middle of a lesson, so he invited me to sit in. As I listened, I witnessed the passion and wisdom with which he approached Antonín Dvořák's Cello Concerto, giving his student a better understanding of this beautiful work. At first, he simply explained fingerings and bowings but then focused more and more on musical phrasing and expression. He interrupted the student's playing again and again, questioning her approach and explaining specific passages. He then played these parts and encouraged her. As I sat watching all of this, my gaze fell upon an inspirational quote on the wall across from me, hanging in a small, classic frame, and constantly in view of his students. "Your practicing amounts to nothing, no matter how often you try, if it does not come spontaneously of its own accord."

Conservatory Training

It would be a terrible mistake to approach faith, purpose, and calling according to this saying. What is deeply meaningful can be learned only through *practice*. Practice is the source not just of the right sound but also of the right life. If the interpretation of a cello concerto demands such care in daily practice and serious study, should our life's sound, deeply entwined in daily tasks and relationships, require any less from us? As music makes the composer's thought audible and thereby touches our souls, so the tasks of daily life can sound out the meaning of our lives. That requires self-dedication, walking the path of practicing and studying like the student who trains day after day to be a good musician. She does not count on co-incidence, hoping that her intonation or interpretation might "come spontaneously of its own accord."

The world-class violinist Anne-Sophie Mutter, whose charity foundation does so much to support young violinists around the world, was once asked about the next generation of musical talent:

> Anne-Sophie Mutter: In Germany—well. More and more it is the East Europeans and Asians who are coming into the fore-ground: Russians, Japanese, Chinese, Koreans.
> Question: How can you explain this?
> Anne-Sophie Mutter: They have a greater capacity for suffering.
> Question: That sounds like solitary confinement with an instru-ment. Isn't there a nicer word you can use?
> Anne-Sophie Mutter: No, that comes with it and it is not meant to be negative. It has to do with passion, demanding something of one's self.[1]

We confuse grace with chance when we assume grace creates au-tomatic success without our participation. It is a cheap and low view of our humanity. The power of "grace" in the Bible never replaces our practice and work; it only affirms them. I cannot imagine any serious path of human existence worth our while that would simply leave us to enrich our knowledge without leading us to put it into practice. A philosophy or a religion that stops at knowledge tempts us to reli-gious or intellectual self-glorification. In this chapter, therefore, we'll look at *what we do*—and therefore what sounds through our lives.

To Be a Person

I would like to tell you about a friend. Ingolf Turban is a wonderful violinist who performs solos with great orchestras. As I was talking with him not long ago in my workshop, he told me that he loves his violin (a 1721 Stradivarius) above all "because it has a special, captivating voice." Those who experience his playing have the impression that the instrument has become a part of his body. Once as he was trying out one of my new violins, he said that on the high notes he did not feel like he was playing a violin but singing.

What Ingolf says about the "captivating voice" of his violin describes what it means to be a *person* in a special way. This word has much to teach us about the nature of our purpose as human beings. The word *person* comes from *per* (= through) and *sonum* (= sound). To be a person is *to sound through*. Linguists have explored the roots of this meaning. The Greek word *prosōpon* means face, appearance, expression, as well as mask or role—also figuratively, the social or moral role that a person takes on. The Latin word *persona* is probably derived from *personare* (through-sound) because in antiquity, theater masks had a horn to enable the actor's voice to penetrate through the mask. According to this concept, what makes us recognizable as people is that which is active, visible, and audible through us. It is that which comes to sound through our lives.

Existence and Presence

God does not replace our presence with his. Rather, he seeks our presence to bring it to fruition in the same way a musician sounds an instrument. It is not as if the musician's sound is "here" and the instrument is "there," nor is it "me" here and "God" there, but *both in one*. As the instrument and musician join together, so God joins himself with the fragility of our love. His gentleness is reflected in the respect with which he meets us, his presence in our attentiveness, his righteousness in our relationships, his truth in our conduct, his mercy in our unwillingness to hold a grudge, in learning to forgive each other.

In this way, God lets us participate with him in life. God is there. He asks, "Where are you?" and we say, "I'm here!" Only through overwhelming, incomprehensible love do we partner with God and understand: He is here. When the musician finds his sound in the violin, the musician and the violin are not each half there but both are wholly present. The musician does not become a violin, and yet he becomes completely united with it. A single, unified sound emerges that cannot be divided. No one would come up with the ridiculous idea that "This half of the sound belongs to the instrument, and the other half belongs to the musician." We are aware of the difference between the musician and the instrument (identity), but still they cannot be separated (unity). Only when both are wholly present does the sound emerge.

This shared sound is the essence of unity. Martin Buber said, "Unity alone is true power."[2] The relationship between instrument and musician shows the most intimate form of unity. It is striking that humanity's great books of wisdom all speak about unity. As *The Book of Changes* says: "An enlightened ruler and an obedient servant—this is the condition on which great progress depends."[3]

The joining of a musician and an instrument is a picture of this unity. The instrument gives itself completely into the hands of the musician, and the musician is fully immersed in the instrument's sound. Many scriptural illustrations describe such collaboration as the essence of faith. One example is the well-known parable of the "True Vine," in which Jesus describes his relationship with his disciples: "Abide in me as I abide in you. Just as the branch cannot bear fruit by itself unless it abides in the vine, neither can you unless you abide in me. I am the vine, you are the branches. Those who abide in me and I in them bear much fruit, because apart from me you can do nothing" (John 15:4-5).

A branch does not produce fruit if it does not remain in the vine, but we are too quick to overlook the reverse: neither does the vine produce fruit if it has no branches. This is both the humility of God and the humility of being human. The awareness of this mutuality is essential for a Spirit-filled life. *Abide in me, and I in you*: the instrument wholly in the hands of the musician and the musician entirely in the sound of the instrument. Within this experience of becoming one, the meaning of our existence is fulfilled.

Something incredible happens for the instrument and the branch when combined with the musician and the vine, but neither is bypassed! Indeed, the musician makes no sound without the instrument, and the vine without branches has no fruit. We should observe this mutual dependence and not allow ourselves to be misled into not taking ourselves seriously because of God's greatness.

Life's unspeakable beauty is found in this interplay. Heaven's grace longs to play our faith as a musician plays her instrument. Indeed, "faith" means placing yourself in the hands of grace and allowing "music" to be played through you. Unspeakable beauty emerges where the bow touches the vibrating string. It is a vulnerable undertaking. The place of contact between the musician's bow (grace) and the vibrating string (faith) is overwhelmingly vulnerable—but that is exactly why beauty can be formed. All beauty emerges out of vulnerability. That is why it is so important to recognize the vulnerability of our relationship to God as something precious.

The images of the instrument and the branches depict unity and synchronicity: the musician and the instrument make one sound, the vine and the branch bear one fruit. As Ingolf said about the voice of his violin, so the fulfillment of human life comes when God can say about us, his instruments: "With him or her there are moments when it is no longer like playing the violin, but like singing!"

God Plays with Us

As a musician does not separate herself from the instrument when she is playing, just so, God does not separate himself from our life. God does not enthrone himself over life but plays within it. It is not a cynical game; as the Talmud says: "The Holy One, praised be he, does not play a mischievous game with his creation."[4] Rather, this is like the musician's self-abandoned playing—wholly and completely enveloped in the sound of her instrument while giving voice to the composition. The sound of the violin is the violinist's voice. The sound of our lives should be God's voice.

Faith has breathtaking significance in this game. This is what Friedrich Schiller was talking about in regard to humanity's aesthetic formation: "Man only plays when in the full meaning of the word he is a man, and he is only completely a man when he plays."[5] God does not need me to be God, and yet God is only completely God when he plays with me. Faith is the willingness of heart that I bring to this game. Life's heartfelt, searching, questioning, meaningful play develops through faith. For God is not only facing the world; he is sounding through the world.[6] The world is his instrument. We can learn to hear his sound.

In moments of doubt we wonder why we do not experience God. But that is like asking during a concert why we do not hear the violinist but only the violin. We will only hear the sound when we understand that we are God's instruments. We do not hear the "pure" voice of God; we hear one through the other. When we become God's instruments for each other, we learn to tune the sound that our calling desires.

We find God, not by bypassing the world, but "in" the world—in tasks, encounters, beauties, and difficulties. When we pray: "God, you are too far away from me!," God answers: "Where are you looking for me? Open your eyes and your heart to the things for which I made you, and don't look past them! I did not make you to let you ignore the world in loving me, but to find me in learning to hope, believe, and love. Start looking at the world through my eyes and you will recognize who I am. Then you will stop saying that I am far away." We become a person in this world. We are called to this. Martin Buber captured the *per sonum* in the following wonderful words:

> One must, however, take care not to understand this conversation with God . . . as something happening solely alongside or above the every day. God's speech to men penetrates what happens in the life of each one of us, and all that happens in the world around us, biographical and historical, and makes it for you and me into an instruction, message, demand. Happening upon happening, situation upon situation are enabled and empowered by the personal speech of God to demand of the human person that he take his stand and make his decision. Often enough we think there is nothing to hear, but long before we have ourselves put wax in our ears.[7]

From Form to Sound

Inner listening is an essential requirement in the development of a violin. I hear the sound with my inner ear long before the instrument is finished. That's the only way for me to know how to shape the wood. The obvious result of my work is a wooden form, but in reality, I am calling sound to life. The form will transform into sound, it will turn into music. The instrument is so much more than visible wood: it is a powerful personal sound.

In the same way, every person has his sound: we consist not only of visible *matter*, but, mysteriously, also of a *consciousness*. This gives rise to the marvelous question: how does our consciousness enter into this matter?[8] Our brains are not only flesh that thinks, but a self-aware, active spirit. And we are able to reflect upon this truth. Our consciousness is entrusted to the thinking brain like the sound is to the reverberating wood. We are—as expressed in a play on the ancient Hebrew words—'*Adam* (the human) created from '*adama* (the clay from the field). That is the tension between sound and form. The creation story describes a mystery in which unconscious physical particles and unconscious chemical processes can develop a conscious spirit. Those who are not amazed by this must have never considered it.

> Then the Lord God formed man from the dust of the ground, and breathed into his nostrils the breath of life; and the man became a living being. (Genesis 2:7)

You are made from '*adama*, and yet you are aware that you are more than clumps of matter. Adam, human, you bring forth art and science; you feel love and hope; you suffer from limits and finality; you are able to compose a symphony and then create and fund an orchestra to play it. You experience fear and joy; you are capable of sinning as well as showing faithfulness. You ask yourself who you are and what you should do; you question yourself and wonder if you matter. You send out your intellect to investigate the world; yet, try as you might to observe yourself, you remain a riddle. And then comes faith—that mysterious fire of the human consciousness! The world was formed by material forces, but consciousness is breathed into us. Clay from the field, spirit from breath, form and sound.

~

The most powerful *self-confidence* in which one can live is this: *I am loved.* But in addition, a *"sense-confidence"* must come alongside, namely, that *I am called.* My life makes sense. These are the two principles of our existence. They touch grace on the deepest level. Through these two words—love and calling—we first come to understand the logos of our existence.

The essential things in life must be refined. For that to happen they must be smelted from the hard stone of our "me." Only love possesses enough fervor and fire for this task. Being nothing but "me" indicates a decision to live impoverished, locked away in one's self. It is the decision to ignore one's calling. This impoverishment is tangible; we experience it in our interactions with others. Lack of meaning in life turns into greed for material things. Lack of certainty makes us greedy for security. Lack of authority becomes greed for power. Lack of character becomes greed for competence. Lack of recognition turns into greed for applause. The list can go on and on. We grow rich in this world in proportion to our inner poverty; we refuse purification and try to numb the mounting pain of meaninglessness. People who do not have meaning within search for it in vain without! In that search we overtax the world and make it our prostitute—as if the things out of which we live could be bought. In this confused, self-absorbed quest, we value the wrong things. Chuang-tzu's famous parable of the ferryman ends with the sentence: "He who looks too hard at the outside gets clumsy on the inside."[9]

Calling and Poverty

We are grounded in these fundamental truths: you are *loved* and you are *called.* That is, *you are* and *you should.* In these words, Adam is created out of *'adama* and wood turns into sound. But this truth makes us vulnerable. We are forced to recognize that the ground of love is also the ground of suffering. Without vulnerability, there would be no love; it would not be necessary. We need love, and therefore we are entrusted to one another. But in our neediness, we can be hurt, which leads to suffering. If we, the essence of this world, were unable or unwilling to suffer, then there would be no room for love.

Two aspects of the same truth are present here: on the one hand, need, on the other, calling. We do not overcome sorrow by overcoming the neediness of our existence, but by becoming people who love. Only the one who loves is in fact enlightened. He devotes himself to his calling. It is the light that brings him out of darkness. He who has no needs does not long for enlightenment; he has merely squelched his vulnerability, dulled his need to be loved. This is not enlightenment but an inflated cowardice of the spirit, the fear of one's own nature.

A piece of rabbinical logic sums up this tension in an impressively simple fashion. Israel Salanter said: "The material needs of your neighbor are your spiritual concern."[10]

True spirituality is not expanding our consciousness but concentrating our consciousness on our calling to be a loving person for the sake of our neighbor's—and also our enemy's—needs. There is no manifestation of God's grace in us more powerful than living this out. However, if we do not animate the calling within us, our hearts will grow dull, as will our faith.

Therefore, faith does not simply mean believing that God is good; it entails the discovery that God entrusts something good to me. We should turn our life's tasks into gifts. That is why it is important that we not simply ask, what do I trust in? but also, what has been entrusted to me?

The spiritual seeker must clarify one question above all else: whom or what should my life serve? This has nothing to do with the arrogance of trying to exploit God's secrets for our own ends. No, it involves a personal humility that allows itself to be present for the sake of the world. This needy world was created for the sake of our calling!

Fulbert Steffensky asks: "What is a spiritual experience? It is the experience of the eyes of Christ in the eyes of a child. It is the experience of Christ's nakedness in the naked beggar, meeting Martin;

the experience of the hungry Christ in the hunger of our brothers and sisters. The French Bishop Galliot says that he who dives into God resurfaces next to the poor. There is no awareness of God without awareness of the poor."[11] We must acquire a taste for what this means.

The Violin-Children of the Himalayas

Some time ago I met Silke, a young violinmaker with a strong sense of purpose. Her life's path fascinated me. After her training, unlike most alumni of her school, she decided not to look for an internship in a respected workshop but to move to a Gandhi Ashram school in India for a year. This "House of Learning," founded by Jesuits from Nuremberg, is extraordinary. As a part of their studies, every student there learns a stringed instrument.[12]

Silke had found out about this school and learned that the instruments were in terrible condition, in urgent need of repair. Some of her classmates and colleagues, who could not understand her decision to go there, kept on asking her, "What will you get out of it?" They believed she would be better off finding a prestigious position that would advance her career. Plus, she surely would not have much opportunity to work on many good instruments there. To work on such "wood splinters" instead would be neither fun nor rewarding. She confessed she was dumbstruck by such lack of understanding, but she remained unswayed by the comments. So she traveled on her own dime to the mountain town of Kalimpong in the foothills of the Himalayas and set up a little violin shop inside a school. There she worked for a whole year for about fifty Euros a month, using her learning and skills to make the rundown instruments sound—to make them technically playable, good, and attractive.

In one of her newsletters, she wrote about her experiences with the students, about making music together and working in the school's little restoration workshop. A well-known German manufacturer who makes fine, specialized tools for violinmakers was so moved by her dedication that he filled an overseas package with the finest tools and accessories and sent it to her, gratis. Because of her, this school came to have decent, functional equipment.

Only the poorest children are accepted at this school. And you should see their glowing self-confidence when they are making music! It gives these barefoot children a sense of worth, building them up. Some of the children come to practice violin before school begins, and often stay long afterwards. (The violins usually have to stay on school premises.) The Gandhi-Ashram becomes their home. Its founder, Jesuit priest Father McGuire, is convinced that playing music nurtures the intellectual ability of growing children and strengthens their self-esteem. For most of them, music comes to play a central role in daily life. The fact that they get three hot meals a day at school is understandably important to their parents, for many of them, farming fields on the mountain-sides of Kalimpong, do not produce enough to feed the family. They earn very little money through their hard labor as "Kulis" (load carriers).

$\sim$

Silke spent her vacation time in my workshop, preparing violins that had been donated to the school. While working, she told me about the self-confidence and openness of the students. The mountain tribes considered it to be a great honor and quite a sensation that she, a young blond woman, would hike over the beaten paths and makeshift bridges to visit students in their villages. The people lavished her with such friendship that she could hardly pull away from their hospitality, often staying overnight in their huts. These usually consisted of two rooms, without running water or electricity. The relationships were simple, and yet the feeling of human closeness was significant. In the morning she often woke up surrounded by the younger siblings of her students, who had cuddled up in bed with her and fallen asleep.

As Silke spoke of this, there was a light in her eyes only found in those who have experienced the meaning of their existence. When we seek the happiness of others our life rises "above and beyond" our individual existence. *That* is the transcendence to which we are called.

Kushmita, one violinist from Kalimpong, was recently accepted to the Richard Strauss Conservatory in Munich because of her extraordinary talent. And even though this is a notable accomplishment, Silke doesn't take it to be her greatest effect. Almost all of the graduates of this school are warmly welcomed at institutions of higher learning in their own country. The desire to have these talented students in orchestras around India has opened the door to a better life for them.[13]

Talent and Interest (BE.IN)

You do not have to venture to far-off places like India to experience this sort of joy. As a special-needs teacher, my wife, Claudia, works at a school for children with learning disabilities.[14] She has always had a warm place in her heart for disadvantaged children and so she jumped at the opportunity for a career in this field. In 2007, she founded a project that garnered the enthusiastic support of teachers and students alike and has since become a permanent program in the school. The project's name, BE.IN, stands not only for "be in" but also for *Begabung und Interessen* (Talent and Interests). Inspired by the contacts that we and other teachers have with artist friends and craftspeople, we were able to bring people with expertise to the school to share their enthusiasm and talents with small groups, providing inspiration for career and lifestyle options. With most children, it's usually the parents who encourage and facilitate artistic, musical, creative, or sports-related involvement. The students in these special schools, however, are usually excluded from such opportunities because they are either too expensive or require organizational or social skills their parents might not have.

One must bear in mind the kind of environments some of the special-needs students come from. My wife once failed spectacularly when presenting a math problem to her students. It had to do with calculating the entrance fee to the zoo, for which parents and children were charged different amounts. The students were supposed to add up the price for their own family. One student became aggressive, and upon being questioned he scoffed: "How am I supposed to know how many parents my family has? My mother and her boy-friend? Her ex-boyfriend? My father, whom I don't know? I don't know how many parents I have. This problem cannot be solved!"

Numerous children come from broken families. My wife knows of one student whose father drinks up to eight bottles of beer every night and forces the children to watch horror films with him. Other children are from Kosovo and are severely traumatized by war experiences. One of them sought my wife out after class to talk and said: "My father has done very bad things . . ." My wife could not even bring herself to tell me what he said.

Many are being raised by single parents, some of whom are unemployed. Some students have had run-ins with the police and the law, and families often lack the financial means and social competence to support their children. The BE.IN project was developed with these children in mind. Artists, actors, musicians, craftsmen, and other helpers offer courses for them at the school for a small stipend.

One concert we presented featured a customer of mine who is a violinist with the Bavarian Radio Symphony Orchestra. She arrived at the school with a friend of hers to play Mozart duets for violin and viola, bringing music to the children. Most of them had never seen a violin before and had never listened to classical music. After the concert, two thirteen-year-olds approached my wife. With gleaming eyes, one of them said that he had never heard anything so beautiful in his entire life.

Another student learned to juggle and perform circus acts in the BE.IN project. He became quite a master at it and, overjoyed, said to my wife: "Mrs. Schleske! I am so happy that the BE.IN project exists. Otherwise I would never have found my talent!"

For Clemente, another student, the future had become clear at the end of a project: "I know now that I will be a tile setter!" He had taken part in a mosaics workshop and had worked on decorating a wonderful fountain.

Through BE.IN, artists and course leaders (some of whom are well known in their field) offer creative projects that would not normally be part of the standard curriculum at a special-needs school for lack of time and resources. These projects included digital photoshopping, soccer, silk painting, mosaics, singing, woodworking, drawing comics, English language, painting on canvas, acting, science labs, PowerPoint, street boogie, Jiu-Jitsu, videos, gardening, modern dance, and silversmithing. The worth of these projects is perfectly summed up in the words of the educator Andreas Flitner: "Children need physical access to the world through their senses. Children are little craftsmen, painters, musicians, runners and skippers. Their senses are organs for world-exploration. Their learning must be accompanied by artistic, crafty, motor activities."

Without BE.IN, these students would have never come into contact with such enriching experiences. Instead, they would have had a lot of screen time or spent time on the streets. Thus far, the school has repeatedly had luck in finding sponsors on which the project depends. Numerous individuals as well as a renowned big-league soccer team from Munich have donated generously to the initiative. They are motivated by the knowledge that they can participate in preventing the aggression and bullying that these children often experience and bring healing instead. Discovering talents, encouraging people, relieving distress—these are the direct sorts of things that give our lives meaning and define our calling.

Our relationship with God is like the relationship between a composer and the musician interpreting the music. The musician becomes the *mediator* of the music. Through him, what has been composed is made audible.

The international concert pianist Ronald Brautigam once offered a remarkable testimony to his mentor Rudolf Serkin: "He made it clear to me why you should place yourself in the background and make sure that your sole purpose is to bring out the composer's intentions. This humility must come from the deepest understanding—it cannot merely be an attitude. You must be able to recognize that the composer's ideas are better than your own."[15]

When we understand God's work in our lives, our humility is found in expressing God's loving intentions. God's ideas are better than ours. Jesus's life was permeated by the humility of bringing

God's intentions to the forefront. This humility was simultaneously his authority, as he said: "Very truly, I tell you, the Son can do nothing on his own, but only what he sees the Father doing; for whatever the Father does, the Son does likewise" (John 5:19). And in another place: "I do nothing on my own, but I speak these things as the Father instructed me" (John 8:28).

If we, lacking trust in God, simply go our own way, we will damage that which is holy—that to which we are called. Brother Roger, the founder of Taizé, said: "What is fascinating about God is how humbly he is present. . . . Any authoritarian gesture would disfigure him."[16]

Reinhold

As this chapter is drawing near its end, I want to tell you about a good friend and amazing role model, Reinhold. Many people can speak with sophistication and put on an impressive display for the world. They are smooth, but they do not do what is good unless it serves their self-interest. The exact opposite is true of Reinhold. He created scandals and poked fun of unnecessary conventions in friendly ways. His small pre-fab, concrete apartment was a catastrophe of "furniture" items picked up at the Munich recycling center. The two rooms were not at all beautiful, but they ingloriously and unintentionally demonstrated that possessions are not as important as many of us think. Reinhold was a warm, quirky person. When I was with him, he always had a list of things that he wanted to discuss written on cardboard or a scrap of newspaper, with bullet points. Among these were notes about his specially formed chin rests for violins. He had once been a concertmaster in Palermo in southern Italy, but that was years ago. Now he was in his early sixties and had been unemployed for years.

How was Reinhold a role model for me? Because of the faithfulness and passion he displayed anytime and anywhere he saw a need he could alleviate. He rejected the church and struggled with faith. He was at the lower end of society in terms of material possessions but was indefatigable in organizing care-packages for the people in the Ukraine whom he visited each year. Because he was a Russian language-teacher before becoming a musician, he had contacts there. He made sure that some of his Ukrainian friends suffering from the effects of Chernobyl were able to come to a clinic in Munich for operations. He chased down donations to cover their travel costs, and quite a few times he was persistent and so supremely convincing that Munich's medical professionals declared themselves willing to operate on his friends for free. If, after all of that, there were still medical bills due, he gave benefit concerts.

I must mention his reinvention of the Baroque curved bow for his own use. It is ridiculously hard to play in this style because the chords are not broken—all four strings sound at the same time. For the left hand, intonation is almost impossibly challenging. The right thumb can be used to tighten the bow hair if desired and thereby one can still play spiccato. Listening to him give a concert in my workshop, we heard Johann Sebastian Bach's Sonatas played in an unusual, original, and authentic manner. A single violin can play *four parts* at once, filling the room with a vibratoless calm and grand sound, as if it were an organ. Our concert guests enthusiastically donated money for Reinhold's work. Even then, he could never quite make ends meet. It was a great burden on him. He planned to change his ways, yet he could never quite manage it. He kept meeting new people whom he could not resist befriending. He made friends quickly wherever he went. I'll help just this one or that one, he would say, and then quit. It was so stressful for him. But he never did stop.

I remember how he once laughed incredulously as someone started whining: "The need is so great out there. You're only making a drop in the bucket." Exposing that cynical attitude, he responded, "You cannot add up the needs of many people. For one person it is always his entire need. It is ridiculous to look at the needs of many people and think that it is one enormous pile. There is only the need of the individual. And if someone will help him, he is completely helped."

Reinhold died completely unexpectedly. I'm glad to say that I saw him four weeks earlier, and we spent more time together than usual, swimming in the Würm River that flows by the east wall of the workshop I had at that time. Swimming at full strength against the current, we could last about two minutes. We would then let ourselves be carried 200 meters downstream under a ceiling of sun-flooded leaves and climb out. Finally, we went out for pizza. That night, we talked together about matters of faith more than usual. He listened, but I do not think he could accept it for himself. In his eyes the church had negated itself through its wealth and harshness, and hundreds of years of abuses.

By chance, I learned of Reinhold's death through a brief obituary in the newspaper. He had died alone. There was no service, no songs, and no sermon at the crematorium. There were far too few people there. He certainly had not kept any organized address book. Who could have informed the people who knew him? His friends in the Ukraine, who could not come of course, honored him with a service there. As I prayed for him, I thought: "He has done more than enough to earn a place with you!" Of course, I know "earning" is an irrelevant thought by any token. Who would or could earn the love and presence of God? And yet, it is special to have known a person who believed much less but did so much more than I. It was his way of embracing life. And in it there was faith, a phenomenal faith. In prayer I placed him before Christ and saw him standing in spirit with those people described in Matthew chapter 25 who meet Christ on the last day and say in surprise,

> "When did I feed you and when did I visit you? When did I bring you clothing and shoes? When did I see your sickness and do whatever was possible? When did I see you in a Ukrainian province in the tortured brown bear in that hopelessly dirty cage that was too small and find a zoo on the other side of the country with a big, friendly space? When did I give you a violin in that little impoverished but musically gifted Ukrainian girl, whose mother, even though she was officially employed by the state as a violin teacher, had not been paid for seven months and collected vegetables off the ground, barefoot, at the end of the week's market in order to feed her two girls?"

The typical self-righteousness of a religious person was missing in Reinhold. He was more likely to laugh helplessly and groan over the fact that he could not let something be. He could not stop helping others. These lines are written for him, because no sermon was given in the mortuary chapel and there were only a handful of people there. In remembrance of him the words of Isaiah 58 well up, words written thousands of years ago, bearing a special significance that will never pass away:

> Shout out, do not hold back! Lift up your voice like a trumpet! Announce to my people their rebellion, to the house of Jacob their sins. Yet day after day they seek me and delight to know my ways, as if they were a nation that practiced righteousness and did not forsake the ordinance of their God; they ask of me righteous judgments, they delight to draw near to God. "Why do we fast, but you do not see? Why humble ourselves, but you do not notice?"
>
> Look, you serve your own interest on your fast day, and oppress all your workers. Look, you fast only to quarrel and to fight and to strike with a wicked fist. Such fasting as you do today will not make your voice heard on high. Is such the fast that I choose, a day to humble oneself? Is it to bow down the head like a bulrush, and to lie in sackcloth and ashes? Will you call this a fast, a day acceptable to the Lord?
>
> Is not this the fast that I choose: to loose the bonds of injustice, to undo the thongs of the yoke, to let the oppressed go free, and to break every yoke?
>
> Is it not to share your bread with the hungry, and bring the homeless poor into your house; when you see the naked, to cover them, and not to hide yourself from your own kin?
>
> Then your light shall break forth like the dawn, and your healing shall spring up quickly; your vindicator shall go before you, the glory of the Lord shall be your rear guard. Then you shall call, and the Lord will answer; you shall cry for help, and he will say, Here I am. If you remove the yoke from among you, the pointing of the finger, the speaking of evil, if you offer your food to the hungry and satisfy the needs of the afflicted, then your light shall rise in the darkness and your gloom be like the noonday.
>
> The Lord will guide you continually, and satisfy your needs in

parched places, and make your bones strong; and you shall be like a watered garden, like a spring of water, whose waters never fail.

Trusted and Entrusted

Why is it so hard to understand that we do not *have* life? We neither made ourselves nor wished ourselves into existence. We did not determine our life's circumstances and we cannot prevent our own death. No, we do not *have* life. It is not a possession. Life is loaned to us for a short time. In death we will give back what never belonged to us. If it belonged to us, then it would be unjust that we cannot keep it. We are lent out to life for a short time.

Our possibilities are fragile and our time withers. Our years dwindle and many dreams fade without ever being lived. What assurance should then guide and lead me?

Each day our lives are entrusted to us. But more than that, Life *calls* to us. Someday we will recognize how we responded to this expectancy and trust. If I seek after the happiness of my neighbor and God, my life is well-lived. If I think only of myself, then I lose everything. My life was given to me so that I will see, respect, promote, and love life in others. By examining ourselves regularly, we might ask, "*Per sonum!*—What is sounding through you? Answer me!"

A little while ago I spent three quiet days in the Propstei St. Gerald monastery in the Great Walser Valley. It was a warm day in May, and I walked up the short, steep path to the monastery's pond. As I looked at the mountains, I felt the warmth of the spring sunshine on my face. I listened to the brook and saw the sun lighting up the young, green thicket of trees in front of my eyes. Then God spoke a word in my heart: "Look at it! See, feel and hear it: I made all of that for you. You alone—it is you alone that I did not create for you!"

07

The Closed Sound

Belief in a Loving and
Therefore Suffering God

Let both of them grow together until
the harvest!

—MATTHEW 13:30

I ONCE HEARD A WISE JEWISH SAYING that God has two chambers in his heart, an outer and an inner. In the inner chamber he hides his pain and weeping. Sometimes God lets us glimpse his inner heart, but he shrouds it in metaphors so that we can bear it. The metaphor of the closed sound is about this pain.

Sound Adjustment

A violinmaker's job is not confined to making instruments. It also includes caring for ones that people already have. Adjusting an instrument's sound is one of the most difficult jobs that a luthier must face. Here we are talking about tiny details, but they are quite sensitive in determining matters of the sound. A good instrument responds quickly to the smallest adjustment of the sound post, tiny corrections in the bridge, the finest of fingerboard stripping, microscopic differences in the glue, changes in humidity and the temperature, and much more. Even the most valuable of instruments can make the musician's life difficult by posing serious problems from time to time. (Some instruments are exceptionally high-maintenance divas.) Violinists, violists, and cellists come to me in search of help. Often, as they lay their instrument on my workbench, they have a slip of the tongue and say they are bringing their instrument to my clinic. They quickly correct themselves: "Not the clinic, of course, workshop." For many musicians our meeting is indeed like a doctor's appointment, and if they have to leave the instrument with me for a few days they get quite upset, as if their child is to be anesthetized to undergo an operation.

It requires knowledge and experience, good ears and—most importantly—steady nerves to deal with musicians and their instruments. But it is also the most exciting job. I first learned to hear through these encounters.

~

One day a cellist came by. He was a soloist with a top German opera orchestra. I knew him from previous encounters and was always overwhelmed by his exceptionally sensuous, singing tone. Back then my workshop was still in the top floor of an art nouveau building in the Lehel quarter of Munich. From the window of the atelier you could see the vegetable gardens of the St. Anna Cloister which are hidden from view at street level. The other window had a wide, sweeping view over the roofs of downtown Munich.

The cellist rang the bell and dragged himself slowly up the stairs to the fifth story. He plopped down into a chair, looking exhausted. As he started to talk, I quickly realized that his problem was not due to climbing the stairs; it was his cello. He had to play an important solo in a few days (I think it was Tchaikovsky's *Swan Lake*, but I can't remember exactly), but the A-string on his cello was completely closed. He could not get the tone clear. The sound remained dull. This hadn't happened before; the tone had always bloomed effortlessly, shining in the highest registers. He could not play the solo like this. Again and again, he would stop and look at me to make sure I understood him. He had tried everything with the instrument and was truly shaken.

The way in which he poured out his sorrow and played passages over and over for me—he seemed like someone with a disability! The instrument of such a musician is like a part of his own body. The way he described his cello's sound, he might as well have said that his right arm was paralyzed or his fingers were in pain. Such a musician has grown together with his instrument. It is a part of his identity because he expresses everything inside of him through it. It is his voice.

I was shaken as I looked at this cellist sitting there in desperate need, playing his cello; I felt how much he suffered because of his instrument. Times like this are revelatory moments. Through the musician's sorrow in that moment, God spoke to my heart about one of his own characteristics. I saw God reflected in the cellist. The episode became the basis for a metaphor about the closed sound that I now, years later, would like to develop. It has accompanied and shaped my relationship with God.

I knew this particular cello well. It was the work of the old Italian master, Giovanni Grancinno (Milan, ca. 1666-1726), with a bold pattern and wonderful deep-golden varnish. This extraordinary masterpiece was worth hundreds of thousands of euros. And I heard that the sound of the A-string was, indeed, not satisfactory. It had a closed sound throughout all of the positions, against which the cellist had to fight with all his might to produce only a shadow of a beautiful tone. It sounded anything but free.

The cellist explained that he had already tried every possible brand of strings, to absolutely no effect. I was his only hope. Could I help him? I said yes, the problem could certainly be solved—and was immediately startled by my own courage, because I was not sure how to approach the issue. You cannot have the slightest assurance in such cases; the problem is too complex for that. But prior experience gave me hope that the sound could be adjusted by changing the sound post and putting on a bridge that had been carved differently so that the string would be open and free again.

A free, open sound is what every musician longs for, and rightly so. No one wants to work against a dull, muted, sluggish instrument that does nothing, no matter how hard you try. The instrument must be able to react, allow its tone to effortlessly dim, blossom, glow, and, when necessary, cry out. Sluggishness and tightness are simply torture.

The musician left me alone with his instrument. I put it on the workbench and looked at it for a long time. The bridge did not seem to be very amiss to me; the sound post was also in the normal place. What was wrong? I recognized that this was a unique case. As I said, it is often just little things that have changed or shifted, and yet they can ruin the tone. As usual, when I was at the end of my rope, I left the workshop and went to the St. Anna Church. It was just two minutes away: a magnificent space, wonderfully cool in summer, with an enormous mosaic of Christ in the apse. I was alone. I sat down on one of the pews and searched for deep insight and inspiration. These times had often been refreshing and strengthening for me. It was a place of retreat and, next to the workshop, my heart's home. And so I listened inwardly.

After a good fifteen minutes I went back to the workshop and mustered the courage to loosen the strings and start working on a new sound post and bridge. In Italian violinmaking the sound post is called the *anima*, or the soul. It is the little, round piece of wood that is placed between the back and the belly, connecting these two vibrating systems together. The resonances start to link up and (solely in this way) get their necessary asymmetry, while the bridge meets the resistance it needs to vibrate and dance on the front of the cello.

I had worked for barely twenty minutes when the telephone rang. It was the cellist. He did not want to disturb me and was quite sure that I would resolve the problem, but if I were not successful, I should please keep the old sound post and bridge so that the instrument could be set up as it was before in case of emergency. The call did not improve my self-confidence. I calmed him down and said that, even though it surely would not be necessary, I would hold his items for him.

Less than fifteen minutes later the telephone rang again. He just wanted to note one more thing. He had once taken the cello to a luthier that he respected greatly; yet the cello came out sounding like a buzz saw, and was I quite certain that . . . I assured him that the cello would most certainly sound good and that I had a very good idea of what needed to be done.

The cellist had come into my workshop like an injured person that I had to help. I saw his face, his movements, his overwhelming problem with the sound. As I saw him playing the instrument, it was as if God had shown me something of his own suffering. It was clear to me: just as this cellist was disabled by his instrument, so it is with God! He is disabled by people—by us, we who are his instruments. The same sorts of questions arise: "Why can I no longer find my way into your sound? Where are the times we used to have? You were once open, but now your soul is dull. Why are you aloof? Why this resistance?"

All of this was not mere thinking, but an inner listening and feeling. It was as if I felt for a moment what God feels—his sorrow, his vulnerability. Since then it has become more and more clear to me that there is something exposed, yes, almost tender, in the Spirit of God. I am convinced that to become people who love we should focus not on the powerful but on the gentleness and humility in the Holy Spirit. We must, in fact, see some of God's sorrow. Even if the following train of thought falters, I want to try to lay it out. It will become clear that this sorrow is mutual. For we, as well, suffer from God. It is simply impossible for it to be any other way.

The Open Questions

Before I take up this allegory, I would like to carve out some niches along the steep path we have to climb. How can we fully comprehend this metephor?

It is by far the longest parable in this book and, more than any other, it gets to the heart of key interpretations of the Christian faith. I witnessed some of God's suffering in that cellist's face and in his interaction with his instrument. This led me to ask many questions.

What exactly does it mean to speak of God's suffering? What kind of suffering is this—should we be worrying about God? What is it that we see in Jesus Christ when we say that he is the "Servant King," the "Suffering Righteous One," "the Servant of God"? Would God, if he is almighty, allow his Son to perish on the cross? Does God need that for himself? He did not intervene; instead, in what happened on the cross, the full power of an evil triarchy—angry aggression (the Romans), cynicism (the pious), and resignation (the disciples)—breaks in. How can one believe in a God of love if he does not intervene in such a case? What does it say about God's omnipotence if he *cannot* intervene? Is he unable, or unwilling? Or was he absent when all this darkness descended?

People have always asked, just as they do today, how did you come up with the preposterous idea of finding salvation in the horror of a death on a cross? Isn't such a thought a relic of a long-superseded era thick with cults of sacrifice and religious dread? Can we, as enlightened, reasonable people, really hold to an understanding of a God and a religion whose core faith rests on salvation by means of cruel torture? Does God need the offering of the Crucified One in order not to be angry at the world? How do the Bible and non-Christian teachers of wisdom (Plato in the West, Lao-Tse in the East) interpret these questions?

A more personal question also needs to be asked: how does this suffering and vulnerability change me—my worldview and my relationship to God? I am convinced that all these questions go to the heart of the Christian faith, and that answering them from the heart and by the Spirit is necessary for a spirit-filled relationship with God.

Weeds and Wheat

In the Sermon on the Mount as recorded in the Gospel of Matthew, Jesus said: "Be perfect, therefore, as your heavenly Father is *perfect*" (5:48). It is understandable that we have trouble accepting this command. It is even more surprising that Jesus assumes a self-evident perfection in God! Does he not see all the suffering and evil in this world, both then and now? If an all-powerful, good God exists, where does all this evil come from? This is an honest question, not a wicked doubting of God, for a faith without questions, a faith that closes itself off from the world, may be pious but will never be real. Where does evil come from, all the things that make life difficult, that humiliate, injure, threaten and destroy, if, in fact, a perfect God made everything?

Jesus told a parable about a farmer who scattered good seed on his fields. But in the night, an enemy came and scattered ryegrass seeds among the wheat. Ryegrass is related to wheat and thrives particularly well in wheat fields. It is almost always infected with a dangerous fungus. If it is consumed along with the wheat, it can cause dizziness; in extreme cases, it can be deadly.

The farmer's servants are indignant: "Didn't you sow good

seed?" they ask. "Where did all these weeds come from? The crops growing in the fields are no longer good!" And the farmer replies: "An enemy did this." The servants suggest a solution: "Shall we go out and pull up the weeds?" The farmer says: "No. You would pull up the wheat along with the weeds. Let both of them grow together until the harvest; then collect the weeds first and bind them in bundles to be burned, but gather the wheat into my barn" (see Matthew 13:24-30).

The farmer does not pull up the weeds. He holds back. Not out of indifference, however, but out of wisdom. He acts out of conviction. Jesus does not tell us what caused the evil, but he does long for us to understand why God holds back. The reason lies in our very existence: weeds and wheat are often quite close together in us, as well. Our strengths have their shallowness. We know nothing of the underground network of roots in us, the abyss of our own hearts. "The heart is hopelessly dark and deceitful," says Jeremiah, "a puzzle that no one can figure out" (17:9, *The Message*). The farmer's "no" is grounded in the fact that *we* cannot comprehend the human heart. If we were able to, then Jesus would let the farmer in the parable say to his servants: "Get to work! Rip up what is bad! Let's go!" This is precisely the motto of religious fanaticism!

Jesus's parable teaches us something different. The ryegrass and the wheat are too similar: faith and superstition, true humility and false modesty, being truly carefree and naively reckless, holy serenity and sinful indifference, true freedom and covert fear of commitment, real hope and cheap comfort, necessary reverence and cowardly subservience, upright love and fearful concession, saving faith and paralyzing customs, true confidence and false security—deceptive similarities that are different from the root up. But who can see what is hidden and who knows the root? Jeremiah gives an answer: "I the Lord test the mind and search the heart" (17:10). In other words, you who are human cannot do it! So, no matter how upset we may get about it, God does not place a hoe in our hands. We are not called to judge each other. In this spirit, the farmer says "no" to his servants. A faith that takes up the hoe of power and condemnation helps fulfill the aims of the one who sowed the ryegrass in the first place: that the self-righteous indignation over evil will come to destroy the good.

The farmer sowed good seed. Both wheat and weeds can grow in the field. We are called to bring forth wheat, to be people who serve the lives of others like life-giving grain: strengthening the needy, lifting up the weak, directing those who are searching, not breaking the downcast, and understanding that the flickering flame, as weak as it may be, should not be extinguished but encouraged and kindled by love into new life.

The Heart

Wheat and weed roots grow together in the field of human calling, the one for strength and life, the other dizzying and sickening. All the great cultures of the world know this "field" and have described it for ages as "the heart."[1]

"The sound" of our humanity radiates from the heart. As with every valuable instrument, our hearts also sometimes need a "sound adjustment." The social and moral climate in which we live, the blows dealt to us in the demands and disappointments of life will not leave us untouched. Lao-Tse says: "A man's heart can be oppressed or it can be agitated. The oppressed is like a captive, the agitated like the mad man."[2] Just as the sound of a cello can be dull and closed or coarse and shrill, and therefore in need of an adjustment, so our inner world needs the work of a master because we, too, suffer from things that oppress or upset us in our daily calling.

There is a reason that we talk about a person's "attitude." It determines our "sound." The value that we never lost will be restored by the adjustment, just as the instrument did not lose its worth but simply could not open up anymore. In this way our calling can be distorted if our sound is dull and full of pride, fear, mistrust, and resistance.

As the cello's resonances take their stimulus from the musician and transform into sound, so the human heart has a mysterious resonant soundboard within. The heart is not a place of intellect, but of intimacy. All the truths by which we live are "internalized" there; it is the site of encounters and calling. Here, an inner burning that does not consume us is possible, and so here must be said the same thing that was spoken from the burning bush: "Remove the sandals from your feet, for the place on which you are standing is holy ground" (Exodus 3:5).

But the heart is also the place where we can deny ourselves what we should do and be—where we can either meet or avoid God's message and actions. The prophet Jeremiah says: "The heart is hopelessly dark and deceitful, a puzzle that no one can figure out" (17:9, *The Message*). One could say the same thing about the cello: what a puzzle! (That cello sure did rattle my nerves!) "Dark and deceitful," says Jeremiah. Some translations say "cunning and corrupt." It is a cunning puzzle, like the image of the intertwined roots. In this verse, the two basic inclinations of the heart are fear and pride. Through them a heart will go unavoidably out of tune. As Lao-Tse says: fear pushes us down, pride stirs us up. These inclinations rob us of the sound of our calling.

Faith means handing oneself over to God. It is the willingness to seek a moment not just of blessing but also of criticism. I, as a luthier, had to be critical of that cello—not because I was rejecting it, but because its sound had been distorted and I had to adjust it. This is the only way to overcome an instrument's "cunning puzzle." We can learn to find access to our heart in prayer so that the sense and nonsense, the will and work, the words and deeds of our existence will become clear. Our resonances are given to us by and for God; in them there is grace and dignity. Discovering this gives us ears to listen deeply.

～

The cellist's suffering over his instrument is like the father's suffering in the parable of the prodigal son. The son had demanded his inheritance but failed to use it in a meaningful way. He distorted the "sound of his life," alienated himself from his calling, and robbed himself of his dignity. Then he repented and decided to return home. "While he was still far off, his father saw him and was filled with compassion; he ran and put his arms around him and kissed him" (Luke 15:20). Jesus's view of the father resembles the prophet Hosea's description of God's burning heart: "My people are determined to turn from me. Even though they call me God Most High, I will by no means exalt them. [Yet] How can I give you up, Ephraim? How can I hand you over, Israel? . . . My heart is changed within me; all my compassion is aroused" (Hosea 11:7-8 NIV). The prophet Isaiah speaks of God as a woman who is expecting: "Now I will cry out like a woman in labor, I will gasp and pant" (Isaiah 42:14). How could one speak any more radically about God's suffering and his passionate will!

As a violinmaker, I too have the job of bringing audible life into the world and of correcting sound that has become distorted. My wife, who helped me with the bookkeeping during the first few years of my business, witnessed how musicians acted in my workshop. She often could not bear to watch as we tried together to restore an instrument's sound. She had to leave because, as she said, it was like a birth—and sometimes a very difficult one.

∽

God suffers from certain tone colors of our life—from the way we permit ourselves to behave, from the relationships we live in—just as that cellist suffered from the sound of his instrument. God's love is disabled *by us*. God's history with the world is not one of conquering, but one of calling. That is the sorrowful story that God shares with the world. We have the power to reject our calling.

A good commandment can clarify what is rightly required of our lives, but the *decision* to practice it with our heart and soul cannot be taken away from us by any power. That would entail the oppression of our heart. If the beloved is subjugated by the one who loves, he is thereby destroyed. If God were to force our calling on us, he would ruin not just the mutuality of his love but the love itself. Love has a built-in disability: it cannot replace the love of the beloved *with anything else*. That is its sorrow. Paul describes the essence of God's love in 1 Corinthians:

Love is patient; love is kind; love is not envious or boastful or arrogant or rude. It does not insist on its own way; it is not irritable or resentful; it does not rejoice in wrongdoing, but rejoices in the truth. It bears all things, believes all things, hopes all things, endures all things. (13:4–7)

The pivotal sentence is: *Love does not insist on its own way.* If it were to insist, it would force the love with which it loves and in so doing destroy itself. The farmer does not pull up the ryegrass; the father does not chase after the prodigal son. The cellist did not break his instrument, either, but he suffered because of it. "God is love" (1 John 4:16). "Love does not insist on its own way" (1 Corinthians 13:5). The connection between these truths reveals God's suffering: God does not insist on his own way! Therefore, things take time with us and with the world. Only ripping things up happens fast.

The Parable of Judas

A world in which God insisted on having his way would look different. There would be no room for anything outside of God. The story of Judas Iscariot, a disciple of Jesus, reads like a "parable of outrage" against the apparent weakness of grace. Judas collides with Jesus's gentleness. His hidden injunction to Jesus is: "Assert yourself, already, and take God's rightful place!" He is disgusted by evil, spies the weeds, and has had the hoe (against the Romans, against immorality, against everything evil) in hand for quite some time. When the devil "put it into the heart of Judas son of Simon Iscariot to betray him" (John 13:2), it is with the same train of thought in his heart: "Step up already! You have the power! God's kingdom can and should come through you! I will betray you. Not because I want the evil, but because I want to move you for good! My betrayal will force you to assert yourself. Don't you see the weeds? I will provoke you for good. In this way God's kingdom, which we are all expecting, will come. And with it you will have the power. My betrayal will force your hand!"

Judas cannot endure the fact that grace does not set aside those whom it calls. The metaphor of Judas's life gives us an idea about how evil might arise not from "evil" itself but from the effort to turn the history of the world's redemption into a story of subjugation—subjugation to what is good. We suffer from God as Judas suffered from Jesus. Judas was indignant because the power of God, which he saw in Jesus, was not ready to be asserted—not on behalf of human faith, nor of love's calling, nor of the reign of grace. No subjugation! Judas was not prepared to accept the apparent powerless of Jesus. For he tragically—more than any of the other disciples—saw the potential power of God that stood behind this powerlessness. He wanted to chain the Son to the Father's power. He wanted to shake up his Jesus for the sake of what is good! Godless life should finally be forced to submit to the good.

This is where pious fanaticism has always had its source. In all the alleged good he aims to do, the fanatic changes himself into a Judas because he brushes the person aside and makes himself a prosecutor for God and the good and thereby makes himself an accuser of mankind—a Satan.[3]

The Parable of Jesus

In Jesus we witness more than mere human sorrow. In the end, the *basis of all sorrows* is visible in him. It is the sorrow that is in *God himself*, the same sorrow that I saw metaphorically in the face of the cellist. I want to explore the reason for this sorrow.

First we need to clarify the proper tone to use when writing about such topics. There are things that we cannot say *about* God, but only *to* God—much better, in fact, *in* God. As thoughts we would classify them as *about* God, but as prayer they become worship, a profound listening that can best be described as "contemplation." Those who know this kind of love understand the Psalmist when he says: "I think of you on my bed, and meditate on you in the watches of the night" (63:6). Or: "I commune with my heart in the night; I meditate and search my spirit" (77:6).

"In the beginning God created the heavens and the earth."

So says the book of Genesis (1:1). What did you relinquish when you gave breath to the world and called something into existence that was not you yourself? What happened when you said: "Let there be," and something other than you was created! What did you lose in that moment when you decided not to be everything for yourself? I am not you! The I AM, omnipotent for all of time, becoming the One who loves in the act of creation. Being vulnerable. That is the world.

And so, something other than God has been created. Now the breath of God is in the world. Out of a love that does not hold on tightly to itself something has come into existence that is not God: our world! For in the beginning was the Word, and it says: I will *not be everything* for myself. That is love.

~

Now God enters the other that he created. He is the love that consists of relinquishing itself. This Logos (meaning) *is* God. That is why John says: "In the beginning was the Word (Logos), and the Word was with God, and the Word was God" (1:1). The Logos is love that surrenders.

So now you enter the space you created. It is a world that does not *have to* love, even though it was made by love's self-renunciation. But that is precisely the essence of love. It calls, but it does not subjugate. We want to be free, we do not want to be subject to anyone, and yet we suffer from our own ability to free ourselves from love and thereby not be subject to it. It is possible for us, we who want to be loved, not to love. Everyone who loves has to bear the sorrow of his own freedom. For as people who love freedom, we must decide if we will allow ourselves to be harnessed in order to be serving, upright, truly present people. Freedom suffers from love when we begin to be servants of our calling. But this means that those who make their freedom the most important part of their existence will lose their purpose (Matthew 16:25).

The world is not subjugated to its Logos but rather called by it. The opening of John's Gospel says: "The world came into being through him; yet the world did not know him. He came to what was his own, and his own people did not accept him" (John 1:10-11) because "people loved darkness rather than light" (3:19).

What happens with the Logos when it must be lived out in a world that is not God? When love must be lived in a world lacking in love, the path of the one who loves will *of necessity* be a path of sorrow! That is the path of Jesus. He is the One the prophets saw coming, and they called him God's servant.[4]

Taking the image of the good shepherd, Jesus says: "I lay down my life in order to take it up again. No one takes it from me, but I lay it down of my own accord. I have power to lay it down, and I have power to take it up again" (John 10:17-18). Indeed, the secret of this Word is that it is exactly what was spoken at the creation of the world. It is the Word that created the world. Jesus's statement echoes the mighty Word that God himself spoke so that something could exist that is not himself. It is the Word of creation: "I lay down my life in order to take it up again. No one takes it from me, but I lay it down of my own accord. I have power to lay it down, and I have power to take it up again."

~

"The passion" is typically used to name the sufferings of Jesus before and in his death. Creation itself is an enormous passion, because it means that God has left his invulnerable being in order that there can be a world, a development. The early church fathers recognized that the passion happened long before the incarnation! By limiting himself, God created the world, and so we are able to meet him in the world. That is the essence of the humility and gentleness of which Jesus spoke: "Take my yoke upon you, and learn from me; for I am gentle and humble in heart, and you will find rest for your souls" (Matthew 11:29). Limiting oneself for the sake of another is a yoke, and yet it is the essence of life as well. For all life springs from life that is given. In each act of self-limitation lies a creative power and wisdom, but always sorrow as well.[5]

In Jesus we see *God's own* passion. The word "passion" holds a mysterious connection between pain and love. Everyone with even the slightest understanding of love knows that we cannot simply live in love without pain. For love manifests itself precisely in the act of not holding on tightly to what is its own. Just so, God does not hold himself tightly but relinquishes the Son "who is close to the Father's heart" (John 1:18). John speaks of Jesus as the Word and as the original moment of God's self-renunciation: "I lay down my life in order to take it up again." Therefore, the Word says: "I am the Alpha and the Omega, the first and the last, the beginning and the end" (Revelation 22:13 and Mark 8:33). The beginning is the moment when he laid down his life, and the completion comes when he takes it up again. And so when the Word says: "I lay down my life in order to take it up again," he has, besides the obvious, spoken of the beginning and end of all existence.

~

In this section I continue to pursue the basis of suffering and what I saw in that cellist's face. A "closed sound" is as if the instrument were to lose all love and consistency. The face of the cellist is like the face of Christ—the suffering of love itself.

God's willingness to place limits on himself was present at the creation of the world, a will that became incarnate in Jesus. God relinquished himself and took on the form of a servant, in the infinite, voluntary odyssey of time. He joined the space that is not God and therefore does not have to be like God; a space that can love but does not have to love. Jesus is born as an image of God revealing himself. In him the servant of God is embodied. He is the One who, at the time of creation, was already nothing other than God's act of self-sacrifice! Jesus becomes the most phenomenal metaphor for this event, a metaphor of God's self-sacrificial love, not captured in words but made flesh as a person.

The early church father Origen noted this when he said: "If he had not already carried our sorrow long ago, he would not have come to share human life with us."[6] John's words about the Logos make it clear that the world has meaning in God's love and its foundation in God's suffering! God shows that he can suffer, too—and because he loves, he also *will* suffer. It is an infinite sorrow born of free will. The world could come about only through this Logos and can subsist only in it.

God's sorrow is like a partial in the musical tone of an unending love. Just as a violin would unavoidably become ordinary without its overtones, so would love be unspeakably mundane without the ability to suffer for the sake of the loved one and the called. The Logos of love would not have been able to sound either in heaven or earth, without the overtone that is God's sorrow.

Indeed, a god that is incapable of suffering would be primitive! He would lack a decisive characteristic of love. Here as well, it is as Origen said: "What was this passion which [Christ] suffered for us at the beginning? . . . He suffers a passion of love."[7] "Then they led him away to crucify him" (Matthew 27:31). How are we to understand this in light of what we have just discussed? If the world is, in fact, something other than God, then ungodly things will happen—neither "actively willed" nor "passively allowed,"[8] but simply as a result of the divine self-sacrifice in which the world has its origin. God gave his Son—it is the same outpouring in which God gave himself at the creation of the world. Jesus says: "No one has greater love than this, to lay down one's life for one's friends" (John 15:13). The secret of the world's creation is hidden in these words.

And so Jesus experiences God's self-sacrifice! God's sorrow falls upon him. One can say that God's act of self-relinquishing that occurred "before all of time" now repeats itself in the flesh. He experiences the sorrow that is *in God*. He, the servant of God, goes to the extreme; he suffers from that which constitutes the world, and yet he enters it completely. He suffers from God's sorrow, but he does not separate from him, but instead makes himself one with this godly sorrow.

The Tone Color of Necessity

Jesus suffered because of God's self-sacrifice, for a God who showed that he is able to not be everything; and he also suffered for a humanity in which everything is "for itself," demonstrating how very much it can be without God! On the cross the horror of separation from God was revealed—and with it the very heart of our world. Here, the reason for my existence is shown in God relinquishing himself, as well as the extremes to which I can go to be outside of God. Therefore, on the cross the *foundation* as well as the *abyss* of our world are revealed.

Because of this, I must understand the dreadfulness of the cross as a *necessity*—neither the active will nor the passive allowance of God. God's suffering is obviously *necessary* in order for the world to be a world and not have to be God!

We hear necessity's tone color in the words of the Risen One as he speaks with his disciples on the way to Emmaus: "Was it not *necessary* that the Messiah should suffer these things . . . ?" (Luke 24:26). Yes, it was *necessary*! It is a voluntary suffering on which the world is founded and an unending, perfect love in which its meaning is fulfilled.

~

The claim stated on the cross can be perverted by the faithful as well as relativized by the faithless. Both happen. There is something wretched about reducing the being, work, and suffering of Jesus to his death. It is not his death but his dedication that is the core message of the cross. Jesus says: "The Son of Man came not to be served but to serve, and to give his life a ransom for many" (Mark 10:45). This expression of dedication ("give his life") does not mean "offer his life to death" but rather "make it serve a purpose." The fact that he "came not to be served, but to serve" shows a quality that one can give only with one's own life, not with one's death.

What does it mean to "give his life"? At the risk of exaggeration, as a violinmaker I understand this to mean that I offer my life on the workbench—not by killing my life but by dedicating it. I give the time, strength, thoughts, feelings, efforts, and creativity of my life for the emerging instrument, for its sound. I know what purpose I am serving. That is what is meant by an "offering." In the Christian faith, the meaning of a "living sacrifice" is embedded in the word "offering" (Romans 12:1). It is the life-long dedication of love. People who buy an instrument have also dedicated themselves to earn the money necessary to that end. We serve each other with the life we have received. We give each other a part of our lives.

The idea that a person must sacrifice something in order to be reconciled to God is overcome through Christ. The cult thinking that a godhead needs a sacrificial offering is a primal reflex of the human soul. This is precisely the misguided notion that is overcome through Christ. God does not need an offering to do something *for himself*. The dedication at hand has to do *with us*.

Love is willing to suffer in order to save. It is important not to confuse this truth by thinking that suffering is, in and of itself, a saving power. No, it is the love. It would be a fatal error to glorify Jesus's death—as if martyrdom had worth in and of itself, as if suffering were a form of serving God, as if Jesus just waited around for the opportunity to die for us. That would be the perverse religious glorification of suicide.

Klaus Berger writes: "He who insinuates that God needs death and violence for salvation has not understood the undergirding statement of the Bible's depiction of God. . . . No, God does not need the spite of the Romans, but he uses it. He did not need the violence and spilling of blood, but he encountered it. He is not bound to the path of brutality, but he transforms it into its opposite . . . he does not bind forgiveness to violence, but he answers violence with forgiveness. He does not freeload on the murder of Jesus."[9]

In Jesus, we are not dealing with the saving power of suffering but with a saving love that is willing to suffer! Suffering does not have the power to save, but love does. And love is ready, when necessary, to suffer. The saying "he suffered for us" does not glorify Jesus's suffering but shows how far his love had gone! My response is adoration of his vulnerable love that overcomes me. I stand under the cross, shaken by this necessity, look at him and say: You loved me into heaven! To know this is the strength and praise of my life.

Jesus makes it clear that there can be no love without this form of self-surrender. A person who seeks love but is not prepared to suffer for their loved one has not grasped the essence of love! It would be pointless to try to lead one's life in pain-free insignificance. This would result in a life without note.

The founding event of faith in Christ is the cross. It asks: do you value matters of faith only when they seem pleasant? Why do I see you hopelessly trying to make a sculpture out of dry sand? It is crumbling already in your hand! Why will you not take the moist clay? And I answer: The clay gets my fingers dirty. The sand is nice and warm! This is a deep image reminiscent of something Lao-Tse once said: "Truthful words are not beautiful, beautiful words are not truthful."[10] Does faith have to be warm and beautiful, or can it be dirty and true?

In the Messiah's Workshop

Pure religious dogma will play on our guilty conscience, but it does not open our eyes or ears. It is like someone trying to master intonation on an instrument without a sense of hearing or trying to paint a picture while blind. Mechanically moving your fingers over the fingerboard or dipping the brush in the paint will not be meaningful or fulfilling because you can't hear or see! We can make religion into a blind and deaf sport of a guilty conscience, but to live from the spirit and love of God is something else. Mere religiosity is not enough. It is mechanical.

This same analogy is expressed in a parable of Chuang-tzu: "You do not question the blind about a painting nor invite the deaf to a celebration of singing. Blindness and deafness are not only of the body; there are also souls that are blind and deaf. You, I believe, are afflicted by this infirmity."[11]

The cellist was able to suffer for his instrument only because he loved the sound that had been lost. As a violinmaker, I felt the closed sound and shared in the musician's suffering. In this empathy lies a unique power that changes everything. The musician shared the ugliness of the instrument with me, and I shared his sorrow. The apostle Paul caught this when he said concerning Jesus: "For our sake [God] made him to be sin who knew no sin" (2 Corinthians 5:21). Jesus shared in sin in a radical way, took part in life's bad sound. But he testified against it by remaining completely in love. He continued to be what he was from God. His life was thrust into death, but his existence was protected. This existence is what sustains our being, as the letter to the Hebrews says: "He sustains all things by his powerful word" (Hebrews 1:3). He remains the loving one; therefore, his name is *I AM Who I AM*. In this, he became one with God's proper name![12] As he continued to be the One who loves, he was one with God. So, the crucifixion tells my heart: "Even through disfiguration I am and will remain the One who loves, the beginning and the end of all of existence. Your sin will mock me and disfigure me, but it will never destroy me. I AM Who I AM."

Just as I shared the musician's sorrow, so Jesus shared in God's sorrow! Jesus suffered from the dull, closed sound of unbelief that closed itself off from God, full of opposition and mistrust. We see this sorrow in his tears: "As he came near and saw the city, he wept over it" (Luke 19:41). We hear it in his disappointment: "You faithless generation, how much longer must I be among you? How much longer must I put up with you?" (Mark 9:19). We understand it in his impotence: "He could do no deed of power there" because of their unbelief (Mark 6:5).

The work of the Messiah could not be self-glorifying, an omnipotent snap of the fingers. It is neither possible nor permitted for him to ignore the faith of those he seeks. To do so would be to abandon the suffering of God's love and exchange the faith of the beloved for a command. But that is exactly what the people of the time had in mind with their mundane expectations. They were waiting for a Messiah in whose reign they would see God's omnipotence. The superstitious belief in an all-powerful God who forfeits his love to force his will is shattered on the cross. On the cross I see a loving God who loses his power in order to allow his love. In the great hymn recorded in Philippians 2:6-8, one of the earliest hymns of the church, we see the renunciation of the servant of God who appeared in flesh and blood. The beginning of the hymn carries an echo of the self-renunciating act of creation by which the world came into being.

> Though he was in the form of God,
>> [he] did not regard equality with God
>> as something to be exploited,
> but emptied himself,
>> taking the form of a slave,
>> being born in human likeness.

And being found in human form,
    he humbled himself
    and became obedient to the point of death—
    even death on a cross.

What happened in Jesus is the most powerful parable that could ever be told. It is the metaphor of the perfect, dedicated love of God. He narrated it with his life.

Crucial Vulnerability

We will begin to take God *and ourselves* seriously only when we understand the vulnerability of God's presence. In the process of making music, there is always something vulnerable in the contact point between the bow and the vibrating string, and yet this is exactly where the sound is formed! Too much pressure and the tone will be grating; too little pressure and it will whistle; too near the bridge and it will break; too far away and it loses its strength. The reciprocity is essential. Vulnerability is crucial in important matters.

We experience faith as a *mutual vulnerability* because we are not the only ones who are exposed. God is too. To share in God's presence creates an endless vulnerability in our existence. It is a *vulnerable partnership* as well because if the matter were merely one-sided—if the decision were made only by God or only by the person—the essential things would simply not be taken seriously, namely, the vulnerability and beauty of the relationship!

The true (we can even say holy) heart of a relationship is shown in what the one party concedes to the other. Grace is the space we make ready for each other. It is a fragile beauty to which we are called, and therefore deeply "charismatic." *Charis* (grace) is also defined as "the charm of beauty." The grace that God seeks in us is the grace of searching, listening, and loving. These three activities reveal the beauty of the inner life. If we do not prepare space for God in our lives, we will not experience him, either. God's love can be experienced only by taking part in it. It is a holy participation, a shared sound, synchronization with God. God reveals himself to the searcher, speaks to the one who listens, bears witness through the one who loves. This alone is the fulfillment of our moment. Thereby we will understand when God says: "I am not *explaining* to you who I am, I am *testifying* to it!"

Faith gives God space. But God gives me space, too. This vulnerable relationship is not about power. What kind of pleasure would God find in making a counterpart only to subjugate it? And what benefit would God gain by subjugating a world that could not resist?

Power-plays put us on the wrong track. We gain a whole new understanding of God's omnipotence when we remember that he was prepared to *share his power* and create space! The space of time. Room to live. The interplay between grace and faith creates a surging field of holy potential. Only the one who truly does not understand the Maker believes that God has a desire for power.

Omnipotence

God's omnipotence does not claim to be everything for itself. Such a "sole power" would be not only disgusting but absurd. It would be, as Hans Jonas says, "a meaningless concept, contradicting and cancelling itself." For "power is a relational concept . . . [and] must be shared in order for it to exist at all."[13]

Power can have an effect only when something opposes it. God's power may be as superior as one can imagine, but if God were not to share it, then everything apart from himself would cease to exist. It would cancel itself out, because what would it have to refer to if nothing other than itself existed? Omnipotence, in the sense of a sole power, cannot exist.

The Bible does not speak of a self-glorifying, sole power belonging to God, but of the calling of humankind. If God chose not to be everything by creating the world, then the time span of our world is not under an almighty decree but is fulfilled in a holy interplay. The Bible uses the term "salvation" to describe a heartfelt

collaboration between God's time and ours. Salvation is the fulfilled time![14]

Zacchaeus's story provides an example (Luke 19:1-10). We do not
know exactly what happened on that evening, but a luthier would
call it the epitome of a "sound adjustment" and the Bible "salvation."
The wisdom that we see here in the Messiah can rightly be described
as that of an "artist" or "master craftsman." A person's previously
ruined and closed sound is transformed. Zacchaeus recognizes something holy and takes part in healing, but it all begins with Jesus saying: "Zacchaeus, hurry and come down; for I must stay at your house
today!" Zacchaeus's actions say: "I must change my heart and my
actions *today*!" He grasped that his time was fulfilled. That *kairos*
happened during a shared meal. It struck deep in the man, and a new
sound emerged. Thus God does not numb us with an all-powerful
song but searches for a new sound in our hearts. He also calls us to
new grace in our actions, as when Zacchaeus says: "Look, half of
my possessions, Lord, I will give to the poor; and if I have defrauded
anyone of anything, I will pay back four times as much." Then Jesus
said: "Today salvation has come to this house." This is the mastery of
the Messiah at work: listening and acting, the holy and the whole-
some, unified by Jesus.

If God laid aside his sole power, then the world is not subject to an all-powerful song. It creates a sound like a musician
with his instrument, vulnerable and holy in a shared tone! This
is synchronicity. This alone is presence. I must see and respect
this interplay. In this we are given to life—given to the world for
which we were made.

~

The cellist suffered for his instrument. But he did not alleviate the
pain by simply singing while the instrument sat there in his hands!
In the same way, God's omnipotence does not begin by singing into
our world but by bringing us, his instruments, to sound!

Yet, how often must God speak into the closed sound of this
world! It happened in Jesus's life: "Because of their unbelief, I could

do nothing!" He was refused and disabled. For me, faith is asking what God can do, recognizing which time is fulfilled. I need to maintain an ambivalent attitude toward God's omnipotence! Why? Because it is not my calling but my godlessness that needs to be shaken—my lethargy, my cowardice, my pride, anything that is not able to watch and pray, everything that coarsely separates the effects of God's grace from human actions. It would be absurd to push off the calling that has been entrusted to us onto God's omnipotence. As Klaus Berger puts it: "The strict division between God's actions and the actions of humans is modern and, from a Biblical perspective, completely absurd."[15]

Speak from the Heart

Every sound adjustment requires that the violinmaker and the instrument touch each other. Faith also lives from this touch. You must close your eyes, be still, and feel this power embracing and covering you with blessings. Then stand up, go forth slowly, and know that this day we are walking in fellowship, synchronized with God. This process, however, is always preceded by a moment of sound adjustment. For me, that moment is my ritual of a morning quiet time when I withdraw in order to open myself to God's presence.

As a master, I must learn to interpret the cello's sound and explore its resonances because it cannot speak through anything other than its sound. The Holy Spirit listens to the sound of our hearts more than the words of our mouths, and he knows how to interpret it. The Bible can teach us to speak with our hearts! In these intimate moments of retreat, very little is asked of us. Rather, we learn to allow ourselves to be observed, to listen and to question. This is how we find the words our hearts can speak.

> Search me, O God, and know my heart;
>> test me and know my thoughts.
> See if there is any wicked way in me,
>> and lead me in the way everlasting. (Psalm 139:23-24)

All the messianic moments that occurred through Jesus—the story of Zacchaeus and all the rest—make one thing clear: it is not an *all-powerful reign* that is dawning in our world but the *kingdom of God*. An all-powerful reign would amount to a cellist singing out an ignorant and trivial song over his instrument, but the kingdom of God is the sound of the instrument; it is about its adjustment.

Herein lay Judas's epochal mistake! If his betrayal would have succeeded in fulfilling his power fantasy about God's rule through Jesus, he certainly would not have killed himself. Tragically, he came to understand the essence of God's kingdom too late:

> When Judas . . . saw that Jesus was condemned, he repented and brought back the thirty pieces of silver to the chief priests and the elders. He said, "I have sinned by betraying innocent blood." But they said, "What is that to us? See to it yourself." Throwing down the pieces of silver in the temple, he departed; and he went and hanged himself. (Matthew 27:3–5)

Where was this disciple when Jesus sat and cried over Jerusalem a few weeks earlier? Judas could have repented in this moment! He would have recognized God's limitations in Jesus's tears—a love that is disabled by people's unbelief because it does not ignore what it has been denied! Judas either did not see it or could not bear it. He, who daringly dreamed of the powerful and glorious manifestation of God's reign—the subjugation of evil under an all-powerful, good God—would have heard the powerlessness in Jesus's words as he cried over Jerusalem: "How often have I desired to gather your children together as a hen gathers her brood under her wings, and you were not willing!" (Luke 13:34). He would have seen in these tears that Jesus is the Lamb of God. He would have sensed that God's hands of power are tied in order to unify the Holy One with the essence of love. But he could not bear that love does not force the good that it desires. A religious power that wants to lead and guide like God and yet tries to remove the limits that God has laid on us will become a Judas, a Satan, sooner or later. Such a person is not able or willing to respect what is crucial: God does not subjugate. He calls.

He Who Explores Life

In one of the most beautiful chapters of the book of Job, God is described as a seeker: "Then he saw [wisdom] and declared it; he established it, and searched it out" (28:27). A similar passage depicts the Holy Spirit as an explorer: "For the Spirit searches all things, yes, the deep things of God" (1 Corinthians 2:10 NKJV). God explores and probes life; by that, we are granted our very existence. I long for God's explorations to create a daring, fearless faith in me, enabling me to truly experience life.

This exploration is to be seen in working with a closed sound. The task demands the utmost wisdom, a love that is willing to suffer for the loved one but also the ability to be happy for him or her. Joy is present here. There is no changing in God (James 1:17; 1 John 1:5) because he *remains* in love, but precisely this fact indicates that the love of the beloved *will change him*! Otherwise it would not be love. And so, I believe in a God who both remains the same and changes because he is love.

Love is capable not just of willing things but of letting them grow. Love makes time, gives the gift of time. Sound is the back and forth over time, the periodic vibration of thickening and thinning air over elapsed time. Love gives time, making sound nothing other than audible love. If there were no movement through time, everything would be wrapped in a cosmic silence. Psalm 148 encourages all of creation to harmonize in the song of love that sustains all things.

Our calling is to transform elapsing time (*chronos*) into existential time (encounters) and in so doing, *fulfill the time* (*kairos*). This alone is presence. On Zacchaeus's night, the time was fulfilled.

Interaction with the Holy One

The metaphor of the closed sound will clarify our relationship with God if we understand that music is not a one-way street. As was said about Wisdom: "I grew up as a child by his side, laughing and playing all the time" (Proverbs 8:30 ERV). Now, we cannot compare the musician (the wisdom of grace) with the instrument (the called person). They are completely different categories—like God and humanity. But that is only half of the truth. The other half lies in the interplay between the two. It is only through this interaction that our faith becomes mature, authoritative, and alluring:

A musician whose instrument I take care of was invited some years ago to audition for a prestigious German radio orchestra. The opening was section leader of the second violins. He did not have a violin of good enough quality for this position, but, because it was such an important audition, I was able to secure a beautiful instrument for him to use—a 1712 Stradivarius that belongs to a customer of mine. Michael practiced for some days with this violin. He had never played anything of such sound quality before. He played outstandingly at the audition and won the position. His reaction was completely humble. No, it wasn't he or his abilities that won; it was the instrument's wonderful sound. I contradicted him. The instrument's wonderful sound is shrouded in a mystery—a mystery that played out between him and the instrument. Such a sound sets something free in the musician; you play unfettered, as if you had wings. "There is no fear in love," says John (1 John 4:18), nor is there with the sound. The tone colors create something new. From a breathtaking synchronization of gentleness and power emerges a space completely free of fear. You find yourself in a sound cloud of possibilities. They inspire the tone and let it soar.

The Stradivarius allowed the violinist to play differently. Of course, the musician brings out the sound of the instrument, but the sound also changes something in the musician. Separating the musician and the instrument in order to compare them to each other or to actually pit them against each other gets you nowhere! It is a shared sound. That is the interplay.

I want to cooperate with holy grace in every moment of my existence. Learning this is the calling of Jesus's students. Faith in Jesus brings the courage to be transported into another world. But through our faith, God also relocates himself into another world—ours, to be exact! Faith grants him admission (see Revelation 3:20). This faith proves that you are being taken seriously; therefore you should take *yourself* seriously as well.

A Primitive God?

God's sorrow puts the primitive notion of an all-powerful God in question. But regarding the question concerning omnipotence, I have no answer! Of course not. If godly omnipotence is described by the prophet Daniel: God acts "according to his will" (NASB), "there is no one who can stay his hand or say to him, 'What are you doing?'" (Daniel 4:35), then the thought of the Loving One will not contradict this confession but will offer the reply: Yes, he acts according to his will, but he will not want everything! Love *cannot* want everything! That is its strength. Only those who don't love want everything. Their freedom from the Loving One is found in this power and in this will. The one who does not love can control others by force. The Loving One cannot do this. He calls and advocates, knocks, appeals, truly listens, perseveres and waits—and, in the end, makes decisions as well. Yes, God acts "according to his will" (Daniel 4:35), but his will is consistent with love.

With hoe in hand and twelve legions of angels, God could have prevented his Son's crucifixion, along with the whole train of crucifixions and crusades all the way down to the Holocaust. The ryegrass would have been cut down, evil uprooted, and humanity controlled by what is good. In the process the world would have lost its rights and room. God would have instilled good in those who did not want it against their will; every threatening boot would be burned and every stiff neck broken. What remained would be tied to the strings of an all-powerful, all-kind puppet master. But would this not destroy the human dignity of repentance?

We are not tied to a puppet master's strings but should be led "with cords of human kindness, with bands of love" (Hosea 11:4). It is only through the interplay of love that development receives its inner order. Some things require time—time to repent and time to heal. Trust leads us into the Messiah's workshop where his first touch will be forgiveness. That will help us, for our part, to forgive the people and circumstances that have made us suffer. But nothing will heal in a self-righteous heart.

God cannot give sanctuary when a heart is presumptuous. People who have no insight will desecrate their lives, but the listening person God will lead back to the place where he abandoned his path or was pushed off by circumstances or people. Then moments of repentance and forgiveness occur. We have the power to be receptive or to resist during those holy moments when it becomes clear that something is being offered to us—an offer to give up our bitterness and be healed. Then we enter the "cords of love" with God.

Each person has a promise to pursue. What is holy is always a cloud of possibilities. We may want to participate in God's work cautiously, but this caution could cause us to miss our calling. Therefore, let us ask and act.

What is faith? That which takes part in God's adventure. What is love? That which takes part in God's resolve. What is hope? That which participates in the world's loving and faithful development. In all of this we must see the vulnerability of God; only then will we take ourselves seriously as God's counterpart. If we do not see God's suffering, then there is no truth in us that can reconcile us to him— nothing that can reconcile us to his resolve to allow this world to be, to suffer for it, but also to courageously and faithfully shape it. We should not worry about God's self-imposed limits in this world. He wants it that way. He gave up being everything so that he can "take it up again" in his time.

~

How often have people waited in vain for God to intervene, to break the arm of evil and sustain the righteous, to bring an end to their suffering, to hear their cries and see their misery and free them from fear and need. How often have they hoped that he would lead them out with a mighty hand and an outstretched arm! But no sign or wonder occurred, and he did not lead them out. Nothing happened. Only silence.

But sometimes things do happen. People are carried off by floods or force; out of thin air lives are uprooted, incomprehensibly and without discrimination between the righteous and the unrighteous, no distinction that would allow the pious to speak of God's firm but comprehensible justice. Should it not matter to God that "I have kept my heart clean and washed my hands in innocence" (Psalm 73:13)?

Indeed, to the contrary: how often do things work out for the unrighteous, whose "eyes swell out with fatness; their hearts overflow with follies. . . . Such are the wicked; always at ease, they increase in riches" (Psalm 73:7, 12).

The apostle Paul struggled to understand these hard questions, only to give himself over finally to praise: "O the depth of the riches and wisdom and knowledge of God! How unsearchable are his judgments and how inscrutable his ways! 'For who has known the mind of the Lord? Or who has been his counselor?' . . . To him be the glory forever" (Romans 11:33-34, 36). That is, these sorts of questions do not lead to a solution but to praise. The inexplicable cannot be answered by logic because then it would not be inexplicable.

The servant of God will always be set over against the question of God's omnipotence. If I cannot see that—especially after Auschwitz—then "God" will be my downfall. If we do not want to fall into a dark silence opposing God, then it is necessary to see what the servant of God is showing us: that there is more than just sense and senselessness! There must be a counter-sense, which consists of seeing our own responsibility and God's vulnerability. This vulnerability is in the Logos who renounces his being and removes his godliness in order for the world to exist. He gave himself to the world so that we could discover, develop, and live in it.

God does not replace the sound of his human instruments by an all-mighty song. God does not identify with the great, the limitless, and the strong. He has united with the small, the unimportant, and the weak. He knows what it means to be disrespected, neglected, and defenseless for our sake. Therefore, Hebrew wisdom states: "Whoever is kind to the poor lends to the Lord" (Proverbs 19:17) and in the Gospel of Matthew: "Just as you did it to one of the least of these . . . you did it to me. . . . Just as you did not do it to one of the least of these, you did not do it to me" (25:40, 45).[16]

Does God not intervene in this world, then? Ignatius of Loyola recommended that we live in a holy contradiction: "Pray as if God will take care of all; act as if it is all up to you." Living in this blessing-rich tension means allowing life to be ambiguous, and therefore beautiful; it means you will see the inseparable interaction between God and humanity.

As we saw in the metaphor of the calling in Chapter 6, when the instrument sounds, the musician and the instrument are both *wholly present*! Resolving the contradiction logically is neither beneficial nor judicious. We should rather understand it as a creative force. And this creative tension inspires me to live and work by listening and praying, and pray and listen by living and working. The two intertwine and do not cancel each other out.

And so, our heart must keep a two-fold rule. Otherwise we use the license of God's "omnipotence" to sneak out of our responsibilities. We underestimate God when we glorify his strengths but ignore his self-sacrifice, which in turn becomes our calling. Paul said: "God's weakness is stronger than human strength" (1 Corinthians 1:25). This is no ordinary sense of God's strength that would force itself on us. We must recognize God's weakness giving us room and authority to show who we are.

~

Every beautiful thing is an anthem to hope, the hope of what will be when God will someday gather us to himself and complete what happened to him in this world. We will see what glorified him, but also what disfigured him. We will then see what will be accepted and what will be surrendered. Wheat and weeds. It will be clear what we were to him, we who saw him at his weakest and served him, in that our strength bows down just as God's strength bowed down for the sake of life and the existence of this world.

Consequently, I have to ask myself how much reverence I can sustain. When we turn to the hurt, the weak, and the broken and acknowledge that life has the right to expect something of us, then the kingdom of God is near! The future world speaks to us now: "Have courage! For we already see the beauty among us today, awakened by your faithfulness and belief" (compare with John 15:8, 16).

This is the only way I can understand Jesus. He did not bring a power-obsessed Judas fantasy into the world. On the contrary. He went so far as to say that a person can do violence against God's kingdom! (See Luke 16:16.) Humans are capable of harming God. We must respect this. Otherwise our view of God will turn bitter.

"Christ" with Plato and Lao-Tse

When I encounter something foreign to me, I do not want to see only that which is my own. Instead, it is like building up the layers of a gorgeous violin varnish: I cook the pigments from different substances and shade it with metal salts, then put it in my little mill and grind it all up into the finest of grain-sized pieces. (More on this in Chapter 11.) If you apply another thin glaze of orange over the first coat, the shade will be intensified but will leave the color rather garish and commonplace. So I borrowed a method from a painter friend of mine to rein in the orange using its complementary hue. No one will ever see that wispy layer of blue, but it will give the orange a wonderfully mellow quality and depth.

Likewise, it is important not just to reinforce our thoughts with what is already like them, but to seek out complementary hues and thereby help gently to mature our grasp of the truth. This deepening is joyful when this other new element sounds familiar, and stressful when it departs from your views. But both are necessary: to allow yourself to be strengthened and to allow yourself to be held back. You can tell when a person associates only with like-minded people; his truth can be loud and garish. Only those who let themselves be irritated will truly learn.

Great masters outside of the Hebrew school of thought have recognized deep truths concerning the servant of God. No one would claim that the wisdom from all the major world cultures is all the same, but when Paul says: "In [Christ himself] are hidden all the treasures of wisdom and knowledge" (Colossians 2:3), then it would be a sign of indifference or carelessness not to lift up these treasures and give them due attention and respect! When we lift up this treasure we encounter Christ, even if he is not called by name. And yet he is clearly visible.[17]

In Christ we find things reversed—a counter-meaning. The ancients hallowed the glittering victor and glorified the ruler in his godly pretensions and power. They also knew that whoever hangs on a cross is cursed! The founding event of the Christian faith—the crucifixion—turns this around completely. It glorifies God's servant as the victor and sanctifies the self-sacrifice of the

One who loves. This counter-meaning is entirely new.[18] Yet, Lao-Tse and Plato, the greatest teachers of East and West, sounded similar themes.

Plato

Plato (428–348 BC) drew a picture of the crucified just man. It comes in the second volume of his *Republic*, in a discussion of how to imagine the entirely just and the entirely unjust person. "Make each of them perfect in his own line," he has Socrates say, "and do not in any way mitigate the injustice of the one or the justice of the other."[19]

Glaucon, whom Plato presents as Socrates's conversation partner, argues that being just is not appealing, and that the "just" person will not remain so very long in this world. The seemingly just man, according to Glaucon, practices righteousness only because he cannot get away with doing injustice. If someone were to enable him by some special trick—say, giving him the power of becoming invisible—he would succumb to temptation and act unjustly. He would behave "like he was a god among men," would kill randomly, satisfy his needs recklessly, and pursue his advantage whenever possible. He argues: "No one is just of their own free will."

For his part, the totally unjust man always acts properly so as to maintain a respectable reputation. He will become rich, call the shots, and benefit his friends and harm his enemies. He is hard to fathom because you think he is just even though he is really exactly the opposite.

With the entirely just man it is completely the reverse. He does not care how things appear, he cannot be bribed, he does not exploit things for his own benefit, he remains true to justice; yes, he will even allow himself to be slandered "so that we can test his justice and see if it weakens in the face of unpopularity and all that comes with it."[20] People speak evil of him and the respectable regard him as unjust, even though he will never malign justice. People simply will not tolerate the just man.

Glaucon argues: "Someone in possession of a supernatural freedom who does nothing untoward with this power would be considered very difficult to understand."[21] The just will finally be perfected in being clothed in injustice; he will be misjudged and persecuted and yet will not abandon the path of justice. In the end, as Glaucon paints the picture, he will be tortured and crucified: "They will say that the just man, as we have pictured him, will be scourged, tortured, and imprisoned; his eyes will be put out, and after enduring every humiliation he will be crucified."[22]

The entirely just man will die the shameful death of a slave, for in Greece, crucifixion was reserved solely for slaves. Using it on free men was considered barbaric. When a free citizen was sentenced to death, all unnecessary savagery would be avoided. Glaucon expects the just man to suffer the most insulting treatment possible. That's the way the world is.

The rest of Plato's dialogue attempts to prove that the opposite is true, that the just man will be happy in the end and the unjust grief-stricken. That corresponds with the actual convictions of Socrates, whom Plato uses as Glaucon's conversation partner in this work.

Plato wrote this text some 375 years before Christ! He could hardly have imagined that his fictional description of the extreme would one day come true. Yet remarkably, hundreds of years later, these characteristics would be deeply incarnate in the words, deeds, and fate of Jesus—the essence of the just man!

Jesus said: "If you love those who love you, what credit is that to you? For even sinners love those who love them. If you do good to those who do good to you, what credit is that to you? For even sinners do the same. If you lend to those from whom you hope to receive, what credit is that to you? Even sinners lend to sinners, to receive as much again. But love your enemies, do good, and lend, expecting nothing in return. Your reward will be great, and you will be children of the Most High" (Luke 6:32-35a).

The reputation that preceded Jesus can be seen in the way his enemies put him to the test. They began a trick question with the words: "Teacher, we know that you are sincere, and show deference to no one; for you do not regard people with partiality, but teach the way of God in accordance with truth" (Mark 12:14). In the end he died the death of the despised, of the unjust man.

Like Plato, the Book of Wisdom sees human resistance to righteousness in the rejection of the righteous man. Written about fifty years before Christ's life, it says:

> Let us oppress the righteous poor man . . . let our might be our law of right for what is weak proves itself to be useless. Let us lie in wait for the righteous man, because he is inconvenient to us and opposes our actions. . . . He professes to have knowledge of God and calls himself a child of the Lord. He became to us a reproof of our thoughts; the very sight of him is a burden to us, because his manner of life is unlike that of others, and his ways are strange . . . he calls the last end of the righteous happy, and boasts that God is his father. Let us see if his words are true and let us test what will happen at the end of his life; for if the righteous man is God's child, he will help him, and will deliver him from the hand of his adversaries. Let us test him with insult and torture, so that we may find out how gentle he is and make trial of his forbearance. Let us condemn him to a shameful death. (Wisdom 2:10-20)

In the end, Jesus's death was accompanied by a cynical test of insults, as the Gospels report: "Save yourself! If you are the Son of God, come down from the cross! . . . He saved others; he cannot save himself. He is the King of Israel; let him come down from the cross now, and we will believe in him. He trusts in God; let God deliver him now, if he wants to; for he said, 'I am God's Son'" (Matthew 27:40-43).

The fourth song of the servant of God in Isaiah also predicts that the just man will be completely misjudged, with shocking consequences: "We accounted him stricken, struck down by God, and afflicted. But he was wounded for our transgressions, crushed for our iniquities." Yet a pivotal change is prophesied to come *after* death! "He shall find satisfaction through his knowledge. The righteous one, my servant, shall make many righteous" (Isaiah 53:4-5, 11).

Jesus's life and end correspond with the prototype of the entirely just man of which not just Plato, but the Hebrew Scriptures, too, knew long before he came. His end makes it clear what he was *all throughout his life.*

Lao-Tse

If we go halfway around the world to the East, we will come across another "old master." Lao-Tse (sixth century BC), who lived in the province of Honan, wrote down his teachings at the end of his life. In the *Tao Te Ching*, Lao-Tse, too, caught the inner truth of God's servant marvelously:

> Nothing in the world is softer and weaker than water,
> yet nothing surpasses it in conquering the hard and the strong.
> Everyone knows that the soft overcomes the hard,
> and the weak conquers the strong,
> but none are able to act on this.
> Therefore the sage has said:
> He who takes the degradation of the nation
> upon himself is lord of all sacrifices;
> he who bears the misfortune of the nation
> is king of the world.
> True words seem to be reversed.[23]

When God's Servant, the "King of the world," appeared hundreds of years later, he lived out this role reversal. "True words seem to be reversed." In reference to himself Jesus says: "You know that among the Gentiles those whom they recognize as their rulers lord it over them, and their great ones are tyrants over them. But it is not so among you; but whoever wishes to become great among you must be your servant, and whoever wishes to be first among you must be slave of all. For the Son of Man came not to be served but to serve, and to give his life a ransom for many" (Mark 10:42–45).

"Whoever wishes to become great must be your servant." The perfect form of righteousness turns things upside down! Jesus lived this out and is therefore the Just One. That is what was meant by the sacrifice of his life, a life that is aware of heaven. In this spirit of devotion his mother Mary accepted her calling and predicted the same reversal of things in her song of praise (Luke 1:46–55).

The Reversal

Jesus's death was not the goal, but the consequence of a life of serving. The joy of the Lord was in the Just Man, not in his death, just as the offering was not his death, but his life. He was the One who reversed the world's relationships, the One who gave worth to the downtrodden, the gospel to the poor, freedom to the captive, redemption to those in fetters, sight to the blind, encouragement to the broken—so that people can stand upright and be free from their chains. That is the spirit and essence of the Messiah (Isaiah 61:1-2; Luke 4:18-19). "The spirit of the Lord God is upon me, because the Lord has anointed me" (Isaiah 61:1). The Anointed—his name is Jesus.

Jesus's message about ransom ("I give my life as a ransom for many") is foreign, abstract, and difficult to understand. The pious reflex often acts in us too quickly. We must slow down and ask: to *whom* in fact should this ransom—the life of the Just Man—be paid? Did God put humans in bondage so that we would have to have our freedom purchased from him? If we think that God demands a ransom, then we are calling him a thief, a blackmailer! God does not need a ransom because he has not trapped anyone.

No, the ransom paid by the Just One goes somewhere else! It is paid where we are imprisoned, and we are imprisoned by our concept of God as an enemy. We must be freed from everything that unsettles and corrupts our hearts, wherever our backwards thinking robs us of our life. We must be freed from our distorted image of a cynical god who will not intervene, a revenge-seeking god on the hunt for a victim, an absent god who wants nothing of us. The cry of God as an enemy has echoed in our lives as far back as we can remember. But it simply lives out the active triumvirate of evil that we have in our hearts: cynicism, resignation, violence. From *that* we need to be set free! The reversal of cynicism, when lived out, is faith; the reversal of resignation is hope; and the reversal of violence is love. As Lao-Tse says, the truth turns things around.

This reversal happens only through repentance. Jesus is the incarnate, gentle, humble power of God that changes my scheming—the tangled roots of my heart—so that I can relearn a daily turning toward him. Jesus's righteousness is so powerful that it can justify each and every person that it touches. "Justified" not because I am doing something, but because something inside me is breaking; this is the power of repentance. Just as the tar and asphalt of a street break simply because a tender plant is pushing its way up in search of daylight, so the heart's enemy concept of God breaks when the tender plant of God's love opens an inner path to the light.

We will overcome injustice in the same measure that we allow Jesus to overcome us. He is the Just One. The willpower of insight is not good enough. The necessary strength can be mustered up only through love, love for a person. This is spiritually deeper and fiercer than love of a mere idea. It gets its intensity from the devotion of the loved one. By turning back to him who is love, love gains the strength to turn our situation around. The reversal through love is calling me. Redemption can occur only through this "turning": then we will overcome fear through faith, indifference through love, guilt through forgiveness.

When Martin Luther said: "For the will of God is efficacious and cannot be thwarted since it is God's natural power,"[24] one may answer: Of course, a person cannot hinder the will of God. And yet you can. Because God decided for himself to restrain his will. That is why Jesus taught us to pray, "Your will be done" and not "Your will is being done." Not everything that happens is God's will. If it were, then this prayer would be ridiculous—and all other prayers along with it. The will that called everything into life is seemingly weak in the world. The Most High is the Most Humble. It is the humility that longs for unity between the musician and the instrument. This unity with God is our calling. It is as vulnerable as love itself. In Lao-Tse's words:

> Nothing in the world is softer and weaker than water,
> yet nothing surpasses it in conquering the hard and the strong.

It is not difficult to see: this is the water of the Holy Spirit.

God's Depression

The song of God's Servant makes visible the necessary suffering of God's love. This is the key thought of this allegory of the cellist. Now let's change the tone color a little. We don't have to trouble ourselves about God's sorrow. God is resilient. He can deal with it. It is strange to talk like this, but it is necessary. After all, isn't it a narrow, fearful, bitter, joyless faith that feeds on a hidden feeling of somehow being responsible for God's sensitivity? As if to say: "Let's live right because otherwise our holy God will have a hard time. Everything depends on my arguments, because otherwise the incomprehensible God will have no lawyer to defend him!"

The metaphor of the loving and therefore suffering God can be terribly misunderstood if we do not realize *the nature* of God's suffering that we see in Jesus. Perfection is not only to be found in God's love, but also in his suffering! He does not suffer from shortcomings but from love itself. It is a necessary suffering. Please note: God lacks nothing. Our faith will be resilient only when we realize that we can place our burdens on God.

There is a kind of faith that is like the heart-rending pain of a child who feels responsible for his parent's mental illness. He thinks: "My mother is not really there. She seems so far away." The child begins to try to cheer up his depressed, tormented mother by being immaculate, perfectly well behaved. The child wants to animate his detached mother, give her joy, extract some kind of emotion or praise from her. His collective behaviors cry out: "Look how good I am! Now you have something to be happy about!"

Some faiths are just like this. These processes of the child-like soul are not imaginary. My sister Gisela—a consultant in child and youth psychotherapy—can speak volumes on this subject. When I learned about this inner process of the child's heart, a painful image immediately came to mind of a similar kind of faith. In it, the believer ("a *child* of God") suffers from God's absence. But it does not stop there; he feels responsible for God in the end. A life in such a faith can be burdened by feelings of guilt. Such a "faith" tries to encourage God to finally come out of his shell ("*to feel God*"). A crazed piousness develops. The child of God feels responsible for God's absence and believes he has to work or love the presence of God into existence through commendable morals, strong praises, or some kind of fervent faith. This builds up an unbearable pressure against oneself. The absence becomes an accusation.

I would like to shout out this creed into such a heart-rending world of faith: "You are not responsible for God!" It needs to be repeated often, for faith will be lively and free only when we learn the opposite through and through: we must learn to be a burden for God. We do not need to cheer him up; he does not break when we do not please him. What mother would say to her child: "I am not your mother anymore because you did something wrong"? It would break a child's heart. What kind of father would threaten: "If you do or don't do this or that, I will go away and no longer be your father. I won't want to see you anymore!" If we can sense how sick it would be to say something like that, can we seriously believe God is like that? God does not break our hearts, and he is not sick. We must learn to cast our burdens on him, to be a burden; we can be like a child who has this assurance from his parents.

Jesus did not say in vain: "If you then, who are evil, know how to give good gifts to your children, how much more will your Father in heaven give good things to those who ask him!" (Matthew 7:11). How little we understand about God—we are not responsible for him! And yet this guilt-laden faith exists. It feels responsible for God in the depths of its soul. It is a faith made of incessant moral demands and constant lawyer-like arguments. Outwardly it is harsh, cold, and combative toward other people. Inwardly it is fragile and feels overwhelmed and guilty. A person with this kind of faith suffers from a false impression of God. It is a faith that is occupied with trying to justify God to others and attempting to put God in a good mood, favorable toward oneself. As if God needs us to do either of these things!

No, God lacks nothing. His sorrow is of a different nature. It is the suffering of love itself. It is a love that cannot love anytime or anywhere that we reject God's presence! Because God's presence is love, it is fragile. But God's being is resilient, also because it is love.

Life's Primal Principle

The primal principle of life is self-sacrifice. It is the foundation of all creation. For what have we taken that has not given its life for us? Food, natural resources, water, provisions, time—whatever I am that is good I am through the sacrifice of others; and whatever good that I should be, I can become only through self-sacrifice. Dedication is the ground motif of a developing and growing life. Such dedication is found in God. When we live out this commitment, then we live "from God." We receive this gift in the same measure that we give it to our neighbor.

The world lives from the sacrifice of life. To not surrender one-self—or at least to not make an effort—is ultimately a revolt against the most holy power that gives life to all living beings. A mother makes sacrifices for her child. She sets aside her time because the child needs her and her time. Our world is like God's child. God speaks through this tone color: could I ever abandon you? As the prophet Isaiah heard, it is the cry of someone in labor, giving her life to the world.

This is how I see the age-old story of the Servant of God. God "gave his only Son" (John 3:16). As is said in Romans: God "did not withhold his own Son" (8:32). So he subjected the Just One, the One who loves completely, to us, we who are humans. The statement that God gave his Son is not passive, because Jesus is not only broken by people. He is broken by God, broken by the Father's suffering, broken by the unavoidable sorrow found in God's love. He is crushed by the necessity of the love in which the world had its origin. The Son surrendered himself into God's devotion.

Jesus identified completely with God's suffering and united himself perfectly with God's longing to transform the world through love. In seeing this we recognize God's love for the world as a path of calling. It is a path of transformation, never of oppression. God cannot force us; that would destroy him. He *cannot*? Is there anything that God *cannot* do? In fact, the New Testament has something surprising to say about this: "If we are faithless, he remains faithful—for he *cannot* deny himself" (2 Timothy 2:13). Yet there is strong evidence of the essence of the Almighty hidden in this verse, and it is not a picture of omnipotent power. "In *every* circumstance, I am and will always be love." Immersed in utter impotence as he was, *this* is the power that is visible in Jesus on the cross! He remained who he was to the end, the One who loves, and in this he is completely united with God: "As you, Father, are in me and I am in you . . ." (John 17:21).

The cellist's experience related in this chapter casts a new light on many things that Jesus said. Jesus's profound words found in John 14:6, "I am the way, the truth, and the life," are certainly not an expression of triumph, but of passion; truth is a *relationship*, and this is exactly why truth is an extremely vulnerable occurrence. As the bow touches the string and awakens a vulnerable series of vibrations, so it is between the impetus of grace (the bow) and the answer of faith (the string). All the beauty of our calling lies in that vulnerable interplay between the invisible realm of grace and the visible realm of creation. The action of our spirit allowing this interplay is called "faith."

It is possible to nullify the vulnerable interplay between truth and beauty—the closed sound is precisely that. We can do this. We have the power to ruin our calling and send God away. It happens when we harden ourselves in our pride and hide ourselves in our fear. There are times when we are frighteningly free. This is evident in the moment when Jesus asks his disciples: "Do you also wish to go away?" (John 6:67). He knows that he is not allowed to break the will of those he calls. Our lives remain the story of our calling.

~

Responsibility is the freedom to which we are bound. Simply stated, what kind of life am I devoted to? Am I able *to bind myself* and thereby *be there* for other people, for other creatures, tasks, and things? That is loyalty. A covenant displays outwardly the inner principle of love *that binds itself*! That is why Jesus talks about a new covenant.

If God were not able to bind himself to a covenant, how could he be the Loving One? Here again, heaven's freedom has bound itself to my limits. The words that instituted the Last Supper speak of God's covenant: the covenant that created the world, permeates all things, and manifested itself in the crucifixion is now *"given for you!"* I am overcome; something I intrinsically know enters me in the bread and wine. The truth that gives me life is the suffering love, the bound love. "This is my body. This is the blood of the covenant." An indestructible vulnerability has bound itself to my response. What else can I do but accept it? I let myself be overwhelmed by this, God's first love, because without it my life simply has no horizon. There is only a dot-shaped tight circle of "me," incapable of self-sacrifice or forming commitments.

The Eucharist is a thank you for God's vulnerability in which I begin to take myself seriously. In the Eucharist I lay down my own power and consist solely of thankfulness. I must allow myself to be permeated and shaken. If I cannot be frightened by God's vulnerability that is revealed here, then I will probably not come to have faith—not in the deep places, which is exactly where God may draw near to me.

The terrifying fact remains: I can love, but I don't have to. I have the power to turn God away, the power of which Jesus spoke when he said: "Father, forgive them; for they know not what they do" (Luke 23:34 RSV).

The end of the Servant of God is the beginning of a new existence. This love does not just suffer, it forgives! The truth of this perfect love finds its resonance in my faith. Therefore, I devote myself to God in communion, not because I have to but because this love has overcome me. It is Love's perfection that has the power of resurrection.

"Get up! He's calling for you!" Like the blind man by the side of the road, I want to allow myself to be called (see Mark 10:46-52). That is my faith. And I know: after the sound adjustment comes the concert!

The New Sound

Every musician longs for a free and open tone, and rightly so. The instrument should react; it should allow the tone to be formed, to blossom and glow, and also to retreat whenever the composition calls for it. The beauty of playing an instrument is to explore the resonances. You can form the sounding tone and knead it like clay in the hand of the potter. I love powerful instruments and enjoy an intoxicating fortissimo. But it is not about the volume; rather, it is about the feeling of uniting your own strength with the instrument's opposing power. It is this thick, rich tone that curbs the bow as the instrument takes the energy that you give it.

So what happened in the story with which I started this chapter? Two days later the cellist came back to try his newly adjusted instrument. As you can imagine, no matter how confident a violinmaker may be, such a moment evokes conflicting emotions. There is great tension. For no doubt-free, perfect sound exists, no objective yardstick with which you can measure. The situation is much more demanding: the sound must match the musician! You are not really working with an instrument but with the voice of the musician. The tension is relieved only if the musician exclaims how wonderful the instrument is now.

The first test usually lasts no more than one or two minutes. In this case, the cellist sat down and started playing specific passages: Dvořák, Schumann, Shostakovich—all the greats. I closed my eyes and felt myself enter the tone. He did not stop playing. A good twenty minutes went by before he laid his bow aside! Instead of stating his opinion, he looked at me and asked: "Mr. Schleske, what do *you* think of the sound?"

This was unexpected. I was nervous and started to hunt for a favorable answer but then decided to just be honest: "I am mostly satisfied. The A-string is much freer, beaming, open. The D-string is good. There is no break in sound when crossing strings. The C-string has gained potency and strength. It purrs at a velvety piano and is warm in the deep tones. But the G-string is a problem. You do not feel comfortable there."

He stared at me, speechless for a moment. Then he replied that now and then someone would tell him quite accurately what he was hearing, but he could not remember a time when someone had told him how *he* felt when he played. But it was just as I had said. The G-string was still a problem. So we spent another full (and stressful!) hour making tiny corrections until the G-string started to dovetail into the sound spectrum between the C- and D-strings.

He gave a wonderful concert a few days later. Listening to it, I had the impression that he had almost grown together with his instrument. Every movement was thoroughly natural and authentic. He was searching humbly for a truly singing tone.

Afterword

If we fully recognize the Servant of God, we will no longer be able to flee to our inner retreat in the role of a victim. As sad or painful as our lives may seem to be, it is still abject self-abasement to view ourselves as continual victims—victims of circumstance, people, fate. This self-abasement loses its rights to cynicism in Christ. We should lay aside the role of victim that we so love to play, for with it we squander away our lives. It is not we, but Christ, who is the Servant of God, whom God sacrificed on our behalf. That makes us the recipients of a gift, not a victim! Christ says: "I have given myself to you so that you can receive, so be the one who receives me! This will be your strength and dignity."

In his thoughts about the concept of God after Auschwitz, Hans Jonas said: "The concept of God can be pursued, even if there is no proof of God."[25] We don't have to share his concept of God, but we should not avoid the heart's search. The question "Is there a God?" requires a quick movement of the lips. You say either yes or no. It is entirely different to ask: "What is God like?" This question has power. For faith is to answer this question with your whole life.

A Personal God?

In the metaphor of the closed sound, I silently assume that God is a "personal God." The Bible shows that God not only exists, but that God is "a person." One can rightly say that God is the main character of the Bible. But can you seriously believe in God as a personal God? Can you talk about him as if he were an individual? Should we imagine God as something like a person *alongside* other people, like an oversized mega-person, a maximized individual who is behind everything?

There is a psalm that can point us in the right direction. It says: "He who planted the ear, does he not hear? He who formed the eye, does he not see?" (Psalm 94:9). Along this line of questioning I ask: "He who made each human as a person, should he not at least be a person?" I am convinced that God can be no less than what I am: active, effective, thoughtful, capable of suffering and loving. God is the love that makes a person out of us. To recognize God is to become more like him—and that means becoming one who loves.[26] Martin Buber said: "The concept of personal being is indeed completely incapable of defining what God's essential being is, but it is both permitted and necessary to say that God is *also* a Person."[27]

Even if it is never enough to understand God as a person, it is also impossible to think of him as anything less. If I quit thinking of him as a person, then my faith instantly becomes "godless," for that approach turns God into an idea. An idea can perhaps "be loved," but it in and of itself cannot "love." It must be thought into existence, but it has no life in itself. But this is precisely what Jesus says of God: "The Father has life in himself" (John 5:26).

∼

Just as the string beneath the cellist's bow finds resonance in the instrument's body, and the cello responds to the vibrating string with color, resistance, strength, and radiance, so the individual responds to God radiating these same qualities out into our world. Faith is God finding resonance in me. Trust means I resonate in this world with God's meaning, dignity, and power, in spite of all that is incomprehensible, troublesome, and powerlessness. Therefore, I do not believe in a great pantheistic something but in the "You" of God. He is the Holy One for the sake of my fallen nature, the One who loves for the sake of my homelessness, the One who forgives because of my lack of love, the Eternal One for the sake of my mortality, the Holy Spirit for my longing to receive. Yes, I am convinced that for the sake of my "me," I can call God "You" in a personal way. Everything comes together in this shared sound: God is the love that makes each of us a person. Something I cannot explain makes me a person and, in so doing, an image of God: this is love. Love alone breathes the Spirit of eternity. That is my confession. I believe in a loving and therefore suffering God. I believe in myself as a person, and therefore also in a personal God.

08

Reworking the Violin

The Pain and Crisis of Faith

The human spirit will endure sickness;
but a broken spirit—who can bear?

—PROVERBS 18:14

*I*T WOULD BE ABSURD to describe the "sound of faith" as true and enlightening and then ignore crises and darkness. I want to write about my own painful experiences, events that have crashed into my life and shaken my faith. A metaphor is hiding inside. But first, an attack.

Self-Centered Doubt

I have often asked myself by what right we consider ourselves "saved" when we see the kind of things that happen in our world. Do we have some kind of special faith-filled place far from violence and poverty, trials and crises? Are we God's special favorites simply because the grace to believe in him was granted to us? Is not God there in the places where crises come crashing down? Do I close my eyes and hold fast to my own faith as long as nothing affects *me*, but stop believing in God when hardships hit my life? Then why don't I stop believing when troubles hit others? Are the problems of strangers not a good enough reason to doubt God? Isn't it pathetically narrow-minded to operate by the conviction that "God is good if he is good to me. But if things are not going well for me, then he has abandoned me, or worse, he doesn't exist!"? Then why in the name of everything holy did he exist before, when things were good for me, but others were in distress?

I have often asked myself why the hardship of strangers does not make us doubt. True, maturity and dignity demand that I not allow my sails to waver in the storm of my own distress. In the midst of *my own* troubles, I should strengthen my faith and calm my soul; but in the midst of the hardships of *strangers*, I should fight, wrestle with God, be a comfort, help, and balm for my neighbor. We are entrusted to each other: this is where we are put to the test.

Is it not childish and small to try and make one's faith crisis-proof based on the idea that, up until now, nothing bad has happened *to me*? Such a faith, closed up in its own happiness, is based on ignorance, selfishness, and fear. If it is not a faith that looks openly and honestly into the world and sees what is happening, if it is not a faith that is ready to inquire about the truth of God and to search for him fervently with the world in mind, then it is no faith at all.

If God takes us seriously as his counterpart, and if he thinks that it is right to question us about our lives, then I know that it is also right for me to question *him*. If he makes it clear to me in my microscopic existence that I am not his advisor, then I will tell him in his vastness how strangely hidden he sometimes is, how incomprehensible his silence, how unbearable the ambiguity in which he often leaves us hanging. "Where were you when I laid the foundation of the earth? Tell me, if you have understanding," God asks of Job (38:4). Then I will cry out to him: "I never claimed to be smart! Why are you talking like this? If you ask me this, then I, being made in your image, will return the question: Where were *you*? Where were you when I could find no meaning? Where were you in the face of the unfathomable? Why were you silent? Why did you remain so painfully hidden?" I will not be denied the right to ask God these questions. Nor will I dodge the opportunity, because I know how I have searched for God in everything and the painful extent to which he owes my spirit an answer.

"God, I would not want to be in your skin!"—this was the last prayer of a woman whose faith crumbled as she looked at pictures of innocent, starving children. That cry of faith I can relate to. This brokenness, years later, would be transformed into new faith in this woman's life, but not through answers, rather through comfort in the face of suffering that she experienced *in her own body*. If we do not creep into silence but rise up and face God, if we cry out to him in the helplessness of our faith, then we will be able to stand upright before him and ask everything for which there is no answer today. And one day, we will be longing for these answers no more because we will stand before him and see him. We will be saved, will be enveloped by his comfort, and will experience what it means to meet a God who knows infinitely more about tears than we do. "God will wipe away every tear from their eyes"; so says the book of Revelation about the gentle and bright crossing over from the sorrow of today into the tomorrow of a new world (7:17; 21:4). Tears are not foreign to him. That is what the rabbi meant by the idea that God has two chambers in his heart, an inner and an outer. "In the inner chamber he hides his pain and his weeping."

The Fire

My faith was most severely shaken when I was eighteen years old. It was January 9, 1984. I was in my second year at the luthier school and lived in one of the oldest houses in Mittenwald. One afternoon, I had two of my classmates, Eckhard and Guido, over for coffee in my room. I had just gotten a designer coffee maker as a gift. Like many fondue pots, the coffee pot had an alcohol flame burning underneath. The flame went out because the denatured alcohol needed to be refilled. I took the bottle of alcohol and carelessly approached the burner, which was apparently still smoldering. The result was an explosive flash-fire. With violent force and a loud whooshing noise, a ten-foot long, eighteen-inch-wide flame shot out of the bottle that I was still holding in my hand. The room immediately caught fire. I did not yet know that the two young men who were sitting across from me were badly burned. They ran out of the room. The ceiling tiles were on fire; the bed was on fire. I stumbled to the sink, filled a tub with water, and in a panic, threw it up against the burning ceiling (all the while screaming out the Lord's Prayer). The fire was extinguished with one splash but continued smoking. In my state of panic, I did not realize how strange it was that I was able to put out the fire with just one tub of water.

Minutes later the police investigators were interrogating me. I heard that my classmates had been badly injured. This was all my fault. I could not accept the fact that, although I had caused the accident, I myself was not hurt in any way. I found out that the student in the next room had called an ambulance right away. My friends had run outside into the cold, injured though they were, and were now being taken to the nearby town of Garmisch by ambulance. A mobile intensive-care unit from the hospital met them on the way and took over, due to complications that they were experiencing. Guido had a lung embolism. Their condition was too serious to be treated at the hospital in Garmisch, so they were sent on to a trauma center in Murnau—luckily, one of the two burn centers in all of Germany at that time. And so, just one hour later, my classmates were receiving expert treatment there.

My father was the only one who knew how serious the situation was at first. The doctors mistook him for a colleague because of his title and shared the details of the complications that my classmates were experiencing. It was not clear if one of them would survive, and the other might end up blind. In retrospect, it was like a second miracle that both Guido and Eckhard ended up healthy and did not suffer any long-term injuries or disfigurement.

On the evening after the accident a neighbor informed my parents that she thought I was an acute suicide risk. That was not at all true, because for the first few days I did not have the strength to do such a thing. But I do remember that there was nothing I wanted more than to never have been born. This desire burned deep down inside me. I kept repeating it to myself. My parents took my neighbor's warning seriously, and so my father picked me up from school and drove me home. I quit violinmaking studies for a while, and my father had me work on home-repair projects around the house for the next few days.

Upon arriving home, I went to visit my friend Steffen right away. I need to take a moment to describe this friendship, which proved so important for my survival after this crisis.

The Friend

Steffen and I had developed a strong friendship as a part of a spontaneously emerging "youth movement" in the little city of Beilstein. We were driven by a passionate love for Jesus. We had been influenced by youth gatherings, street music, compositions, rehearsals, and concerts of our Christian band. My brother, Michael, played drums, Bernd was on bass, and Steffen and I played electric guitar. My parents were surprisingly tolerant when we rehearsed three times a week in our basement, shaking the foundations of our house with our amps. (I had built the tube amp one free afternoon with my physics teacher, Höhnberg, a genius with a passion for electronics.) When working even on the third story of our house became impossible, my father would always call out: "I'll bet you could play quieter!" We called our band *Aufbruch* (Awakening), which was certainly the spirit of our entire youth. We wrote our own songs, gave devout concerts in left-wing youth housing, and often played—but with acoustic instruments and more participants—in the pedestrian zone of Heilbronn and sometimes in other cities as well.

Many young people joined our Jesus movement in Beilstein. We had cookouts in the forest park, baked campfire bread, and delighted each other with Bible devotionals (with probably highly questionable interpretations). It was very exciting, at least for us. There were hardly any older people who could have led us in these matters. The discoveries that we young people made in the Bible were the only authority that we were ready to acknowledge.

Sometimes we all went to Schwäbisch Hall on Sundays to celebrate a church service with the inmates at a juvenile detention center. Apparently, one of our friends had stumbled across a passage in Matthew (chapter 25) and was shocked to read: "I was sick and you took care of me, I was in prison and you visited me . . ." The prison was not far away, so we could put the word into action. The main thing was to take things seriously and try out what we were reading in the Bible. We felt so alive; Jesus was near, and we were his disciples.

The long walks through the vineyards of Beilstein—especially with Steffen—were defining moments when we discussed pressing questions of faith, shared our experiences, told each other about our discoveries, and wrestled for answers. These strong, youthful struggles with my friends were a counterweight to the discussions that took place in my parents' house. Since I had caught on fire for Jesus two or three years earlier as a thirteen-year-old at a youth camp on the Isle of Arran in Scotland (I was the only German among about eighty Scottish boys) hardly a meal went by without an argument. I felt that I was being cut down in my convictions when my father, who was a professor and had far superior debating skills, wanted to know how one could even speak of truth in light of different religions and worldviews, or how I could believe in a "loving God" given all of the suffering that takes place in the world. My father had been a believer in his younger years, and now he is again. But what had happened to "God's chosen people" during the Third Reich had dissuaded him from believing in God. That was one reason he gave me at that time. When I asked him what he believed, he once answered that he was a nihilist. At the age of thirteen, I did not know what that meant.

After these impassioned discussions, I usually retreated to my bedroom on the verge of tears, Bible in hand. A Scottish student from Cologne, whom I did not know personally, had sent me a little red Bible "in today's German." Malcolm, one of her Scottish friends who was pivotal for me at that time, had told her about me. She inscribed a verse from Romans chapter 8 in the front as a blessing. It continues to be a life verse for me even today. I would sit in my room and start to read, beginning with the letter to the Romans, a candle burning constantly in front of me. I often felt a holy presence as if Jesus was standing right behind me, laying his hand on the shoulder of the thirteen-year-old searching for God, and illuminating the texts as I read them. This had an impact on the conversations I had with my father as well.

In the beginning, I did not know any Christians in my area. The more I read during those years, the more the text in all its truth, strangeness, and beauty pulled me along in its wake. It was "my first church," and it still is. When I was fifteen and sixteen years old, there were days during which I disappeared into the Scriptures for hours at a time—not because I felt it was my duty to read it, but simply because I could not stop! The Bible became my spiritual home.

As a young person I rarely, perhaps never, went out and about without my Bible in my tattered pants pocket. It was a treasure that I carried along—in the Beilstein vineyards, hiking, in the waiting room at the train station, or wherever I was. I sat and read in the invisible tent that it erected around me against the outer confusion. I felt a holy nearness and powerful peace—God was talking to me, and I began to understand things. I memorized certain passages (mostly from Isaiah and John) because I had read them so many times. Steffen was on the same path of faith. He shared my passion.

When we got together, with other friends as well, we shared our concerns and our questions: What have you discovered? What have you experienced? What have you stumbled upon? What is God doing with you, and where do you notice it? We were excited for each other, and, of course, we also had considerable ambitions. We wanted to compare ourselves to each other and find out what we, ourselves, had to offer.

Later, during my civil-service time, I of course had no money but shared a bank account with Steffen. We had come across the part in the book of Acts where it says: they "sold their possessions and goods, and divided them among all, as anyone had need" (Acts 2:45 NKJV). We each put in what we had and took out what we needed. Steffen would later become a pastor, and I a violinmaker.

But after the fire, with him still in high school and me in my second year at Mittenwald, a true catastrophe with real consequences had brought my life crashing down around me. This was the first massive blow for me, and I was terribly afraid for the two young men who were lying in intensive care in Murnau.

～

As I mentioned, my father had picked me up at school and brought me home. Steffen had, of course, heard the whole story. So when

I sought him out, without saying much he took his guitar and we drove to a familiar place in the forest. The things he said to me sparked the strong conviction that this was a message from God. We felt that God was suffering over the situation, and we knew that he was present with my classmates in intensive care as well. I have never experienced hours like that since then. My *own* faith was no longer there; there was nothing of my own to summon up. But as we sat there in the forest with the guitar and prayed for the boys, God's presence was close and tangible with an intensity that I have never experienced since. Complete despair and praising God, both so extreme yet without touching each other; fear and certainty; broken faith and God's presence—this is not humanly understandable, but we could sense God's presence and assurance, so strong and enlightening that we began to sing songs of praise. Of course, such a thing seems completely absurd and unexpected; yet alongside the fear and inner turmoil, there was also the nearness of God that we could not explain. It was like a holy presence. We knew that healing would occur. But on the other hand, I was also completely devastated. The inner shattering and strong assurance did not extinguish each other.

My mother was worried about my faith during the next few days. She asked herself what would happen if my sense of assurance was deceptive. I knew what purple burn wounds looked like and was terribly afraid that my friends would carry these marks forever. It is like another miracle to me that neither of them ended up with permanent injuries or disfiguring scars. The doctor in charge told my father that the clinic had just received a new medicinal compound that they had never tried before and that the results were better than anyone could have expected.

While still in intensive care, Eckhard asked for me to call him. That telephone conversation was an indescribable relief. Eckhard said that, even as he was lying in the mobile intensive care unit, he was wondering what could have happened to me. He said that he did not think I was at fault, that it was just an accident. In that moment I realized how vitally important it is for a person to live by forgiveness. I asked him to talk to Guido, too. The next day Eckhard told me that Guido had basically said that I was such a nerd. That was his way of forgiving me, and without it my situation would have been unbearable. With every week that they had to stay in the clinic (and it was a long time!) I grew more and more aware of how serious the situation had been.

From the very beginning I knew one thing with remarkable clarity: if I were to ask the question as to why this situation occurred it would be the end of me, for I knew that the question "why" leads to death. Death is the logical answer to this question, because life doesn't offer any answer. It became clear to me that I was not allowed to ask this question, and so I did not do so.

The students at Mittenwald were strongly affected by the whole situation. Classmates, some of whom I hardly knew, rose to the occasion during those weeks. There was an atmosphere of humanity, awareness, closeness, helpfulness, and friendship as had never been before. And yet the months after the explosion were still a terrible time. It was like being hurt over and over again as the picture of the explosion flashed in my mind completely unexpectedly during everyday activities. Over and over the image of the burning room put me in a state of shock, panic, and fear.

But almost every time, I experienced something else surprising, too. As the picture of the fire flashed in front of me, another image would appear that made the fire fade away. It was so real that it felt like a memory. Without wanting to, I saw a picture of a story from the Gospel of Matthew. It was always the same, and I did not have to do anything to evoke it; it was as strong as the memory of the fire:

> But when he noticed the strong wind, he became frightened, and beginning to sink, he cried out, "Lord, save me!" Jesus immediately reached out his hand and caught him, saying to him, "You of little faith, why did you doubt?" When they got into the boat, the wind ceased. (Matthew 14:30–32)

This scene was inside me as if I had experienced it myself. I saw the hand taking hold of me, and it was lit up as brightly and powerfully as the fire. One scene would replace the other—as if I had experienced them *both*.

A few weeks later I was officially charged with extreme negligence resulting in personal injuries. My parents protested the charges because a conviction would give me a criminal record. The case went to court. That was an amazing experience, too. I told about the time after the accident, my conversations with my classmates, things that were important to me, as well as the forgiveness that they had given me. My defense attorney said nothing the entire time, and finally the prosecuting attorney (!) stood up and made a request, "considering what he had heard," to stop the proceedings. The criminal charges were replaced by a fine, and I was even allowed to say where I wanted the funds to be allocated. Those weeks were simultaneously better and worse than ever before. Only much later would I notice what deep scars the whole episode had left in me.

The Raised Sword

The self-cursing with which I incessantly beat myself up in the days after the explosion continued for at least ten years. I didn't even realize it, but it became suddenly clear in the middle of another crisis.

Since my mid-twenties I have had severe, nauseating migraines that are sometimes accompanied by impairments to my speech and vision. One day, about ten years after the explosion and fire, it was worse than usual. A friend suggested that, while he didn't like to be dramatic or anything, something deeper might be going on here. He advised me to discuss it with a pastor.

When I was alone, I felt the weight of the world on my shoulders and completely collapsed—not because of the headaches, but because of the enormous burden that I had been carrying for years. As I lay there, unable to get to my feet, I started to pray and was surprised that I called out to God not as "Father" but as "Mother." I had never done that before. Of course, I was familiar with the passage in Isaiah where God says: "As a mother comforts her child, so I will comfort you" (Isaiah 66:13), but I would have never thought of the idea of calling out to God that way.[1] For the next few hours I lay there completely drained and felt an infinitely gentle, strong, comforting presence. I knew that God was with me and was speaking with me. Suddenly I saw the fire again, ten years later!—that whooshing shot of flame and the burning room—but this time without any sense of panic. I was reminded of all my self-accusations and the curses with which I had assailed myself, how terribly hard I had been on myself.

I knew Walter well at the time; he was the pastor of our church and a confidant. He was shocked that I had never spoken with him about the accident before since we had known each other for a long time. We talked for almost three hours. I don't remember the details of that conversation, but it was a path of profound healing. We discussed the matter over and over and then fell silent. It was a communal time of inner listening and prayer. We went through the experience step by step, including my internal accusations that needed to be recanted. Some of the images and words that came to me during this journey of prayer are unforgettable. Walter did not do much. For the most part, he just listened, prayed with me, and recommended ways to go forward.

In one of these internal images I saw the figure of Jesus. It was a sight that was quite threatening and utterly oppressive. He wore a luminous garment and held a blinding, sharp sword in the radiant light. He held it up in front of me as if he was going to strike me with it. This internal movie froze at that point and became like a snapshot. I then heard this question: "What will I do?"

Walter and I fell silent, considering this question. The raised sword fit well with the deep feelings of self-reproach with which I had lived for years. It was pitiless and menacing. In response, I stated what I knew about Jesus, his gentleness and humility, that he said we would find rest for our souls in him. He spoke of an "easy yoke" (Matthew 11:30). As I said all of this, the freeze frame began to move again like in a movie, and I saw Jesus take the sword he had raised and slowly touch my left shoulder with it like a king does when he is knighting someone. So that was the meaning of the raised sword! I understood that in all my inadequacy, what I had to answer for is what and who I think Jesus is. I understood that it is through faith in his gentle and humble lordship that I had become "noble."

In the days that followed, I felt as though I had just undergone a difficult operation. I was weak, but I could tell I was healing. Certainly I was not completely changed, and yet I had a different sense of life. I still tend toward melancholy rather than a carefree temperament; that is a matter of predisposition, and it is not all bad. An old acquaintance once said to me: "How could you possibly want to have a 'thick skin'? Do you think that you would be so receptive and creative that way? You are fine the way you are." No one, in fact, can be and have everything.

Pain

Most crises are accompanied by physical or spiritual pain. What does pain have to do with faith? As long as we live in this world we will suffer pain. We should see a calling in this that does not eclipse our longing for harmony. In this lifetime we will not be pain-free. And yet through the pain, our yearnings will stay alive so that we can, with all our might, practice good "intonation" by our presence.

Perhaps the intonation—the tuning of a musical instrument—can be a metaphor: if a guitarist has not tuned his instrument and starts to play anyway, it is painful. This pain is not bad; it is a signal that something is not right. Pain creates the irrepressible urge to correct what is wrong. Therefore, in pain we should recognize an unerring longing for harmony. What "inner music" would our world have if we knew nothing of this longing? But how can any longing be free from pain? The loss of harmony is the beginning of pain (Genesis 3:16-17), and the restoration of harmony is its end (Revelation 21:4).

The older you get, the more necessary it is to tend to the spiritual task of resolving your relationship with your pain. To give a personal example: pain in my lower lumbar region can hit me like a bolt of lightning. Once it happened while I was operating a band saw. The lightning-quick pain knocked my legs out from under me. I was barely able to pull myself up using the table next to me. The orthopedist gave me shots that eased the pain, and subsequent doctor visits have been a great blessing. When pain like this goes on for weeks, I find myself praying out of reflex: "Good Lord, this back pain!" Once, however, another thought came into the mix: What am I actually imagining? Should every ache and pain stop the second I pray, like waving a magic wand? Would I be happy then? How dreadfully distorted would my life be if I had a God who bent to my every whim?

Even though not all pain is a result of misconduct, nonetheless I recognize in myself all too well the fanaticism of a violinmaker. If I were pain-free and "limitless," I would abuse my body and my time. Is not my back pain a signal to be more cautious and reserved, to take care of myself? Do I not assume way too many burdens and only notice the toll they take through pain? Do I want to just push forward and give God commands to be a healing servant who can make the symptoms disappear, only leaving me and everything else that is out of balance unchanged?

Not all pain is self-inflicted, but I want to meet it all actively. Instead of whining about sleepless nights, I can spend these long night watches lifting up the needs of those I know to God, strengthening them with my prayers. I want to take care of myself as much as possible, but when pain and flaws come in spite of my efforts, I want to learn to accept them as an extreme form of prayer. They should at least be a reminder to intercede for others that I know are in need. And so the pain is not removed but transformed, and my spirit is lifted up to heaven despite it all.

The apostle Paul's example also shows me a unique way of dealing with pain: "I want to know Christ and the power of his resurrection and the sharing of his sufferings" (Philippians 3:10). Pain is not a form of devotion, but coping with it should make us glad that we are traveling the path of maturity and not of resignation.

The Threat

Hard times hit from all sides just after I opened up my own shop in 1996. Trouble seemed to be lurking all around, threatening our very survival. I probably would not have made it through this time had I not had a special experience—the story of my calling—a few months earlier. More on that later.

While I was launching my workshop, my wife was diagnosed with a dangerous disease. We were told that, assuming the diagnosis was correct, she had only a few weeks to live. A doctor friend of ours said that when she read the findings she went weak in the knees. It was an enormous shock and began an odyssey of examinations. We were in a constant state of uncertainty. I do not want to describe this time in too much detail. Suffice it to say that concentrating on work was out of the question. I felt fearful, defenseless, and completely bewildered. I kept picturing myself at my wife's graveside and wondered what it would be like if Jonas—our first son who had just turned three—had to grow up without a mother. My wife, who had much more spiritual strength than I during this time, was in good hands both professionally and personally at a modern oncology center. She had access to the best diagnostic tools available in Germany. I remember our first conversation with the doctor and the peace it gave us. He said that we could feel free to call him day or night with any questions we might have. After a few days they gave us some relatively good news; it was not one of the intensely aggressive cancers but would nevertheless have to be treated.

Instead of feeling strong in the faith, I felt unbelievably defenseless. I am certainly no faith hero and I did not know what I should believe, but we felt the prayers of our friends as never before. It was as if Claudia and I, at the exact same time, although in different places, could feel it when someone was praying for us. We found out later that our friends took turns meeting every evening to pray for our situation and Claudia's health. Fellowship with these friends was like a protective covering during an utterly vulnerable time.

During those seven terrifying weeks, I had two bike accidents and started my company with no customer base. No one came in. In a mixture of self-pity and cynicism I thought: "That's the way it is for you, too, God. You are there, but no one comes." Finances got tighter and tighter. I did not know how we could survive physically or financially. Time and time again I called on an experience that I had had months earlier in Wales. I held on tight to it. In such times you learn to sound out biblical experiences differently and anew. The little but immeasurably important signs of God's goodness were also important for survival. Once Walter called me to say that he had been praying for me that morning. He had a thought to share: "Do not depend on people but put your whole hope in God."

I was happy that he had prayed for me, but I did not know how to take this advice. If anything, I felt like I was being attacked. I asked myself: What's that supposed to mean? Don't I have enough faith? How am I supposed to interpret this message? During this terrible time I simply had no sense of the measure or intensity of my faith. Everything was mixed with fear. I turned this message over in my mind for the next few days, kept contemplating it, but could not come to terms with it.

Then one morning as I was trying to work at my bench, a strange feeling of unease came over me. It was not a typical, familiar sort of discomfort, but a kind of spiritual restlessness that gives the impression that God wants to tell me something directly. So I asked. The answer was: "Go in your office and open your devotional book." I had to look for it first, because I had not read it for weeks. I opened it up and the verse of the day was from Psalm 146: "Do not put your trust in princes, in mortals, in whom there is no help. Happy are those . . . whose hope is in the Lord their God."

I still did not understand it, but joy shot through me in recognizing this simple message: I am with you! It was exactly what Walter had felt compelled to tell me a few days earlier after praying for me.

The prayers for Claudia did not seem to be changing anything, but then one morning, when she was alone reading the Bible, she suddenly felt a great weight come over her. It was so enormous that she had to lie down. She felt a deep calm, as if she were paralyzed, but it was so pleasant and permeated with peace. Then she felt the lymph nodes in her body become hot one at a time. It felt like they were being carefully touched one after the other. It lasted for about an hour, and then she was able to stand up again. Her next exam in the oncology unit showed a strange result. The doctor thought that there must be some mistake but could not be sure because her previous results could not be found in the archives. They had disappeared. He was indignant, because in all his years there, test results had never gone missing. They could not ascertain whether the previous results had been faulty or her physical condition had changed in the meantime. It remained a mystery, but the doctors declared her cancer-free.

My wife remained stable the whole time, much more so than I, but once the immediate threat was over, both of us, especially Claudia, needed a few months of healing for our souls. It was not a pleasant time and it left its mark. We certainly had lost our previous youthful, carefree attitude toward life. All this makes you acutely aware of what life is worth, but also how terrifyingly fragile it is, how insecure our very existence really is.

It was only after these terrible weeks that financial relief came in the form of the sale of my first violin (Opus 24). In retrospect it was very naïve to start my own workshop with so few financial reserves, but there were no other options in sight. We lived hand-to-mouth for the first three years—never knowing if we would be able to pay our monthly bills and provide for ourselves. These troubles cut to the quick, especially since I do not have the psyche of a natural-born entrepreneur. Sometimes I would think that my "service to God" would be to leave the realm of cares and search for the realm of faith. The inner work of trust did not immediately fall into my lap, but I see it as a kind of service to society to create my own business and (in the long run) be able to provide work for other families.

The Calling

These terrible weeks were preceded by something that I refer to as the story of my calling. When I started my own workshop, I had neither capital nor a customer base. I had completed the master's exam for violinmaking with excellent results two years after finishing a master's in physics, but the feeling of self-confidence had not yet kicked in. Owning a workshop is a big job. A few months before I opened my business, we visited my brother, Michael, in Wales.

On Sunday morning, June 4, 1995, we went to the church that Michael attended regularly, Saint Michael's Church—a dignified, monumental structure. The friendliness and openness of the people there touched me the moment I entered. They greeted us warmly even though they did not know us. It was a fairly normal service at the end of which the events of the coming week were announced. One of these was an evening service that same day. Lord knows I'm not used to going to church more than once on a Sunday; I'm usually proud to have made it at all. But on that day, to my wife's great surprise, I had the irrepressible feeling that I should go *again* that evening. So I did.

The service was not like the one in the morning. The church was full again, but it seemed to be a circle of members who knew and trusted each other and were meeting for prayer. I felt quite comfortable, even at home. It was a time of deep, concentrated, musical praise. Since I knew several songs from back home, and the others were not difficult, I joined in.

What I experienced while we were singing shook me to the core. I saw Jesus in my mind's eye slowly and silently coming toward me, brilliant and clear. Then I saw him kneeling in front of me. I could not bear this; I said: You can't kneel down before me! But nothing changed. And so I knelt, too. At that moment I didn't care what the person next to me thought. I knelt, without words. Then Jesus took some dirt—I did not see the church floor, but bare earth—and he took my hands and laid the moist earth in my hands. Then I knew that I was being called to form something, and that it had to do with the violinmaking workshop I was about to start. I asked: What should I make? He took the dirt out of my hands, laid my hands in his, and with his thumbs, pressed the wound marks in his hands into my palms. I thought that I felt the pressure and opened my eyes, but there was nothing to see. But I understood what it meant.

I did not get an answer as to *what* I should form. My calling is about the *how*. It must be *his way*, and it must happen in *his sacrifice*, because that is what his scars stand for. If our actions lack sacrifice, they will not find their way to God. It was also clear to me that I should not try to do everything, but only form that which he put in my hands.

I was shaken. I could never forget that moment; I have hearkened back to it continually, especially during difficult times.

After the singing, they offered the opportunity to receive a blessing on either side of the church, in the side chapels. I was probably the only stranger there. I approached one of the volunteer leaders, introduced myself as Martin from Munich, and asked him to pray for me. He said his name was Paul, and then he laid his hands on me. I could scarcely believe what he prayed for. My closest friends could not have prayed anything more fitting for me. Without knowing me, without having spoken with me, he prayed, blessed, and confirmed my gifts and tasks that no one other than myself could have known. At the end of this time of blessing, I felt a deep peace in my soul as I had never felt before. I wanted to pray silently, but it was as if Jesus was saying: "Be still! Now it is not only you who is doing things for me, but I for you." So I remained quiet. Apparently these occurrences and impressions are not uncommon in this congregation. For me, it was new. It was as if I had seen a seal being placed on my calling.

∼

This vision of my calling would become a tangible reality ten years later when I unexpectedly had a visit from a mother and her sixteen-year-old son from West Virginia. Siegfried, an old friend, called me. These two had just come to Munich, and because the son, Charles, was a fantastic violinist, they would like to visit my workshop.

There was something special about how they had met. According to Siegfried, on the previous Sunday he had the feeling that he should go to church not at 6:00 p.m., as usual, but half an hour earlier. He did not know why, but he went. As he approached the main entrance of St. Matthew's Church in Munich from one side, an older gentleman whom he did not know was approaching from the other side. They met right in front of the entrance, shook hands, and greeted each other as if they knew each other. It was clear to both of them! Somehow, at this exact time and place, they had an appointment with each other. The gentleman had come to spend a few days in Germany with his extended family: two of his children, their spouses, and six grandchildren. Of Jewish heritage, he was lucky to have escaped death during the Third Reich. Now, near the end of his life, he wanted to show his family the land of his youth and had therefore invited them along on this trip. Siegfried offered to be their tour guide for the next few days to show them the city.

The gentleman's daughter and her violinist son, having heard about my work, were eager to come and meet me. Siegfried drove them over. Our meeting was most intense because it was clear that she had a strong love for Jesus. It was obvious in much of what she said. She lived from a listening faith. When I inquired about her father, whom Siegfried had told me about on the phone, Esther shared his story of surviving the Holocaust. At the end, she threw her arms out and said: "He forgave everyone!"

I showed them the shop, our work, and the latest innovations. Esther's enthusiasm was a great encouragement since I was having a hard time, full of setbacks and many unanswered questions. Through her appreciation for what I do, a spark was ignited, and I finally felt a new, thriving joy for the visions of sound that I had been working on for the past few months. Her son, Charles Morey, was a total surprise. He is not only a phenomenal violinist but an impressive composer. He played his violin—a beautiful Mittenwald Joseph Klotz from 1807—and the piece he played was a composition for three voices (!) that he had just written. Among all the gifted musicians that I have had the pleasure of hearing in my shop, I have rarely heard one play such pure chords with left-hand pizzicato sounding at the same time.

His mother explained that he had started playing violin as a two-year-old, still in diapers! She had seen during her prayer time that she should give him a little violin (even though no one in their family had experience with that or any string instrument). She could not have guessed how it would develop. Often, when she would take it from him, he would burst into tears and go to the cupboard where it was kept and cry for it. He was accepted in the Charleston Youth Strings at the age of six, and at fourteen he was the concertmaster of the West Virginia Youth Symphony Orchestra. At that time he was practicing five hours a day as well as composing.

I asked him how he had found this wonderful violin. That in itself was a story of listening faith. Two years previously, it became evident that he needed to exchange his student violin for a professional quality instrument. However, his family did not have enough

money for a violin that would come anywhere near his level of playing. What Esther said after that was a modest sentence, but to me it
sounded like an enormous booming of the timpani against the power
of hopelessness: *"He put it on his prayer list!"*

About a week later, Esther had on a whim gone out to eat at
a local pancake house with her children and husband, something
they almost never did. There they struck up a conversation with two
ladies at the neighboring table. In the ensuing conversation they began speaking about her children, and the strangers found out that
Charles played the violin. The younger of the two strangers said
that her grandfather had played as well. Then she suddenly asked if
Charles needed a new violin. Esther was taken aback and revealed
that they were, in fact, in the market. Upon hearing that, the woman
replied that she had five violins—they were in the trunk of her car
in front of the restaurant! The violins were the reason for their trip.
Her grandfather had been a violinist in New York. He had owned five
violins, but now they had to liquidate his belongings. The violins
were too valuable to ship, so the women had driven to New York
themselves and were now on their way home to Florida with the
violins. They had traveled many hours and had arrived in this little
town in West Virginia by chance that morning. When they saw the
Shoney's restaurant while driving by, they spontaneously decided to
take a break for breakfast.

To make a long story short, Charles played the violin for the
ladies at a nearby church. They were quite moved and placed one of
their best violins in his hands. It was the 1807 Joseph Klotz, which
is appraised at $20,000. They said: "This is yours now!" And with
that, they said their goodbyes. The younger woman said that she was
sure that her grandfather would have been very happy. Charles was
in shock as they drove away. That is how he came upon the violin
that I heard him playing two years later in my workshop. *"He put it
on his prayer list!"*

The meeting with Esther and Charles in my workshop was
so intense that we could not simply part ways. I asked if we could
pray together. Esther was delighted, and after Siegfried and I had
prayed, she began praying a powerful, faith-filled prayer, blessing me, my work, and my family in the name of Jesus. But she

did not seem completely satisfied at the end; she was unsure. She reflected, and then asked her son if he wanted to pray over my hands. Then Charles, who had been silent up to that point, prayed as I had never heard a sixteen-year-old pray before. At the end, he took my hands to bless them, laid them in his own, and lightly pressed both thumbs into my palms. It was exactly the same thing that I had experienced in Wales ten years before in the vision at St. Michael's Church. I had never spoken with anyone about it; it was as if God sent these two people to my workshop to confirm the vision of my calling.

Insist on Living

It would be cynical to use *crisis* as a catchword for maturation, as if it were a mechanical, self-evident process. And yet we can often take the sting out of a crisis if we use it to understand our calling in a new and different way. Sometimes it is like the painful reworking of a violin, when you realize that you have to be brave and open it up again. There is a painful opening up in times of crises, as well. Our eyes are opened to see that we are vulnerable. We want to understand God and the world in order to overcome fear, but we can't. That is what crises communicate to us. Faith does not show us the path of understanding, but the path of trust. That is faith's way of confronting life. Faith needs this holy defiance in the face of life's troubles.

Of course, we would love to live without crises, and we consider it a joy and a blessing when we are spared from troubled times. But in retrospect—looking back from the end of a person's life—a crisis-free life has a much harder time reaching the goal of its calling than a life that was directed and pulled through stretches of weakness and need.

I spent many unforgettable evenings with a friend in the months following the unexpected death of his wife. We shared not only tears, questions, shock, and reoccurring bouts of resignation, but also his experience of profound closeness to God's spirit and a deep, unique kind of comfort. God was near to him in a way that passes understanding, and yet his pain was not simply wiped away. God did not protect him and his children from sorrow, but he protected them in the midst of sorrow and lifted them up. This is a presence that takes your breath away. It is a comfort that penetrates down to the deepest part of you, even if the pain is still there and the questions cannot be answered. Faith also involves our responsibility to stay alive and insist on living.

My wife and I have a good friend whose husband, who was near and dear to us, died totally unexpectedly. Her husband had said goodbye one morning and was dead that afternoon. He left behind a wife and four children. We drove over as soon as we heard the news. Through all the tears, I will never forget the impression she made: her steadfastness, her faith, her prayers. She had the strength to comfort her children and bid her husband farewell. In prayer, she let the man that she loved go. She returned him to the hands of God. What I know to this day is that, above all, the faith that shone through her weakness and dread was not of this world. Her tears are not taken away by it—or perhaps they will be! Her tears will be taken away at the end of time. Then the tears of faith will be transformed into the tones of a holy symphony; they will be turned into precious stones decorating the holy city with their beauty. Our tears of faith are noticed by God, and in the end they will be transformed.

You cannot deny it when you have a faith experience. You can cynically explain it away as "empty promises," but only the one who possesses a better source of comfort has the right to do that! Does atheism have better answers, a stronger consolation? Does it promise experiences that will strengthen us in our weaknesses? What and where is its grace? The apostle Paul in the middle of deep personal crisis received this comfort: "My grace is sufficient for you, for my power is made perfect in weakness." Paul responded, "So, I will boast all the more gladly of my weaknesses, so that the power of Christ may dwell in me" (2 Corinthians 12:9-10). Where, then, is power available in atheism? It is not superior on any level! It does not have more to offer, but less. Therefore, you must deny it the right to view faith as "empty," for in itself it offers no comfort. It claims that godlessness is the more intelligent way of coming to terms with meaninglessness. As Hans Küng asks: "Does atheism explain the world better? The world's grandeur and its misery? Does unbelief explain the world as it is now? And may unbelief take its comfort from unmerited, incomprehensible, meaningless suffering? Doesn't all unbelieving reason have its limit at such suffering?"[2]

~

The deepest witness to our faith happens when we burden God with our trust. "I will not stop being a burden to you, because your carrying me is the essence of your love!" I will not let go of this dignity, and one day I will stand before him in nothing but this unconditional trust. Within its embrace steadfast faith knows that the darkness will someday soften like the morning dew in the warmth of the day's dawning, and we will be called into a safe place that will be as high as the heavens are above the earth, higher than our present seeking, doubting, and reasoning. When that trust illuminates our hearts, the reward is already here; the darkness is no longer dark. That is the reasoning of faith. There is no worldly logic that can transcend all the need and suffering in the world. Faith's logic does not mean that we *understand* suffering, but that we *survive* it in trust.

> Where can I go from your spirit?
>   Or where can I flee from your presence?
> If I ascend to heaven, you are there;
>   if I make my bed in Sheol, you are there.
> If I take the wings of the morning
>   and settle at the farthest limits of the sea,
> even there your hand shall lead me,
>   and your right hand shall hold me fast.
> If I say, "Surely the darkness shall cover me,
>   and the light around me become night,"
> even the darkness is not dark to you;
>   the night is as bright as the day,
>   for darkness is as light to you. (Psalm 139:7-12)

There are times when we decide whether we want to turn to death or hope for life. Often we have no strength left to decide, just emptiness and confusion. Not even the strength to doubt remains, and we stand apathetically in front of emptiness. But even then, I will not turn myself over to destruction. When it is dark and I am falling, I will let myself fall into the hands of God who will keep me from falling. When I know that I have reached my limits and the end is near, then I will know only this: Christ is the beginning and the end. If he established an end, then there will also be a beginning in him, now and in eternity. He is the bright morning star. I want to see the light of a new heaven and a new earth and be picked up in God's love and have peace in it. I will see that it was worth not giving myself up.

And even if I must give up myself, my lifestyle, and all that I loved from my heart, and darkness and fear flood into whatever remains of my life, even then I will still trust God. How small and pale are success and glamour, yes, even happiness and contentment, next to this grandeur: the person who, to the end, faces the fight with faith and surrenders himself to God! I bow down in deep respect before you who are tested to the limits of your existence!

$\sim$

The one unforgettable thing I remember from crises is how people have grown above and beyond themselves when faced with suffering—the people who were standing alongside of us! In these situations we truly experienced "another world," and I had the impression that I was witnessing different people—literally *better* people. This happened at the luthier school, during my wife's illness, and when my business was starting up. Narrow-mindedness retreated; apathy and dullness were overcome for a time. Yes, in the end, only love and suffering can overcome us on behalf of others. We experienced situations that hurt us and opened us up. But this openness also opens the hearts of those who care for us.

As confusing as it may sound, I have the impression that, because misery and evil are possible in our world, it would be *even worse* if we were not capable of suffering! This does not answer for sorrow and it does not and should not justify evil. But there is living proof that the suffering of creation can set something free in us: neighborly love. Only in it do we grow beyond the bigotry and triviality of our "me, me, me." We are entrusted to each other. The only thing that suffering has to say is: Be there for each other! This trust and mutual care make our world bearable. It is a holy power that sustains our life. Therefore, the unshakable idea remains in me: a world capable of evil but not capable of suffering would be unbearable.

09

The Sculpture (I)

The Meaning of Doubt

You have . . . put my tears in your bottle.
Are they not in your book?

—PSALM 56:8 (ESV)

*I*NTENSE CONTACT WITH the human soul takes place during a sound adjustment. Some musicians come into my shop with great expectations, others with a great need. Adjusting an instrument's sound is far too complicated for me to simply say: "I can do it!" When a musician trusts me with his instrument's needs, my only choice is to regard myself as a tool to be used, to believe that my senses will be guided and that my hand will accomplish the right things. There is no easy path to follow, because with sound you are touching a person's voice. The voice is the conduit to the soul. Maybe that is why the powerlessness and exhaustion that come over me after days of this sort of work are necessary. Otherwise I risk hurting others through the arrogance of assuming that something so essential can be *contrived*. You can't force it; you must receive it. Faith is like this, too. Our faith is like a holy and yet questionable instrument.

In crafting a violin, I am working on visible forms. I test them as they take shape. The developing instrument looks like a wood sculpture. Only when it sounds is its true form established: a sound sculpture! In its vibrating resonances the violin reveals its unmistakable essence. I see faith as an inner sculpture. Our inner life is formed and established not only by our gifts and the beauty of life but also by periods of doubt and pain. Just as my tools create a visual form, a certain kind of doubt can sometimes be a necessary tool in faith's development. Our testing and shaping do not take place only through beauty.

The Distant God

There are phases of our lives that are like that moment of working on a violin's arching. The plane goes against the grain so that it can sense its course. The wood rips in some places during this phase; it seems like the wood plane is running about blindly over the wood. If it could speak, the wood would say: "Is the creator's wisdom completely hidden from me? What is happening to me?"

It is truly painful when God seems far away, as if he has completely withdrawn from us. The Bible knows this cry as well: "Lord, where is your steadfast love of old?" (Psalm 89:49). And yet, I will not allow my faith to overcome the pain of God's distance by hardening into a law—incontestable to be sure, but no longer living. Legalistic faith lacks the courage to endure God's remoteness. It is unable to cope with an empty heart, unable to fast inwardly. Such a faith lacks the right to expect anything of me. It is not sovereign. Legalistic faith must obstinately guard against doubt and hold to assurances that fall apart in the face of misgivings. The philosopher Miguel de Unamuno writes: "Those who think they believe in God, but do so with no passion in their hearts, without a tortured soul, with no uncertainty, without doubt, with no trace of desperation even in the midst of comfort—those people believe only in thoughts about God, not in God himself."[1]

~

What is it like when I, as a violinmaker, work against the wood, against the grain? Sometimes this is the only way to accomplish something substantial. Right here, where the fibers rip a bit and show themselves; right here, where the plane vibrates more and the fibers give off a harsh sound; this is where I do not back away from the wood but feel its grain all the more. Sometimes it seems as if all sorts of painful and bewildering things are working against our souls. And yet, in the end, it is the same as working with an instrument.

The wood experiences a crisis when the wood plane is harshly drawn across its grain. But Wisdom is still Wisdom even in the middle of crises. She endures the pain and will ultimately serve the promise and completion of the work. Therefore, I would much rather welcome these rough times, the disappointments, degradation, and powerlessness, than live a habitual life devoid of passion. Perhaps it is precisely these times of doubt that prove that the vitality of our faith comes not only from trust but also from reverence. Mature faith does not just trust but also bows spiritually before the mystery of God. Only when our faith knows the fear of God as well as trust in him will we be ready to face crisis upon crisis. Knowing that my life may be different from what I would like, knowing as well that God may be different from what my faith wants him to be, this is my soul's acknowledgment of God. This is reverence. Fear of God is not separate from my love but a serious part of its reality.

This, too, is like the work in developing the violin. God does not pass over our lives but feels the course of their fiber. Just as physical pain is a hint that something is not right in our bodies, "faith-pains" show us that something is out of balance. Our doubt can be a message from God. We should not fear it. It is not doubt but complacency that must be avoided. Doubt does not make faith easier, but it can make it deeper and more authentic.

Doubt can be a form of faith, the faith that lives through questioning and that suffers because not all answers support it. And yet it still knows that life-giving truth is more than quick, stereotypical answers offered up to us by ignorance. The one who doubts has *no other* answers, no better answers. He has simply chosen not to send his faith out on the thin ice of human ignorance.

Life's queries and our questions demonstrate the profound strength of doubt. People who consider themselves to be free of doubt always put the superiority of answers above the right to question. Answers sound the war cry—usually against other answers. Questions allow us to pause and ponder what we are called to do and to listen to the message being spoken to us. Real questions cannot be answered intellectually. Their answers come through our life experiences.

The Learning Faith

Doubts can be messengers from God. We will not overcome them by constantly checking the internal temperature of our faith's fervor. We should instead check to see if we are learning to practice what we understand. God does not allow our thoughts or feelings to strengthen our faith, only our obedience. Spirit-filled doubt is God's messenger asking us how matters stand in our lives. Its question will simply be, are we *acting on our understanding?*

A person who "practices authenticity" is someone who wrestles with life's "should." When we say, "I should," a promise of revelation opens up. Our authenticity is revealed. The fact that God is close to the deceptive person does not mean that the deceptive person is close to God.

~

In the Gospel of John, Jesus said: "They who have my commandments and keep them are those who love me; and those who love me will be loved by my Father, and I will love them and reveal myself to them" (14:21). The disciples asked: "Why to us and not to the world?" If I understand Jesus's answer to this question correctly, he said in effect: Truth reveals itself only to the one who loves. The world tries to be clever and satisfy its own desires, but it does not try to be obedient. Without obedience, knowledge is nothing more than vanity. The love of truth is lacking; knowing does not translate into doing. Start acting on what you understand, and you will understand more. But if you stop doing what you know you should do, then you will lose that which you used to understand (Matthew 13:12).

A violinist who does not practice will lose her intonation. A gardener who does not water his plants will see them wilt. If we want the sound of knowledge and the fruit of assurance, if we want the wings of spiritual experiences, then we should start to practice what we have been commanded. Through a learning faith we understand life's necessary disturbances and, in them, gain trust; it is like "an eagle [that] stirs up its nest and hovers over its young; [that] spreads its wings, takes them up, and bears them aloft" (Deuteronomy 32:11).

We have knowledge, but that is not enough. We are *stirred up* in order to unfold our wings for flight, to understand and bravely act upon our calling. We are not thrown out of the nest to fall but to learn to fly. God will take hold of us like an eagle pushing its young out of the nest and yet still bear us up on his wings. True power can unfold in the middle of faith crises when we follow the advice of a great Jewish scholar: "Do God's bidding and then you will know who he is."[2]

The essence of faith is *to learn*. People who believe in Jesus call themselves Christians today, even though the term appears only three times in the New Testament. The term *disciple* appears more than 180 times. A subtle difference is evident here: a Christian defines himself by what he believes; he makes that confession the center of his religious identity. A disciple (or an apprentice) defines himself by who his master is and what he learns through him. The faith journey of the disciples did not begin with Jesus inquiring about their confession, but by Jesus calling them to go with him and learn from him. It was not until the third year, after they had learned and witnessed much, that he posed the question: "Who do you say that I am?" (Luke 9:20).

We often ask this question at the beginning. And yet it can only be answered as a result of what has been learned in discipleship, what I have touched, heard, and seen (1 John 1:1). Jesus told his disciples: "Take my yoke upon you, and learn from me" (Matthew 11:29). An apprentice follows his master and learns from him.

As an apprentice violinmaker, I knew who I was because I went into the schoolmaster's workshop and worked on developing violins. My master instructed me, and I tried to hold the tools correctly and practice correct technique on the emerging violins. It was the practice that was important. No one will ever learn to build an instrument by simply watching and amassing knowledge. You have to grasp the tool yourself and master what you are being shown. No eagle will ever learn to fly by watching and taking note of things; he must spread his wings himself. It starts with being shaken up! Just so, mastering one's calling is not a spiritual ingredient added to life; it is life itself. It is learning and trusting through the things that disturb and challenge us. So when we do not understand what is happening to us we should spread our wings of trust to experience the unexpected and launch into our calling.

Does not our longing for certainty arise in part from the sin of impatience? A confession brimming with assurance is like the solution to a difficult math problem. The solution may be right, but if you cannot show the work that led to the answer, what have you achieved? That is cheating!

Therefore, I would rather spend a few minutes every day searching for a quiet spirit before God than read books about it; I would rather forgive someone who hurt me than destroy years of my life holding a grudge. I would rather tidy up my home than purchase more stuff. Our self-indulgence robs our life of clarity and peace. It is the thousands of daily "shoulds" that steal our strength and fuel our doubts.

We suffer most from the untruthfulness, unrighteousness, and self-indulgence that we allow in our lives. Doubts are often the soul's cry that can simply no longer cope with an over-abundance of "shoulds." The return to truthfulness, righteousness, and clarity is a spring cleaning of the soul. We need radical measures to reduce the number of "shoulds." Above all, we need daily rituals to help us *protect* our measure of truth and righteousness. Quiet time in which we collect our thoughts is one such ritual. To not take quiet time, to know nothing of forgiveness, nothing of moderation, is like carrying things into our homes everyday but never taking out the trash. Stuff piles up, space becomes tight; we cannot see around it anymore and it starts to stink of noise, dissention, and excess. We usually know quite well what we should do. Why don't we do it? As Hillel the Elder asked: "If not now, when?"

Truthfulness

Sometimes we complain about not having experiences with God, all the while bypassing the things in which he wants to reveal himself. Therefore, repentance can mean returning to the place where God is waiting for us: "I have spoken with you here and I have been waiting for quite some time for you to act and understand. You have known for a long time. You heard my voice. Why are you complaining, saying that I am silent and waiting?"

If we have been untrue to ourselves, it is possible that God will meet us at the place where he last spoke to us. There are places with invisible doors to heaven. "Let all action or inaction take place amidst deep understanding!" Are not expectations of God sometimes this kind of waiting in which he speaks and then is silent? It is a reminder of the Holy One's humility. There are markers along our path—sometimes inconspicuous, other times obvious. But the trail of truthfulness is clear. That is why doubt can be a blessing if it shows the person who got carried away that he is on the wrong path.

We have time. But this time is more about practicing and less about knowing. We can choose to follow Jesus, but we will know who he is only if we do what he says. We must spend time with him as his *pupils*; otherwise we will not experience him. We will surely belong to God only if we allow ourselves to be shaped into his nature. We will see that there is a perfect God only when we seek the perfect nature of love. Only when we love will we recognize the One who loves. There is no other path that brings us closer to God. He remains true to us, and we should remain true to him. That is why Jesus speaks to his disciples so often about "abiding": "Abide in my love. Remain in my word." Only the *learning* faith can overcome doubt; and only those who *practice* what they have been commanded will be in the position to follow Jesus.

The fourteenth Dalai Lama, Tenzin Gyatso, said: "We do not live to believe, but to learn."[3] On the surface, this statement seems like a frontal attack on a central biblical tenet. The essence of biblical life is believing. It bothers me: why is the Dalai Lama questioning what is essential to my existence? Neither Jesus nor any of the prophets would ever question the fact that we should "live by faith." The prophet Habakkuk said: "Look at the proud! Their spirit is not right in them, but the righteous live by their faith" (2:4). This idea appears in numerous New Testament passages as well.[4] The faith that Jesus had in mind and in which he himself lived emphasized alertness above all. The concept of quiet time is quite similar. It is an essential part of what the prophet Isaiah understood as faith: an alert stillness that observes the work of God's hands. Ultimately, a faithless life is incapable of loving the vital insights revealed by faith. The deeper

I believe in God's truth, the more I should heed the Dalai Lama's advice.

A faith that does not learn is like an answer with no question. Jesus did not say: "Listen to the following definition of God. It should be your faith. Blessed are those who believe that their doctrines are holy. They will give you rest." Instead he said: "Come to me, and learn from me, and you will find rest for your souls" (see Matthew 11:28-29). He quoted the prophet Isaiah, who said that all "shall be taught by the Lord" (Isaiah 54:13; John 6:45). Concerning himself, Jesus said: "I do nothing on my own, but I speak these things as the Father instructed me" (John 8:28). Jesus "learned," too,[5] as is evident from the fact that he could be "amazed."[6]

If a teacher does not teach his students to be amazed, then he is not a good teacher. Our faith should be open to teaching and amazement, not closed down to a list of confessions. Certain questions that life asks us are painful—we call these questions "doubt"—but we should see this pain as the chance to learn. If we have grown too complacent to be amazed by God and this world, then our faith has probably hardened into a "confession." Christ says: "Don't think that you already know me. I've shown you some things and you have seen some things. But do not replace me by your faith! Because how can I go forward with you if you do that?"

What faith implies will not always be the same. There are times when faith means *yielding to what has happened*; other times it is *doing what has been commanded*; then there are times when it means to "lie in wait" for the impetus of grace like an instrument that, having been tuned and thus freed from the dissonance of ambivalence, can *speak life and action* into a situation with an assurance that can only come as a gift from heaven. Other times, faith is to believe a promise and therefore *strike out on a new path* that we see opening up through the eyes of understanding. And so, with Jesus in mind, I admit that the Dalai Lama is right when he says: "We do not live to believe, but to learn." This saying is not applicable to religious controversies, but to crises. When our faith is in crisis, belief must either listen and learn or cease to exist.

No one *has* faith. Faith is not something that you can save or pile up; it cannot be stored in a barn or brought out as if it were a possession. You cannot say: I've stored up faith for all these years, now I have peace. No, we can gain faith only in the moment *when we need it*. In good times it seems like our lives sail along effortlessly. But when doubt lies heavy as lead on us and troubles, pain, fears, and frustrations oppress us, then it is *necessary and therefore possible* to learn to trust. When we ask: Where is my faith?, the answer is: it was never there. It was never property nor a possession. We receive it only when God teaches us to trust him. On the glorious mountaintop we are full of wonder and thanksgiving. That is also faith. But it is in the dark valley that we seek the hand that leads us and the comfort that guides us. Here our hearts learn to trust; as the psalm says: "Those who seek him shall praise the Lord. May your hearts live forever!" (Psalm 22:26).

In the end, to remain a learner requires humility. I would rather be a student of trust than a proud master who no longer lives by faith. For if the master—in spite of all his mastery—does not *begin daily* to live by faith, then he is not even a beginner.

When doubt is a messenger from God, it opposes the proud heart. It is set against the one who thinks he is a master. Doubt can bless us in God's name only by giving us the heart of a beginner so that we will return as learners to the starting point where faith began. Therefore doubt shakes the hardness that was once strength; it shakes the possessions that used to be an assurance; it shakes the inflexibility that was at one time clarity; it shakes the power that used to be charisma; it shakes the pride that was once a blessing; it shakes the fanaticism that used to be passion; it shakes the martyr complex that used to be dedication; it shakes the doctrines that were thought to be true; it shakes up experiences that were once grace; it shakes the words that used to be prayers. In all of this, one thing is consistent: what used to be love is stirred up, shaken, and only that which is unshakable will remain.

But the tears that we cry will be cherished, because if doubt is God's messenger, then it knows what it means to be shaken. This messenger does not have the right to give us an answer or assurance, but it has power to clear out new space for what is holy. Our tears are cherished because God has given them the holy privilege of making our faith young again.

Brother Doubt

One quiet morning I had the following conversation with doubt:

> Brother Doubt, I greet you. You wake me up early out of sleep. Lord knows we have spent good and also stressful times together. And yet I thank you, because without you I would be satisfied all too soon. You rightly demand that I ask and seek. You demand that I be thorough. Without you I would not have become what I am and do today.
>
> But do not be upset, Brother Doubt, if I have little time for you right now. Because I have, as you know, other brothers and sisters, and I must listen to them as well; there is much to do. What they demand ought not be inhibited; I will do their bidding. Later I will listen to your arguments again and, if need be, go another round with you at the crossroads. But you should know one thing: in my calling I will give hope greater rights than you. Then you will ask and I will give an answer; our lives speak through our actions.

Our doubts are answered through our calling. Doubts make us alert in the places where our learning-impaired faith was all too sleepy. Doubt can be a messenger guiding us in our calling. But doubt will take its leave when its time has come. It will bow as it departs but without giving us an answer, because it sees that we no longer need it. We got up long ago to act in understanding and truth.

St. Vincent de Paul (1581–1660) is a glowing example of a man who overcame doubt in just this way and found his calling in the process. Born the son of a farmer, he decided to become a priest. After years in that work, he went through a crisis of faith. This allowed him to discover what his real task was: to help the poor and needy and bring them the gospel. He devoted himself primarily to uneducated country folk, galley slaves, and the thousands of castaways in Paris at the time. But he soon realized that spontaneous help in emergencies did little long-term good. So he began to organize remedial measures in a more professional manner. He founded countless brotherhoods, clubs, seminars for priests, asylums for the mentally ill, children's homes, and hospitals. He founded the Daughters of Charity, who still follow him as a role model today. St. Vincent and his helpers saved tens of thousands of abandoned children from certain death, hundreds of thousands suffering from poverty and hunger. Guided by love, Vincent took on the need because he was convinced: "The poor are your masters. You are the servant."[7]

St. Vincent de Paul did not overcome his doubt with clever thinking but through a heart on fire. What is "God's spark" in you if you do not allow it to set your heart on fire? Which inner fire will light up your calling if you limit the question concerning God to a tiny flicker your whole life? What a gruesome light it will cast upon your dead calling!

How much violence have we inflicted on our calling? We have suffered from our doubts instead of understanding their message. We have allowed our hearts to grow cold in lethargy, cowardice, and pride, instead of stirring up the flame with the fire of God so that we can love God. We cannot force ourselves to come to faith, but we can actively hinder belief.

St. Vincent de Paul says that we are called to burn with a godly fire:

> Our vocation is to go and enflame the heart of men, to do what the Son of God did, he who brought fire into the world to set it alight with his love. What else can we wish for, than for it to burn and consume all things? Thus it is true that I have been sent not only to love God, but also to make men love him. It is not enough to love God if my neighbor does not love him. I must love my neighbor as the image of God and the object of his love, and do everything so that in their turn men love their Creator who knows and considers them as his brothers, whom he has saved. . . . Now, if it is true that we are called to bear God's love near and far, if we must set nations alight, if our vocation is to go and spread this divine fire in the whole world, if it is so, my brothers, if it is really so, how must I myself burn of this divine fire![8]

It was necessary for Vincent de Paul to have had doubts about his faith. Uncertainty is necessary to free us from our narrow-mindedness. Doubt is sending us a message: "Do not confess only what you understand. Do not believe only in what seems pleasing to you. Do not acknowledge only that which corresponds with your favorite thoughts. Do not trust only in what you feel. Be alert to what is happening and look for opportunities to be quiet before God!"

Only when we stop constantly blabbering and checking the pulse of our mental state will the arguments inside of us find an end, and we will begin to truly listen. My faith is not sustained by answers; otherwise I would have lost it long ago. What sustains me is the heart's search. I am poor before God. I must endure this poverty because I know that not what I possess but only what I receive is sustainable. I cannot hold tightly to my faith as if it was an object in my hand.

Doubt is the excruciating pain of faith. As Jean Paul said: "The whole spiritual universe is dashed asunder by the hand of atheism into numberless quicksilver-points of 'me,' which glitter, run, waver, fly together or asunder, without unity of continuance."[9] We, along with Jean Paul, fear that doubt could hurl us into the loneliness of the one who denies God, "whose orphaned heart has lost its greatest Father." Yet further speculation will not help us. The ultimate question of faith cannot be explained through contemplation. The most concrete things dissolve away in contemplation as if it were acid, and the most obvious truths are tattered and torn apart.

Not what we believe, but only what we love will ultimately have the strength to convince us of what matters. In real crises we may have to experience that the cord of truth in which we have come to trust might chafe—and snap in the end! The only rope that will hold us is not the truth that we believe but the truth that we love. After the crucifixion, Jesus did not ask Peter "Do you believe in me?" but "Do you love me?" (John 21:15).

∼

When our nephew was having his first communion, my sister-in-law surprised her relatives by asking us to write about an experience we had had with God—a challenging request! She wanted to create an album for her son out of these letters along with pictures of his first mass. This album would stay with him throughout his life. I procrastinated for quite some time before I finally sat down to write. It was not the mountaintop experiences with God that came to mind but a period of dark months followed by a turning point. I knew that this letter was not for this moment in my nephew's life. The day of celebration was kid-friendly, and rightly so, but the allure of the gift of reflections was for future days.

This simple sentence came to me one night, marking the turning point during a crisis: "Martin, take care to love me! I will take care of your faith!" When I heard it, I turned around, but it was immediately clear that this was not an externally audible word but a sentence spoken in the heart. I had heard the voice of Jesus.[10]

The lesson was plain and simple: I have not been given the ability to believe in God all on my own. My ability consists only in loving him. As severely as doubts may oppress faith and as difficult as it may be to pray "Jesus, I *believe* in you," I am much more able to pray: "Jesus, I have seen how you lived and what you did. I have seen your mercy and truth; your devotion and courage, your love and vulnerability are ever before me. I will *love* you for this. And so, I want to hear what you are showing me and do what you say!"

For some, faith means accepting doubts as a part of belief. You can have doubts about God and still love him. Then belief is a living "*and yet*," and faith is a living choice. Love is like the warmth-giving sun, dispelling the early dew of doubt. In these seasons, it is as Carl Friedrich von Weizsächer once said: "Faith means living like what you believe is true." We should be comforted in painful times in knowing that we do not have to overcome our doubts to believe in God. For believing is not the same as doing. We can control our actions. Faith cannot be forced, and yet it can continue through doubt. God will be with us in the valley of the shadow of doubt. He will walk the path with us; we will go through the unanswerable and yet be comforted. We will not solve the questions, but that is not what it is about! We will end not with a solution but with praise. We must not take anything for granted: what seems to be an enemy on this path may not be an enemy, and what seems to be friendly may not be a friend.

The God-Singer

I love the story of Jacob in the book of Genesis because it illustrates the path to praise. Jacob was a lifelong fighter. He insistently scrambled for victory or sneakily got what he wanted, starting with the right of the firstborn and his father's blessing. But he was really engaged in a much greater fight, and of a different sort. It was a struggle with God. This is the struggle that we have in times of dark doubt, in days and nights full of fear and despair. We become accustomed to constant struggle, but sometimes we sense that it is beyond our strength.

This is the story of Jacob's struggle according to Genesis 32: 23-30:

> He took [his family] and sent them across the stream, and likewise everything that he had. Jacob was left alone; and a man wrestled with him until daybreak. When the man saw that he did not prevail against Jacob, he struck him on the hip socket; and Jacob's hip was put out of joint as he wrestled with him. Then he said, "Let me go, for the day is breaking." But Jacob said, "I will not let you go, unless you bless me." So he said to him, "What is your name?" And he said, "Jacob." Then the man said, "You shall no longer be called Jacob, but Israel, for you have striven with God and with humans, and have prevailed." Then Jacob asked him, "Please tell me your name." But he said, "Why is it that you ask my name?" And there he blessed him. So Jacob called the place Peniel, saying, "For I have seen God face to face, and yet my life is preserved."

Jacob received a new name. Now he is Israel, a title of honor. He is a man who struggles with God rather than with men. Jacob is a father for me, as well, because he teaches me to live by faith until the very end. It is important to note that this episode takes place the night before he is to meet his brother Esau. After all the years of enmity, what kind of meeting will this be? Will it result in reconciliation or retaliation? Jacob is unsure. He approaches cautiously. But Esau runs to him, embraces him, and they weep.

There is a special interpretation in rabbinic Judaism of this night struggle that prepares the way for the brothers' reconciliation. This interpretation cuts to the heart of our reflections on the nature of doubt: the power to prevail is found in praise. This is the interpretation of the Midrash Tanhuma.[11] The fight between Jacob and the angel is interpreted as the duty *to sing*. The poetic text expands upon the biblical story and depicts it as a bargaining discussion.

> The angel said to Jacob: My time has come to sing a song . . .
>
> [But Jacob said:] I won't let you go unless you bless me (Genesis 32:27). Didn't the angels go to Abraham and bless him?
>
> [The angel] said to him: They were sent for that purpose. But I wasn't sent for that.
>
> Then he said: . . . I won't let you go unless you bless me.
>
> And he said to him: What will become of my song, for the time has already come?
>
> [Jacob] answered: Your comrades will sing.
>
> He said to him: Look! My time to praise has come!
>
> He answered: Then praise tomorrow if not today!
>
> Then he said to him: If I go to my comrades tomorrow, they will say: You did not praise at your time, you should not then praise at the time that it's not yours to praise.
>
> And he said: I will not let you go until you have blessed me.
>
> [The angel] said: And who will sing the song?
>
> Then he said: I will sing it for you, as it is said: "He wrestled with the angel" (Hosea 12:5). That is "singing."[12]

The angel asks Jacob to let him go so that he will not miss his appointed time of praise. Jacob remains stubborn and does not let the angel go before he is blessed. Wherein is Jacob's victory according to this interpretation? It is in him singing praises in the place of the angel! In the scriptural text the form of the word "he wrestled" (*wa-yaśar*) is read as "he sang" (*wa-yašar*).[13] A few verses later, Jacob is renamed Israel. By regrouping the consonants, the rabbinic Midrash makes Jacob into "the God-Singer." This is important: the fighter becomes a singer! The desperate struggle is transformed into a song of praise.

This ancient story and its rabbinical interpretation are so important because such a transformation must, in fact, take place. If it does *not* happen, the subsequent encounter with the brother will become a battle. Dealing with the doubts of our own soul with all the expectations that life sets before us is a struggle of faith. But faith should never become a battle against people; it must be a struggle with God, who will give us a new name, transforming our longing into blessing—despite all the hard knocks! Whoever does not leave limping after wrestling with God has apparently not really fought.

Jacob's victory is found in his singing praises in place of the angel. Without praise we would be people whose sad existence consists of fighting with people and doubting God. In the triviality of our thinking, in the hardness of our hearts, in the narrow-mindedness of our actions, our name is "Jacob." It is only through praise that we are given a new name and our world is immersed in a new state of being. Even though we may limp away from this fight, we have nonetheless done the right thing in insisting: "I will not let you go until you bless me." That is the highest form of dignity: that in spite of darkness, fear, and doubt, we say: "I will sing!"

Sometimes our praise of God leads us to interrupt our brooding to write songs, poems, spiritual diaries—or to be still. The further we distance ourselves from the *beauty and trouble* of real life, the less our thoughts are capable of recognizing God's truth, and the less we will have to say to ourselves and to others.

Where are You, God?
He says, and you?
Are you not spirit of my spirit
And the longing of my longing?
So reach out your hand of spirit—your faith!
For I am here.

Many things can show us the life-giving love of God and help us to understand that we are not merely made of thoughts. Early morning walks in the woods; hiking with friends; a bed of herbs in which every plant has its place; making music together; a man's willingness to go to dance classes with his wife[14]–there are many ways to cease to glorify thinking for a time and see "life's gifts."

We should consider not only strong faith but also doubts as a form of our love. It is the aching search for that which remains hidden, heartache because our beloved is so far away. We must first affirm this pain for it to become a form of faith. If we decide to accept the pain of doubt as a form of our love for God, then we have, in the end, chosen love, because true love cannot exist without suffering. It is as Søren Kierkegaard said: "Truth only has victory through sorrow." Even the Holy One affirms this path to suffer for the sake of the beloved. Fulbert Steffensky notes this as well: "Perhaps it is true that one can often only retain a great love in the form of a wound."[15]

My love for God is, of course, a limping love. But it was through pain that I first understood that his hiddenness is not absence. He is there. If we try to emulate the saints, and so we should, then we will accept the pain of distance and hiddenness. We will accept the painful searching for the beloved as love's insatiable and yet necessary anguish. It is faith's lovesickness. For the saint, doubt is not bad, it is a form of love for God; it is love's restlessness that, for the sake of the beloved, will never fall asleep in repetitious actions, the habits that numb the pain and extinguish love.

If we are to search for a mature faith, then we must understand the "chemistry of doubt": it is rarely granted to us to bid our doubt adieu through answers, but they bow to us when confronted with our praise and our courage.

A New Courage

Proximity and distance are neither abstract nor subjective dimensions. But they are realities we experience in this existence. We cannot overcome true doubt with thoughts or feelings, but by accepting our calling to serve each other. It is not our doubts, but *ourselves* that we must overcome!

A violinist whom I know well told me that he usually uses his train commutes between concerts to practice. Most of the time he sits in the family area because it is a little more spacious. If he is not alone, he asks the other passengers if it would disturb them if he were to play the violin. Most of the time they say no—quite the contrary—and listen attentively. (They are unaware of who this virtuoso is or that he is playing on a Stradivarius.) On one such trip, the train made an emergency stop. Luckily, he was not playing at the time but sitting in the main cabin of the express train with many other passengers. An announcement followed: "Due to personal injury, the trip will be delayed." People complained, fumbled through their bags for their cell phones, impatiently made calls, informed business partners that meetings would have to be postponed, etc. The violinist was shaken up. Someone had jumped in front of the train, and these passengers viewed it merely as an inconvenient interruption of their daily activities. After a few moments, Ingolf stood up, got out his violin, introduced himself, and addressed the passengers. He said that he was dismayed that a person whom he didn't even know, whose life had apparently been filled with so much sadness and despair, had lost his life in this way. He announced that he would like to play the first movement of the Beethoven Violin Concerto in his memory. Then he put his bow on the string and filled time and space with the violin's sound. He transformed the busy environment of the commuter train into a concert hall. I am sure that a space of holy admonition and thoughtfulness opened up. This is so necessary for our times!

My sister, Gisela, used to work in a cancer clinic during one of her rotations as an intern to become a doctor. One day she plucked up the courage to get out her cello. She sat in the corridor of the clinic and began to play the Cello Suites by Johann Sebastian Bach. The corridor had fabulous acoustics. One by one, the doors of the sick rooms cautiously opened up and the people slowly came out. Even the doctors and nurses, who were often under a lot of pressure from the stressful schedule, stopped. Many sat down, and within the cello's sound a special space for the heart welled up, a space of absorption and quiet. That is the courage that is necessary to counteract doubt and despair. Our souls need the sound-space of healing, as well. Some sonatas are better played in clinics than in concert halls.

~

At the start of this chapter I talked about the sound of my customers' instruments and explained that you cannot simply *manufacture* a good sound because the sound involves a person's innermost voice. If I am successful with an instrument, it is a result of all my passion, and yet it remains a gift of grace. Some of the best feedback I have ever received about one of my instruments came from a woman who wrote: "The sounds of this violin are like medicine that make you come alive again after a hard day at work."

The sound is like the soul's voice. I firmly believe that music is simply a prayer that is cast in sound. When dedicating myself to the sound and voice of an instrument, I set my hope upon grace. For here I am touching the realms that have been opened up to me. It is powerful when we learn to set our hopes on grace. Anytime we are dealing with people and real life, this hope is more necessary than any clever argument!

I have named three things: our *learning*, our *praise*, and our *courage*. Doubt can be God's messenger, helping us to mature in our calling through this threefold sound. It is surely life's victory when we succeed in transforming our doubts—transforming them rightly into doubt of the notion that life is only trouble, sadness, and sorrow. There is more than that. When we recognize this, the door to faith is already open.

10

The Charisma of the Stradivarius

The Meaning of Grace

For the mountains may depart
and the hills disappear,
but . . . my promise of peace for you
will never be broken, . . .
O my afflicted people,
tempest-tossed and troubled.

—ISAIAH 54:10–11 (TLB)

*I*N ONE OF THE LAST, most intimate conversations that Jesus had with his disciples, he spoke about a powerful "charism": joy. "Charis" means grace; charisma is the gift of grace. But "charis" can also refer to the elegance of beauty, as in a wedding psalm: "Your words are filled with grace (*charis*)" (see Psalm 45:2). The sound of some violins captures the characteristic of grace. They fill space with resonant beauty and lead us from the outside world into the inner space of the heart's joy.

Johann Sebastian Bach

I had the pleasure and overwhelmingly intense experience of hearing the space-filling beauty of the "Schreiber" Stradivarius for the first time in my atelier.[1] The violinist, Michael, played this 1712 instrument—which is also visually exquisite—carefully, with some reserve. He played the Chaconne by Johann Sebastian Bach.[2] From the first chord the room was suffused with a warmth and brilliance that is difficult to capture in words. Even the least educated listener would have noticed it. Seldom have I been struck by such a powerful metaphor for the spiritual reality of grace. The Stradivarius is like a prayer dipped in tone colors. It is no coincidence that Antonio Stradivarius, unlike his contemporaries, signed the label inside each instrument with his initials "AS" underneath a cross. Playing on such a violin is like standing in a cloud of sound. The moments when I am allowed to experience the presence of the Holy Spirit in a special way are like this sound: they exude the exceptional coexistence of gentleness and strength.

This violin has surely been given the power to touch our souls. I had the honor of playing it later and was able to conduct an acoustical analysis. When my wife heard me playing, she said thoughtfully: "When you hear this sound you immediately start dreaming." That is a beautiful description of sound that has authority. It opens up something inside of us and speaks to the soul. You experience it even more intensely when you're playing. Not long ago, a violinist was trying out one of my recently finished instruments, lingering in certain ranges, very intent, deep in the sound. The next day she said: "I noticed how certain tones start to open up when you talk to them. . . ."

The "Schreiber" Stradivarius has been passed down through many generations of violinists. Bach's Chaconne is unsurpassable in capturing the nature of this violin. It is a completely different story with the violins of Giuseppe Guarneri del Gesù (1698–1744). They are made for the resilience and resistance demanded by Johannes Brahms's 1878 violin concerto. On Guarneri's violins you can feel how the tones allow themselves to be "kneaded and formed" under the bow. They almost suck the bow into the string. I strive for this quality in my instruments as well, especially on the G-string. There, the tones feel like fresh-fallen snow that crunches under your feet with each step, a lush, satisfying feeling. The sounds of a good G-String are like that: dense, dark, compressible. Guarneris have a ruddy sound in the lower registers and a silvery shimmer on the E-string. They can be almost archaic, wild, snarling, with a huge tone. It is such a passionate, intoxicating sound.

It would be inappropriate and crude to fight with a Stradivarius in this way. You must remain "underneath" them and heed their nobility; you must feel out their tone colors and potential bit by bit. You cannot force your way here; you have to win them over. That's why the humility and depth of Bach's Chaconne are meant for the Stradivarius. A profound unity of violin and composition is found here; there is nothing obtrusive pushing itself into the foreground.

I will now dig into the Chaconne and consider how this magnificent work came about.

The Work

The Bach Chaconne is filled with a blatant aching. Compared to Bach's other partitas and sonatas, it is unending both in length and intensity. It is superior to every other Bach composition for solo violin. He wrote it in response to the unexpected death of his wife, Maria Barbara.

Just imagine: in 1720, he undertook a journey with the prince of Anhalt-Köthen, his employer at the time. His wife was quite healthy when he took his leave, and he returned to find that she was dead—and already buried. The Chaconne is an earth-shattering composition in which Bach tried to come to grips with this catastrophe. For me it is one of the most breathtaking answers to suffering ever given by the human soul. Pain and remembrance roll on here without end.

Within the vast complexity of this work, I hear a simple theme: pain that in the end finds comfort; hope that cannot be of this world; questions that cry out and finally come to rest in consolation. The Chaconne is incomprehensible. It begins with the violin's desperate rebellion, its driving questions and despair ringing out time and time again. There are these forlorn monophonic sections (such as measures 84–87) that seem unable to escape themselves, only to be embraced again and again by a warm protective polyphony—a voice that does not answer questions but consoles.

In composing this piece Bach must have known of a comfort that exceeds human wisdom. Nothing is sugarcoated in the Chaconne, and yet it is somehow able to dry your tears. You can hear heavenly intercession in it as the violin grows beyond itself, as if someone is reaching down into your world. The violin becomes a pipe organ with all of its tone colors and polyphony. A space-filling, all-enveloping chorale emerges. I believe that the Chaconne is grace interceding in the life of a man gripped by sorrow.

For hundreds of years the chorales that J. S. Bach had interwoven into this piece for solo violin remained hidden. They were only recently uncovered through harmonic analysis:[3] "Christ Lay in Death's Bonds," "Thy Will be Done," "Jesu, Joy of Man's Desiring," "In My Beloved God," and finally "Thy Will Be Done, Lord God." We know from Bach's writings that he consistently attributed spiritual meanings to certain harmonic progressions. And just so, this breathtaking work for solo violin is an "encrypted song of praise." Bach did not quote these chorales formally but called them forth in a veiled way through the sounds of the violin.

The Violin

The violin that I heard playing the Chaconne that day is one of the most beautiful and adaptive instruments ever to have graced this world. It was made at the beginning of the eighteenth century during Stradivarius's "golden era," just a few years before Bach composed the Chaconne. This violin is the antithesis of anything hardened or tight. Its sound seems to completely fill up the room. It is unobtrusive and yet pulls everything in. It does not have to be loud to have this effect. Violins that have a hard, insistent sound cannot speak to the listener's heart. This violin is different: even at the finest pianissimo it fills the entire space and opens you up with its power. It takes nothing, it does not brag, it is never common. Its dynamic range is vast. There is nothing one-dimensional about its sound.

Finding Grace

When the sound of this violin fills a room, it brings an acoustical reminder of the overwhelming spiritual experience of grace. To have grace is to have space. You do not have to take it for yourself. Those who have it have room in someone else's heart. Grace offers space that you *cannot* take. The joy that we have and hold for each other, the trust in which we live, create room for life. You can sense the difference between a person who believes that she must earn and fight for everything and the one who knows that she is the recipient of a gift.

So is our interplay with God. It is a way of living that develops out of real mutuality. Grace is not a one-way street from God to us. God will find room in our lives when we "make" room for him. The fact that God does not simply take this space means that each person has a kind of grace that he can either give or withhold! If God were to bypass the permission that we call "faith," he would simply be taking over our space regardless of whether we granted or withheld it. That would be a frightfully primitive god!

A prayer through which we give God room is: "Hallowed be your name. Your kingdom come; your will be done." This can be a steady, basic theme in our existence. Amid the hectic daily life of the workshop this awareness and trust can be stolen away. Then I step back for a moment and will often pray (slowly and breathing calmly): "All honor be to the Father, the Son, and the Holy Spirit. As it was in the beginning, let it be today, and always from eternity to eternity. Amen." This slow, calm prayer is all that I need. In it I receive a new freedom. Eternity's horizon opens up as a backdrop to the workshop in front of me. A broad space emerges out of narrowness. Prayer is a living interaction in which not only the grace that we have with God can be expressed, but also the grace that we give him through our trust.

Friendship

Setting up my business was a school of hard knocks for me. It taught me to enter this space of faith. Being on the edge financially, barely having enough to live, feed a family, and cover the monthly bills, I repeatedly had to make the decision to leave the inner space of needs and troubles and enter the space of faith.

Yet we must not view grace as something exclusively internal. It comes out most clearly in a good friendship. For in need and trouble we are entrusted not only to ourselves but to each other. We are intended to have space in others, space in their thoughts, sympathy, and aid, and they in us. During my early years of self-employment, friendship became tangible, practical, and financial. One friend who knew about my workshop asked us to accept money from him—and no small sum!—for as long as was necessary to get over the scant start-up years and into the clear. Then we could pay him back slowly (and interest free!). He kept saying: Take your time! As a businessman, Reinhardt knew full well how to get a lot from his money, but a different value was obviously more important to him. Friendship is what we make room for, what we enable in each other, where we strengthen each other and show that we believe in one another. What I experienced with Reinhardt reminds me of rabbinical wisdom: "The material needs of your neighbor are your spiritual concern."[4] We never felt the slightest hint of superiority or patronization from Reinhardt. We probably could not have accepted the money if we had. Contrary to the proverb that "friendship ends where money begins," our friendship fulfilled its purpose in life-giving strength.

A similar thing happened with another friend. Günter, a self-employed dentist, knew that you need nerves of steel during a business's start-up years. If I were ever in dire need, he promised, he would gladly order a violin from me—not for himself, as he did not play, but for some young, talented musician to whom he could loan the instrument. Thus far it has not been necessary to accept this offer, because I have always had enough to do, and for quite some time enough to support my coworkers and their families as well. But it has always been a relief to have Günter's safety net under the high-wire act of art, music, and economic realities. I could tell many more stories of friendship and faith, like of the Swabian investor who, with a father's heart, promoted one of my sound development projects because he believed in the vision.

The grace in which we meet and walk with one another becomes tangible in external spaces where faith and trust, respect and mutual freedom become incarnate. We respect each other and thereby create freedom and space in our friend's heart. Space for time. Space for life. We should understand our life as a "spiritual experience" of friendship and community, and we should reverse course if our relationships have become distant. Friendship is a great source of life's strength because it means that the joy and value of others *lives in me*. It is the certainty of being known, respected, valued, and supported by others. That is grace. Even deeper: it is the knowledge that there are people who have heartfelt joy for others. That is one of the most beautiful reasons to live.

In this same way, Jesus tells his disciples that they are not "slaves" but "friends" (John 15:15). This is the most profound realm of joy that a person can experience: the all-fulfilling joy of God's love. A life of faith means enjoying the joy that God has in me. Living out that joy has more potential than any command, so I have left the other spaces of pride, selfishness, and continual worry for the space that I have found in God.

How much damage do we cause others because we do not provide enough space? Active space generates love and power. If a person is given no room, if he is not trusted, not respected, and not recognized, he is being robbed of that which belongs to him. He can retreat or stubbornly fight back, but he will have a tough time being who he should be. The space we deny each other costs us true friendship. Then we are surprised that our life has so little meaning or occasions for joy. We cannot speak of grace without considering friendship.

Spacious or Narrow?

When the Spirit of God is present, an expanse opens in your heart free of narrowness and fear. Paul says: "Where the Spirit of the Lord is, there is freedom" (2 Corinthians 3:17). The book of Job also speaks of this when it says of God: "He also allured you out of distress into a broad place where there was no constraint, and what was set on your table was full of fatness" (36:16). It is like the violin's expansive sound.

We are talking about the space at the table. The table expresses grace. It is hospitality. Here, a guest may enter another's space, his house, his heart. Fellowship at the table is a symbol of clearing out space to be close to each other; it is necessary for life. It means living in grace, not in an abstract sense, but in daily interactions. The disciples of Jesus "spent much time together in the temple, they broke bread at home and ate their food with glad and generous hearts" (Acts 2:46). I have personally experienced the change that happened when a leadership circle stopped meeting in homes for food and conversation and instead took the practical option of meeting in the church building. When they no longer opened their living spaces to each other, internal divisions broke out; power struggles and jealousy became unbearable.

The hospitality of which the Bible speaks extends to strangers as well. This is a big test. Bigotry and fear keep others away by creating boundaries, but the boundaries that God creates are made of trust and enable people to find space. The prophet Zechariah speaks of this in a vision:

> I looked up and saw a man with a measuring line in his hand. Then I asked, "Where are you going?" He answered me, "To measure Jerusalem, to see what is its width and what is its length." Then the angel who talked with me came forward, and another angel came forward to meet him, and said to him, "Run, say to that young man: Jerusalem shall be inhabited like villages without walls, because of the multitude of people and animals in it. For I will be a wall of fire all around it, says the Lord, and I will be the glory within it." (Zechariah 2:1-5)

The space in our hearts tightens when we build walls to prove our own power. Where pride and fear live, the holy can find no room. Nor was there room for Jesus when he was born. The words sound as an early metaphor: "there was no place for them in the inn" (Luke 2:7). Later, Jesus found them true again: "there is no place in you for my word" (John 8:37). This rejection came from the human heart.

Grace creates space for life above and beyond our own accomplishments and abilities, our frustrations and failures. In our own dissatisfaction, we judge each other, cramp our neighbor, and find ourselves in narrow, hardened relationships. Those who judge this way have not understood the essence of Christ, and the spirit of Christ is not in them. We should ask how we can give each other room so that—in spite of all of our annoying weaknesses—the good in us can find expression. If we bury what is good in others under criticism, we have lost our eyes of mercy. We offend God and rob each other of the grace that God has promised.

~

The witness of John the Baptist clarifies the deepest nature of Christ. "Behold, the Lamb of God, who takes away the sin of the world!" (John 1:29 RSV). The word "take" in this verse can also be translated as "carry." The root of the verb best corresponds with the word "tolerance"![5] Fear and frustration should not rob us of the Lamb's nature to which we are called. He who fixes his eyes on Christ will recognize this sort of tolerance as the most intrinsic characteristic of truth. It is the strength to carry another instead of lifting ourselves above him. The first thing that John the Baptist recognizes about Jesus is not the truth that he brings but the burden that he carries. Following Jesus means asking what he is carrying. It also means recognizing when the burdens of others are becoming too heavy and staying in conversation with Christ to see the measure he gives us to partner with him in carrying others. First and foremost, I will carry my neighbors in prayer. That will change my view of them and give me new strength. I will lift them up to the Lord rather than judging them. If Christ himself declared: "I came not to judge the world, but to save the world" (John 12:47), how much *less* then should we judge others! Whoever judges another loses the strength of Christ. He will notice it in the fact that he is unable to bear his neighbor, and in the end, himself.

A simple but helpful prayer says: "God, I cannot love this person right now. You love him!" That can act as a conduit, allowing some of God's love to jump over into us. It will change *us* as well. It is a mystery that, in God, I can love the people who are hard to love, and love God himself, even though I find myself surrounded by hardships. *Asking* for love in light of our own limits is a tremendous empirical "experiment of faith" that can hold the heart of the world. Loving the unlovable shows that grace exists and is powerful even in our weakness. By rejecting the unlovable you impoverish yourself, depriving your life of its greatest gift.

Responsibility for Grace

Grace, just like the sound of the violin, opens up inner spaces. It takes nothing for itself. It does not brag. It is extraordinarily supple. It seeks to win us over. Many Bible passages work like this. They seek resonance in us. Words that express the sound of grace *read us*; *we* do not read them. Like music that can only be heard through an instrument, they work inside us. You might think that the violin is playing the music, but it is really the music that plays the violin! The "music" of our hearts makes all the difference.

The prophet Jonah said: "Those who regard worthless idols forsake their own mercy" (2:8 NKJV). Every person has *their own* mercy in the same way that they have their own eye color and personal traits. Paul said: Do not "accept the grace of God in vain" (2 Corinthians 6:1). If we lose grace, like the sparkle in our eyes, a fog rises up like a haze over our hearts.

Losing Grace

The extraordinary sound of the Stradivarius created audible space. If grace is above all "space" that we have, we need to consider what it is that takes this space away, making life tight and troublesome. I see four culprits: stereotyping, arrogance, judgment, and knowledge.

Stereotyping

We draw up boundaries to protect what seems to us to be true and valuable. That is how we protect our little spiritual plot as if it was the Promised Land. Should God, who spread out the expanse of the heavens, feel at home in spaces that have become so tight and sickly via insults, indignation, and the need to always be right?

Spiritual or ideological in-breeding sickens what is good. We must associate with more than just "our kind." God is not "my kind." God remains "the other" more than one's own. Experiences with other people, other congregations, other denominations, and other witnesses are life's metaphor for meeting God. Often God will surprise us and meet us outside the camp of our comfort zone in the place where we start to seek more than just ourselves.

The less we allow God to meet us, the more diligently we draw the borders around our kind. This is how the stereotyping of an inbred, familiar, inward culture prevents itself from being disturbed in its sickness. Jesus Christ had to bear living on the outside and dying "outside the city gate" (Hebrews 13:12). We should in turn "go to him *outside the camp* and bear the abuse he endured" (13:13).

To share what is your own not only with others like you but with others who are different is to encounter God. When we are able to respect the differences of others even if we *don't understand them*, our humanity will start drawing from a new source. This is the wellspring of reverence. The familiar seeks our trust; the unfamiliar, our reverence. How many treasures remain undiscovered because we are not able to expand our hearts beyond what we are accustomed to. It requires humility to see that the essential things often take place outside of "our camp."[6]

Arrogance

Truth does not need our tutelage; it is sovereign. But the truth *does* need our love and awareness: "Wisdom hastens to make herself known to those who desire her. One who rises early to seek her will have no difficulty, for she will be found sitting in the gate" (Wisdom 6:13-14). Realizing this opens freedom and deep trust within us.

Wisdom finds you more often than you find her; you stumble upon her, experience something exhilarating that draws you on. You are more likely to be enlightened than to enlighten yourself through your own understanding. We are gripped by what is important, not the other way around. Some realms must open up as if "of themselves" (see Mark 4:28). Through all our *research* we can only access the part of the universe that is within our *knowledge*. But through our *trust* we gain access to something far beyond ourselves, something that simply must be *acknowledged*. You will acknowledge only what you love, and you will experience only the good things that you acknowledge. A person who only wants to understand but cannot trust or appreciate will be unavoidably impoverished. Faith means delving into all of existence sustained by a sense of appreciation. If your searching lacks the humility of love, you stand before a closed door.

Judgment

We criticize each other because we feel called to guide those who have gone astray, to correct the obstinate, to explain things to the foolish. Of course, a spirit-filled person will always accept admonition. Only the stupid are not ready to accept constructive criticism. But as one must tune a violin before playing it, so the one who is teaching or criticizing must first be tuned by God's Spirit— then her intonation will be different; she will be more merciful. The difference between judgment and constructive criticism is mercy. Only mercy allows us to see with the eyes of the heart. A person who is unable to do that—as right as he may be—is like the blind leading the blind. We cannot force understanding, reason, and grace on each other. We can, however, demand mutual respect. Where there is no mutual respect, even the loftiest knowledge is stupidity.

Knowledge

How many people say they love God, and in the same breath judge others who love him in a different way! Should it not be said, based on Jesus's words: "If you only respect others who are like yourself, what reward do you have? If you only give space to those who share your views, what are you doing that is so special?" (see Matthew 5:46-47). We do not usually judge out of a lack of love—we would be aware of that and be ashamed—but rather because we have idolized our own religious and philosophical convictions. As if God were born in theological views and not in the poverty of our hearts!

We battle each other with our intelligence because we are beggars before the gates of experiencing God. They do not open up to those with knowledge, but to those without. The one who is poor in spirit regards all his knowledge as nothing compared to the command to listen to God's Word and serve his neighbor. When we enter, we will not wash each other's heads but each other's feet. In this way it becomes visible that our wisdom is from God.

Heraclitus (sixth century BC) said: "Much learning does not teach understanding." We deceive ourselves if we think that the great teachers of humanity are here first of all to increase our IQs. By all accounts, Confucius (Kongzi) changed his entire outlook on life from the ground up when he turned sixty. His conversion is attributed to an encounter he had with Lao-Tse, who said to him: "You have brought confusion into the human spirit," and "Wash your soul so that it will be white as snow and release your knowledge."[7] This encounter resembles something of the night-time meeting between Jesus and Nicodemus as told in the Gospel of John. The scholar begins the conversation with the words: "Master, *we know . . .*" But Jesus did not talk about knowledge, rather about the effects of God's Spirit: "The wind blows where it chooses, and you hear the sound of it, but *you do not know . . .*" (John 3:8).

"You hear—but you do not know . . ." Perhaps spirit-filled listening and spirit-filled naïveté build a tighter unity than intellectual people like to think. There is a kind of knowledge that drowns out the inward ear and robs us of the courage to deal with God. How often we obscure what has been promised to us by what we think we know! The Chinese proverb about the Tao can certainly be said of the kingdom of God: "One cannot speak about God's kingdom with a schoolmaster: he is walled in by his teaching."

It is a poor replacement if we—squeezed between book covers, addicted to knowledge, and incessantly chasing after new experiences—have lost the emptiness of a listening heart. An example of spirit-filled naïveté is to be found in the unselfconsciousness of children. Eastern teachers say that the holy or enlightened person has "become as a little child once more."[8] Jesus said so, too: "Truly I tell you, unless you change and become like children, you will never enter the kingdom of heaven" (Matthew 18:3).

What is the natural character of a child? A child does not close himself off from the world but maintains his desire to be enthusiastic about life. What fascinates me about my children is their indefatigable questions. Unwitting and uninjured, they do not yet suffer from a closed-up worldview; instead they explore life as it reveals more and more. But whoever insists upon his own knowledge is not open to life's revelations; he has lost the grace of being a child, he is neither a learner nor a searcher. We should turn back to this grace and not replace God's revelations with our own insights. That is to make ourselves God and worship the idols of our own decrees and convictions.

~

We are not called to living long-term on the boundary line of truth. Wisdom is not found at the dividing line. If we stay on defense at the border, the truth for which we stand will corrupt us. If we fight at times and places to which we are not called, we will become hardened. Passion will turn into fanaticism, and the Holy Spirit will find no room in us.

Jesus has not called us to construct walls by the strength of our views. Instead he said: "My sheep hear my voice . . . and they follow me" (John 10:27). If we say that the main thing is to man the barricades and protect the borders of truth, we will remain in place and not follow Jesus. "Woe to you," he says to us, "you zealot who has lost your ears. In your fight for me, you lose me. You are wasting your energy on the dividing lines. How can you believe that you hear me?" Our love for the truth should never be the *only thing* of which we are capable. Wisdom speaks to our hearts: learn to believe in God no more than you are capable of loving the world! Your love must determine your boundaries. At the end of the day, it is not being right that counts but being righteous. We revel in how right we are only because we are not able to hear the sighs of the world and unite with each other in the fight against injustice and adversity.

Self-Respect

Of course, we may be convinced that we believe in the truth, but we should not forget that our truth does not only conform to *God* but also to *us*—our calling, our understanding, our experiences, and our times. The fact that we color the truth through ourselves is not bad in and of itself. A resonant body also colors the sound of the vibrating string with its particularities. Every time and culture has its own sound. God does not neutralize what belongs to us in order to create his image in there—virtually unchanged. As holy as a person may be, we still only see an image of the Maker. God takes form in us, not in place of us, but through us. That God "created humankind in his image" (Genesis 1:27) does not mean that we are godly. It does not even mean that God looks like a person. It rather means that God wants to show himself through us.

With each and every human being, something personal comes into the world. This should lead us to self-respect: we can mature, but we cannot become *someone else*! Therefore, we should receive and accept ourselves and be healed as the person we are. It is not the fantasy person that we would like to be, but who we really are that can mature in our callings, resonating with grace. And so to lose our self-loyalty is to lose the grace that has been given to us—grace that we are no one else, and hope that good things can happen in and through us! We are called to this self-confidence.

How can Christ find resonances in us if we lack loyalty and hope for ourselves? You cannot replace the resonating body with the vibrating string, and you cannot claim that because the string is vibrating you do not need a resonant body. Both have their purpose. Do we want to replace ourselves with Christ? Christ will not play along in this game of self-loathing! He does not seek the *same* sound in every person; he does not reveal himself the *same* way in every person and in every culture. He did not pray that everyone would be *the same*, but that "they may all be *one*" (John 17:21). Grace will never replace a person, but rather be active through him. Grace says: "Don't give yourself up, but learn to respect who you are and to trust what I can do through you. Just as the instrument's resonances color the string's sound, so will my glory be colored by the resonances of your faith.

Does not every instrument have its own resonances?" In the coming world I will certainly not be asked: "Why were you not Stradivarius?" or "Why weren't you Isaiah?" Instead, "Why weren't you Martin?"

The command of solitude is to understand yourself, and yet within any community, comparisons will inevitably arise. Pull away from this! Each heart must be able to ask on its own what it believes and what it should receive. We must be ready to expose ourselves—listening and asking, searching and loving—to God. Solitude then becomes a faith experience. Those who experience this fulfilling solitude will have strength to offer their unique gifts to the community, the strength to live from the heart. Solitude before God is a promise that tells you to make your heart like a blank canvas and ask God to create something that matches both *himself and you*! Make your heart a book of revelation and ask God to describe *himself* in you! Believe that he will bestow on you what is yours. Have the courage to open yourself up and live in trust before God. Have the courage to count on God's grace in your life.

Replacing Grace

Our understanding makes God smile—not mockingly, but like a father who rejoices over his child's discoveries. This means that behind all the truth that we speak and teach, we should always see God's smile. Obstinacy would be childish. We should not allow ourselves to be thrown off course by our thoughts. Nor should we idolize a spiritual doctrinal system because that would mean that we need to stabilize the right conviction about this god—a very shaky god—with our own thoughts lest it fall over. If "right doctrine" could justify us, it would become the greatest attack against grace. A terrible form of "righteousness through works" would sneak in through the back door. It would consist of believing the "right" thing, and orthodoxy would become the most important "good work." Faith would degenerate into talking the right theological talk and the heart would be abased, because you suddenly "have to believe" something. We are searching for truth and safety and hence for "purity of doctrine." But more often the Holy One speaks to us about "purity of the heart."

The pure in heart shall see God. One cannot be taught more truthfully than this.

The heart understands differently than the intellect. It does not understand by thinking about things, but by entering into them. It only understands by living in relationship. We know nothing about God if we do not have this "heart knowledge." And so *prayerful* faith, faith in *action*, and faith that *celebrates* must join in with *thinking* faith. The faith of the one who knows his doctrines but knows nothing of mystery, ethics, and ritual will lead quickly to a dead end; it will end up as nothing more than a dogmatic trivialization of God.

Where Are You?

God is the one asking. You can wish that your faith were certain, but you cannot force it. I can only answer the questions that God asks me, and it is important to know which questions are being put to you at each phase of your life. God is the asking One. What does it mean when he asks: "Where are you?" (Genesis 3:9)? Does he not know where that person actually is? Martin Buber explains: "God calls to every man: 'Where are you in your world? So many years and days of those allotted to you have passed, and how far have you gotten in your world?'"[9]

How will we come to believe if we are not courageous enough to place ourselves before God? "Where are you?" That means: "What have you done with yourself and what has been entrusted to you?" The more we hide, the deeper we entangle ourselves in wrongdoing. Meeting God means leaving our hiding place and confronting what we have known all along. To find God, we must stop avoiding life. In the words of Rainer Maria Rilke, "Do not now seek the answers which cannot be given you because you would not be able to live them. And the point is to live everything. *Live* the questions now. Perhaps you will then gradually, without noticing it, live along some distant day into the answer."[10] Our responsibility before God is the simple, honest cry of the heart. "Here I am! You are right!"

We must finally leave our hiding place and dare to walk the path. Even Taoism, which we have to thank for the famous and often misunderstood saying "The journey itself is the goal," would never describe a path that leads to nowhere as a path meant for the journey. A journey with no goal leads us on the wrong path. It is not sufficient to wander alone in aimless self-adoration. This turns our lives into a lie: the only motion is a revolving around ourselves. God's grace is effective only when we take on our calling and start out upon the corresponding journey. The first step is to recognize what we have *really* known for quite some time. Each journey begins with our own truthfulness. The more we live in opposition to our heart's knowledge, the more our dishonesty numbs us before God and costs us our purpose and our calling. Then, our only hope is to be hit by grace—that grace will knock us off the self-circling path of "me, me, me," so that we can finally stand upright and see the path whose goal is not oneself.

"*Where are you?*" God's first question in the Bible is rich in meaning. In the beginning, God spoke and things happened. But something new happened *through humankind* due to the fall into sin. Adam recognized this and hid himself in fear. Something had apparently also happened to God, because earlier he had simply said: "Let there be . . ." but now God begins *to ask*. Both happened at the same time. The human is able to do something in opposition to God, so God begins questioning the person, to sound out his existence, to scrutinize his actions and inaction. And it is the sound of God's question that pulls the person out of the hiding place! He enters the space before God. A dialogue ensues. It is not merely external but much more an inner conversation. Statements and answers, Logos and dialogue. Where there used to be only instructions and obedience, now there is the first question!

With this new element, something beyond instinct has come into the world. Before, the world was quite simple: God spoke, it happened. But now Adam stops hiding and emerges as someone else. Fearful as he is, he is not a servant responding to a command; he is a person answering God. What makes us human is our ability to take part in this dialogue; the inner speech, the answer that gives your life to the Logos (Meaning), the answer to which you commit yourself. To all of this the question "Where are you?" calls us.

The journey begins with a conversation that allows us to stand upright before God. Being *upright* within and living *righteously* without can no longer be separated. You are worthy to give an answer! Stand up! Walking upright is a symbol. "Now I don't *have* to do good, but I *want* to." When a person straightens up, law is transformed into grace. If leave my hiding place and choose grace, then I have chosen to be in harmony with God's question. We can do this, but it is not forced upon us. Among our many possibilities is the choice to deny ourselves grace—to ignore what God is asking me, to hide myself, to pull back from God and revolve around myself.

In this, what is harsh and narrow shows up just as it does in certain violins. They have no space and they give no space. They do not open anything up. They are like people who numb themselves to the questions, people who do not leave their hiding place and so deny themselves access to grace.

Examples of Grace

Some years back, I became acquainted with Gabriel Weinreich, a renowned scientist in the field of acoustical research. One of our first encounters happened at an international conference. During a discussion related to my presentation, he stood up and clarified the controversy at hand in so sophisticated a manner that no further comments on the subject were necessary. Our meetings after that were usually short and all too seldom, and yet they were always intense. When we met a few years ago in a café in Ann Arbor, Michigan, to talk about acoustical projects, I asked him about matters of faith as well. He told me about his life and some of his experiences.

He felt lucky to have escaped to America after the Germans had invaded Poland in 1941. Over the course of the years, he established himself as a renowned physicist at the University of Michigan, but along with his teaching duties he had also taken up theology later in his career. One could hear him lecturing at the university in Ann Arbor during the weekdays and listen to him preach from the pulpit as an ordained minister at an Episcopal church on Sundays. This was a voluntary post, but he took it as seriously as teaching physics.[11] Gabriel Weinreich not only talked about grace; he embodied it. At the seventy-fifth anniversary celebration of the Acoustical Society of America, he shared the following. He could have spoken about many topics, since the field of acoustics is so vast, but he decided to talk about the phenomenon of the violin's sound, closing with these words:

> There is also a specific excitement in researching musical instruments because so much ingenuity in building them has been acquired by trial and error in the course of centuries if not, on occasion, millennia. We are then given the enormous satisfaction of adding some scaffolding of logical understanding to musical instruments' miraculously singular quality, and to stand in awe of what human beings have, through the ages, been able to develop and harness through the use of intuition, patience, and God's grace alone.[12]

Weinreich looked to the work of the past centuries that still fascinate and touch us today. When thankfulness opens our eyes, we realize for a moment that we are surrounded by works of grace living in people—in their art, service, projects, and research. Appreciating the good in life is a question of character. It can be stated thus: a happy disposition is capable of thankfulness. Not everything that we have unfolded in our world is grace, but we have grown so accustomed to complaining that we often do not even recognize the breathtaking grace that surrounds us and the way past eras and generations have touched and blessed us. It is appropriate for us to acknowledge the accomplishments, wisdom, knowledge, and culture that we have inherited, to which we will add our humble contribution (may it be greater than our sin!) for the next generation.

Good politics are possible in a country only if a large enough number of people know that there is more to life than just themselves. If faith can accomplish this, then it becomes political in the best sense of the word. It will become a formative power, creating what we pass on to the next generation, whether of sin or grace.

Yes, the concept of sin applies when speaking about grace, for just as grace is something that gives us space and enables our calling, the primary definition of sin is deviating from the path and missing the goal![13]

~

I have described two powerful effects of grace found in the 1712 Stradivarius and in the Bach Chaconne, written in 1720. Every violinist who has the courage to tackle the Chaconne knows what it means to kneel before the grace that one man received and then—in spite of profound suffering—poured out of his heart. Explaining things intellectually is not enough; we must express them.

11

The Secret of the Varnish

Reconciliation in the Diversity
of Community

And you shall make of these a sacred
anointing oil blended as by the perfumer.

—EXODUS 30:25

*A*PPLYING THE VARNISH is one of the most visually stunning phases of violinmaking. Here the violin takes on its beauty, its luminous garment. The refraction index of the primer can work miracles: you look deeply into the spruce's tracheids and get the impression that the surface is three-dimensional. A good varnish does not push itself into the foreground but brings the wood to life. The secrets of the violin's varnish tell us a parable about great spiritual beauty.

The Recipe

Many of the ingredients of the finest varnish recipes have been passed down through generations, and good violinmakers have them in their varnish cupboards even today, and with good reason. The fullness and beauty of these materials are overwhelming!

Mastic

Along with amber, dammar, and sandarac, the fine *mastic resin* is rightly considered to be one of the most important resins for producing fatty oil varnishes for violins. Mastic is the resin of the Mediterranean mastic tree (*Pistacia lentiscus*). It flows in little viscous pearls (the so-called "tears of Chios") that are taken directly from the tree. Mastic is a soft, heat-sensitive, elastic resin that is mixed in with other resins as a softening agent. In ancient times it had an important medicinal role as well, but it was primarily used to increase the shine of the varnish's top coat. In the Middle East, due to its naturally high rubber content, mastic was used as chewing gum in harems. These little droplets release a wonderfully spicy aroma, and the gummy consistency of mastic means that it can be chewed for quite a long time without losing its flavor.[1]

We are familiar with mastic from the account in the book of Genesis of how Joseph is sold by his brothers to "a caravan of Ishmaelites coming from Gilead, with their camels carrying gum [mastic], balm, and resin" (Genesis 37:25). Years later, when Jacob's sons had to travel to Egypt for a second time because of the famine in their land, we read of this resin again. The patriarch, Jacob, gives them the finest gifts of the land to bring to the Egyptians: "If it must be so, do this: take some of the choice fruits of the land in your bags, and carry them down as a present to the man—a little balm and a little honey, gum [mastic], resin, pistachio nuts, and almonds" (Genesis 43:11).

Aloe

Another resin is a brownish-colored extract from the fleshy leaves of the aloe plant, a member of the lily family. Pure *Aloë sokotrina* was brought from the coast of Zanzibar and Madagascar in thin, ruddy, transparent layers for trading. Everywhere aloe is mentioned in the Bible, it is mentioned alongside other resins. It is the subject of conversation in one of the royal psalms:

> Therefore God, your God, has set you above your companions
>> by anointing you with the oil of joy.
> All your robes are fragrant with myrrh and aloes and cassia;
>> from palaces adorned with ivory
>> the music of the strings makes you glad. (Psalm 45:7-8 NIV)

A similar passage is to be found in the Song of Songs:

> You are a garden locked up, my sister, my bride;
>> you are a spring enclosed, a sealed fountain.
> Your plants are an orchard of pomegranates
>> with choice fruits,
>> with henna and nard,
>> nard and saffron,
>> calamus and cinnamon,
>> with every kind of incense tree,
>> with myrrh and aloes
>> and all the finest spices.
> You are a garden fountain,
>> a well of flowing water
>> streaming down from Lebanon. (Song of Songs 4:12–15 NIV)

At the end of the Gospel of John we read about Joseph of Arimathea who, along with Nicodemus, takes Jesus's body from the cross. They brought "a mixture of myrrh and aloes, weighing about a hundred pounds. They took the body of Jesus and wrapped it with the spices in linen cloths" (19:38–40).

Aloe always appears with myrrh in the Bible. I do not use aloe alone in my violin varnish because it fades in the sunlight.

Myrrh

The milky sap of the torchwood tree, burseraceae, which flows out through slits in the bark, is oily when it first congeals, then turns into rigid, brownish-red chunks of resin. They have an aromatic, balsamic smell and a sharp, bitter taste. Myrrh was long used primarily for its medicinal properties: internally for chest and throat ailments, and externally to treat gum disease and ulcerated wounds. In violinmaking, myrrh is usually used in spirit varnishes as a strengthening resin.

Myrrh has a special role in the Bible: it is one of the three valuable gifts worthy of royalty brought to Jesus, the newborn king of the Jews (Matthew 2:11) by a group of astrologers (who would only later become referred to as the "three wise men").

Amber

One of the hardest balsam resins is a fossilized reddish-brown colored resin originating from the so-called amber spruces.[2] The only other material this hard is fossilized copal. Amber can be used in violin varnishes only after being melted in a crucible at 550 degrees Fahrenheit. Only then, while still hot, can it be dissolved in linseed oil. Amber varnish (also called glass varnish) is traceable back to the fifteenth century. Due to its durability and transparency it is one of the materials best suited for oil varnishes in violinmaking. "It dries slowly and resists the effects of ambient air."[3]

Dragon's Blood

For the color tinting of my madder-root pigments, I always use a small amount of so-called dragon's blood in my varnish along with the poisonous South Asian golden gamboge resin. Due to its dark red color, this resin was thought to be the blood of dragons during the Middle Ages. It seeps out of the fruit of South Asian rattan palms. High-quality dragon's blood resin is rolled into balls and affixed with a gold seal.

Linseed Oil

The use of linseed oil as a transparent topcoat on wooden objects can be traced back to 3000 BC. The varnishes for my instruments have this as their base. The recipes I use were already common as early as the sixteenth century. I never cease to be amazed that the acoustical characteristics of these varnishes surpass those of all the modern varnishes that I have used in research experiments.

Benzoin

Benzoin resin, which can be red or gold colored, has a fantastic aroma—reason enough to use it as a fine polishing resin. It gives the surface a velvety shine. In violinmaking, it removes the muddiness from the varnish, especially on water-damaged areas. A couple of drops on a polishing cloth make the varnish newly luminous. The Benzoin resin that I use to polish my violins comes from Sumatra and Thailand.

~

There are at least a dozen other varnish resins that could be described, such as dammar or sandarac resin, but what I really want to clarify is a spiritual concept. The decisive factor in every good violin varnish recipe is that no single substance can be used on its own. It is not about one single, fabulous characteristic, but about the communal effect. The true genius is found in the recipe. One of the oldest known varnish recipes is found in the book of Exodus. This recipe, in "the art of the apothecary," is given in directions for making a varnish for the Ark of the Covenant, made of acacia wood, and the utensils used in holy service. The Torah gives us a detailed account of how the varnish was created, including information on measurements and materials. A violinmaker can see that it is a typical fatty oil varnish. It is not, however, based on linseed oil or walnut oil, like later varnishes (which became common around the thirteenth century); it used olive oil as a vehicle instead. We read in Exodus:

> The Lord spoke to Moses: Take the finest spices: of liquid myrrh five hundred shekels, and of sweet-smelling cinnamon half as much, that is, two hundred fifty, and two hundred fifty of aromatic cane, and five hundred of cassia—measured by the sanctuary shekel—and a hin of olive oil; and you shall make of these a sacred anointing oil blended as by the perfumer; it shall be a holy anointing oil. With it you shall anoint the tent of meeting and the ark of the covenant. (Exodus 30:22–26)

Many recipes, like the ancient one quoted here, follow a clear principle. Watin, an old eighteenth-century master varnish maker, expressed it thus: "Indeed, an artist's true secret is to proceed as simply as possible."[4] The old recipes are still referred to by luthiers today. The symbolism they contain often determined the way they were used. Harmony is found in how the ingredients are proportioned to the order of the planets.[5]

Walnut oil was commonly used as early as the first century AD, and linseed oil came into use in the seventh century. Starting in the thirteenth century, amber and sandarac were dissolved in these oils to create widely used varnishes. In the middle of the sixteenth century, essential oil varnishes arrived.[6] Since the sixteenth century an almost overwhelming abundance of recipe collections have been handed down along with other medieval manuscripts that include painting techniques, alchemy, medicines, and the art of varnishes. Spirit varnishes (acoustically inferior!) became popular in the early 1700s due to their shorter drying time.[7]

Some of the important oil varnish recipes originated from the Venetian Jesuit priest, R. P. Bonanni.[8] According to his recipe No. 4 (Rome 1713), a varnish that is still used today for violins, Venetian turpentine and amber were dissolved into polymerized linseed oil by continual mixing. In 1707, Johann Kunckel described the preparation of a "white, good Venetian violin varnish" as follows:

Take one pound of clear linseed oil and let it boil in a kettle. Take a full vessel of Beern or Agtstein (amber). Put in 2 Loth (1 Loth = 1/32 pound) of cream of tartar and place over a strong charcoal fire. Stir with a hot glowing iron until fully melted and then pour in the hot oil and stir. Let cool a little and then add 2 Loth of Silberglett (litharge, or white lead oxide) and 2 or 3 Loth of Postolin (ground porcelain) of the best and cleanest variety. Filter through a cloth. The older the varnish is the better it is.[9]

Nowadays the language of old recipes sounds strange to us, and we are likely to smirk at specific instructions that sometimes pop up, such as "stir the copper pot by no means more than three times over the coal fire." Even the mixing tools are described in detail. But one is quickly humbled upon discovering that it is exactly by means of this specific process that a certain temperature profile emerges upon which the characteristics of the melting resins depend! Venetian turpentine is exactly like this. This fine balsam from larch wood remains sticky and viscous when it melts at 250 degrees Fahrenheit. At 285 degrees it changes so that, after cooling, it becomes strong and flexible. At 320 degrees it becomes brittle and breaks. If overheated, it can no longer be used as a softener to make the oil varnish spreadable and supple.

I pay special attention to the production of my pigments. They give the varnish its color, creating a pigment that has a vivid, intense color, yet is still highly transparent. However contradictory, this is exactly what gives the varnish an attractive appearance: it should never cover up the wood's structure but should allow it to glow in all its depth. On the other hand, the varnish should not be pale, lacking a play of colors. The pigment's refractive index allows the color to vary when viewed from different angles and in different lighting. This interactive color spectrum cannot be attained by simply stirring in a monochromatic aniline dye, as is often done nowadays. This might spare the maker the cost and effort of producing a good pigment, but it loses any attractive visual interplay. In certain lighting a good pigment can turn the violin's color to light gold, and then again give it a red shimmer.

I have not yet found a commercial pigment that can fulfill all these requirements, and therefore, like many of my colleagues, I cook all of my pigments myself. The process takes hours. I use dyer's madder (*rubia tinctorum*) as a ground color. This pigment is one of the oldest Asian dyes for producing red varnishes. It has been used since ancient times in textiles. As a vehicle for the pigment, I use pearl ash and alum. Later, the colors' nuances are refined by adding various salts during the cooking process: ferrous sulfate brings out a brown pigment, aluminum sulfate creates a deep red, zinc sulfate pulls out a luminous golden-orange. This has been known for centuries, and the process is exciting each and every time as I watch to see if the pigment will come out right before putting it in my ball mill and grinding it into a fine powder.

In addition, I check the pigment's quality by listening. When I grind the mixed pigments with the glass muller on a glass slab to give it the correct consistency, a light hissing noise emerges, clearer and clearer. When the initial rough noise softens to a hiss, the pigment has reached the right consistency. This quality is very important later on for the varnish's transparency and illuminating power. Finally, I apply the pigment using a well-known technique from the Renaissance masters. It requires much practice to do this successfully, and a special application brush is called for along with the thickener.

Over the years, I have painstakingly reproduced the cooking techniques of numerous historical varnishes in my little shop kitchen in order to test their acoustic effects on tonewood. It was obvious early on that a flawlessly built violin can take on its ultimate sound refinement through a good varnish, but even the most beautiful instrument can be irreparably damaged by a bad varnish. Encouraged by my mentor, Helmut A. Müller, I began preparing small strips of tonewood to test the tonal qualities of primers and varnishes with a measuring tool that I developed. I measured the eigenfrequencies and damping values of the untreated wood and then again after each coat of varnish.[10] At first, we decided to test between five and seven substances and recipes. But working carefully on it opened up a whole world. The influences of the penetration, the layer thickness, the recipe variations, and many other factors were too fascinating to ignore. So, in the end, I treated at least 300 strips of wood with every possible procedure and recipe. I spent more than twelve years researching their acoustical effect on the wood, focusing not just on the short-term but on the long-term effects as well.

The Anointing

As life continues to amaze us, our joy over nature's secrets has the power to lead us to God. Where do I find the metaphor in the varnish? One of the greatest Christian hymns, *Veni Creator Spiritus*, speaks about the "anointing Spirit." The experience of Pentecost is about the anointing of the soul by the Holy Spirit. We now know about the ointment's recipe according to the "art of the apothecary" in the Old Testament. But ritual alludes to a different anointing—an anointing that we shall experience, that will change our lives.

The Hymn of Pentecost talks about how the Holy Spirit can sanctify, renew, strengthen, free, uplift, and penetrate our lives completely. This is not a supplement for the Christian life but its very essence! Christ is called "the Anointed." We should also be anointed, for this will bring us nearer to Christ. Christ does not only say: "*Where*

I am, there will my servants be also" (John 12:26), but "*How* I am, my servants will be also—anointed with the Holy Spirit. So wait until you receive this power from on high. Then I will send you out."

~

There are Bible passages that read like a good varnish recipe. They show us the diversity of spiritual substances that should fill our hearts with something holy. Here is how the prophet Isaiah speaks of God's Anointed: "The spirit of the Lord shall rest on him, the spirit of wisdom and understanding, the spirit of counsel and might, the spirit of knowledge and the fear of the Lord. His delight shall be in the fear of the Lord" (Isaiah 11:2–3).

The more we get to know the Holy Spirit, the more honestly and faithfully we will call out to him. God says: "Reach out your spiritual hand to me, your faith!" And so our faith can call out: Come, Spirit of peace: Come to me when I am too driven! Come, Spirit of counsel: Come into my scattered state. Come, Spirit of grace: Come into my narrow-mindedness. Come, Spirit of faith: Come into my doubt of God and self! Come, Spirit of hope, you are smooth resin: Come into my troubles. Come, Spirit of strength: Come into my uncertainty. Come, Spirit of reverence, you are purified resin: Come into my entangled life. Come, Spirit of God, yes come, you perfect Comforter! God then speaks over our heart's call: "I will pour water on a thirsty land, and streams on the dry ground; I will pour my spirit upon your descendants, and my blessing on your offspring" (Isaiah 44:3).

Second Timothy also describes the Holy Spirit as a holy anointing: "For God did not give us a spirit of cowardice, but rather a spirit of power and of love and of self-discipline" (1:7). Here again the holy varnish recipe consists of two resins and one oil: the spirit of strength, of love, and of self-discipline.

Such biblical lists of the gifts of the Spirit read like a varnish recipe in which each resin has its own character and strengths that are useful for the whole. Therefore, we should understand and respect each other as recipients of these gifts. The Holy Spirit entrusts the gifts he gives to the individual for the faith and love of *the other*. When we do not believe or respect each other, then we will remain a foreign body, a lonely substance that cannot be dissolved in the varnish. The resins, oils, and pigments, all of the recipe's ingredients, are indeed given to the community *by God*. But the warmth and wisdom necessary to bind it all together as an oil varnish is the love that is required *of us*. The fact that God has entrusted something to us does not mean that he has *replaced* something human in us with something spiritual. The varnish does not replace the wood but brings out its value. In that light ponder the apostle Paul's list of talents:

> Now there are varieties of gifts, but the same Spirit; and there are varieties of services, but the same Lord; and there are varieties of activities, but it is the same God who activates all of them in everyone. To each is given the manifestation of the Spirit for the common good. To one is given through the Spirit the utterance of wisdom, and to another the utterance of knowledge according to the same Spirit, to another faith by the same Spirit, to another gifts of healing by the one Spirit, to another the working of miracles, to another prophecy, to another the discernment of spirits, to another various kinds of tongues, to another the interpretation of tongues. All these are activated by one and the same Spirit, who allots to each one individually just as the Spirit chooses. (1 Corinthians 12:4–11)

The Community

From such words it is clear that the vessel to be filled is not only the heart of the individual but the heart of a community, a community of faith in its togetherness. We are "a dwelling place for God" (Ephesians 2:22). Old Testament rituals show that even the sanctuary needed to be anointed: "And you shall make of these a sacred anointing oil blended as by the perfumer; it shall be a holy anointing oil. With it you shall anoint the tent of meeting . . . and its utensils" (Exodus 30:25–27). If we think that God's Spirit is a private matter between us and God, something internal, a gift of experiencing oneself, then we have not understood the fundamentals. Life's gifts tell us that we are either a hard or a soft resin, an oil or a pigment in the anointing of the sanctuary, each in its way and with its own character. Binding ourselves with others lets the community experience something holy through the wisdom of the recipe.

Just as in the Old Testament the acacia wood fibers were primed with a sanctified recipe of myrrh, cinnamon, calamus, and olive oil, so should the fibers of the New Testament sanctuary be filled and permeated with spiritual substances that we call the gifts of the Spirit. We must recognize the different ways the Holy Spirit works in individuals for our spiritual communities to be brought together. We must explore the life-giving game that the Holy Spirit wants to play with us. Which problems might turn into providence through him? Which gifts should become tasks? Which passions should be empowered through him? Which faith should become an anointment of blessing through him?

~

As multifaceted as the Holy Spirit may appear to us, one common characteristic is always present: he leads us to *what he is*. The Holy Spirit frees us by *fulfilling us*. He fulfills us with what he is: love. That is his way of freeing us from our self-adoration. It does not happen by him forbidding the attraction of selfishness, but by him satisfying us with the beauty of God's love. As Paul says: "God's love has been poured into our hearts through the Holy Spirit that has been given to us" (Romans 5:5). We can request this experience. We should not be wondering "How much can I change myself?" but "Am I ready to ask for the Holy Spirit?" It is often only the little moments of stillness that allow us to breathe again and entrust ourselves to this holy presence. It only requires this simple request: Come, Holy Spirit!

For Jesus, it was a given that God acts through the Holy Spirit: "Is there anyone among you who, if your child asks for a fish, will give a snake instead of a fish? Or if the child asks for an egg, will give a scorpion? If you then, who are evil, know how to give good gifts to your children, how much more will the heavenly Father give the Holy Spirit to those who ask him!" (Luke 11:11–13).

The Calling's "Radiation Damping"

One of the acoustical qualities that the varnish affects most is the amount of *damping* in the wood fibers. Several primers that penetrate the wood change the fiber damping and sensitize it to the sound of the vibrating string. A good recipe will minimize the fibers' inner friction. That way, the violin absorbs less vibration energy on the inside (the loss factor) and instead releases more energy as sound into the open air (radiation damping).

These two very different damping processes are symbolic for our calling. When the Holy Spirit fulfills our relationships, we will use up less energy in "internal friction." The humility and reverence that unfold can turn us into a promised sound in our environment. Our gifts will spend their energy on tasks rather than on ourselves.

Just as the ground resists the spade, so the violin's vibrations turn into sound that meets resistance in the surrounding air. This loss of energy turns the idle air into sound vibrations. Just as the earth costs the spade its power and the air takes the energy from the violin, so we give our strength and energy to our calling.

In experiencing the anointing of the Holy Spirit, we will notice that our calling costs us something. Our tasks make demands on us; allowing ourselves to be touched extracts energy from us. This is precisely the essence of the radiation damping of our hearts. Releasing our sound into our surroundings makes our inner lives audible. If we are not expending energy on this world, we are most likely not living out our calling.

I want to experience the effects of the Holy Spirit in the same way that I prime and varnish a violin, saturating its fibers. The Spirit minimizes internal friction and increases the heart's radiation damping. That turns the question from what power we have to what power we receive. The apostle Paul speaks of this when he says: "So we do not lose heart. Even though our outer nature is wasting away, our inner nature is being renewed day by day" (2 Corinthians 4:16). I do not want to expend energy on myself, but on my calling.

Gifts of the Spirit

If we take a closer look at the makeup of the violin's varnish, we will see that there are four characters present in every good recipe: hard resins, soft resins, oils, and pigments.

This fourfold nature has the genius of enabling a combination of diverse strengths. It is obvious what happens if any one of the elements is missing:

> › Without *hard resins* the varnish will bond well with the subsurface but will lack durability. It cannot cope with climactic and surrounding influences. It rubs off.
> › Without *soft resins* the varnish will be brittle. It will be hard enough but is likely to chip off. It does not have the power to bond. If there is only hard resin, fissures and islands develop; it splits apart.
> › A varnish that has no *oil* cannot make unity out of diversity. There is nothing that can bind the different elements together.
> › A varnish that has no *pigment* will be useful but not attractive. It has neither beauty nor light refraction. Everything is practical and useful but devoid of inner space and generosity.

The genius of the violin varnish will also show itself in a community that decides to regard responsibility as a gift of the Spirit. There are four basic substances in that community.

The Pigments

Pigment people are not officials; they are not recognized for their obvious usefulness. But when they are absent, the community's beauty disappears; it becomes a work club, oriented purely to function. Everything is utilitarian and efficient, but there is no light refraction, no color or illumination. There is nothing wrong; yet at the same time nothing is right. People who are like pigments know how to welcome others and be inviting with their whole being. They have the gift of hospitality and warmth. Pigment people need to be paid their due respect perhaps more than those whose usefulness is immediately obvious. Of course, the violin varnish would function just as well without pigments, and yet one assumes that such a violin is poor.

The Carrier Oils

If the carrier oils are missing, there are no people who can bond diversity together and reconcile differences. Then the harder the resins are, the harder they become on each other. They rub against one another and fight, each primarily for himself. There is no substance present that creates something communal. I have noticed that one particular friend of mine seldom contributes much at a gathering. But when he is gone, we get caught up in our own conceited and sensitive natures, and when he is there, there is an atmosphere of friendliness that encourages assimilation. "Oil" contributes a spiritual power of integration so that we do not remain a collection of separate disconnected substances.

The Hard Resins

The hard resins stand for content, truths, convictions, and ideas. They stick to the creed. Remarkably, they are the only elements that need to be melted in a crucible in order to dissolve—to be enjoyable and socially competent! This is the only way to render amber and make it part of the varnish. There is tremendous allure in its solidity. These people provide orientation. Without them, the community has no resilience and it cannot deal with the surrounding climate and difficult times. Therefore, hard resins are indispensable. And yet they stir up inwardly and are at odds outwardly. They often lack the suppleness and charm of the soft resins.

Some hard resins, when refined, possess a *prophetic* power to be effective in the community and in society. They have experienced what Isaiah spoke of: "The Lord God has opened my ear, and I was not rebellious, I did not turn backward. I gave my back to those who struck me, and my cheeks to those who pulled out the beard; I did not hide my face from insult and spitting. The Lord God helps me; therefore I have not been disgraced; therefore I have set my face like flint, and I know that I shall not be put to shame" (Isaiah 50:5-7).

And yet these hard resins must go through the crucible, because otherwise they will have no sanctifying effect upon the whole. "The crucible is for silver, and the furnace is for gold, but the Lord tests the heart" (Proverbs 17:3). Only in the fire will the unpleasant or even dangerous hardness be transformed into the blessing of necessary stability. It is the crucible of hardships, but also of prayer, that can transform a person's hardness. Hard resins are similar spiritually to fanaticism. The harder the resin, the more humility is necessary to allow oneself to be melted. Curiously, amber does not give up its solidity after it has melted, but the melting allows it to dissolve in the oil. Without the crucible, hard resin is not capable of bonding with other resins. Fossilized resins cannot remain as undissolved, foreign bodies within the varnish; melted, they provide a precious stability and a holy resilience.

The Soft Resins

The soft and semi-soft resins have their own special gifts that are useful to all:

> People who are like *mastic resin* have been given a quality that softens the heart. They are praised for giving the community its sparkle.

> People who are like resin made from *myrrh* have a healing power for sorrows, sicknesses, and injuries. They have the power of laying their hands on others and blessing them. God works through them when he says: "I have seen their ways, but I will heal them; I will lead them and repay them with comfort . . . and I will heal them" (Isaiah 57:18-19).

> *Aloe resin* is like people who rarely work *alone*. They are strong in dialogue with others. They live from and for the community. They build up. They have the gift of helping—especially in practical matters. "I have aroused [him] in righteousness, and I will make all his paths straight; he shall build my city" (Isaiah 45:13).

> › People who are like solid *copal resin* look after spiritual clarity and orientation. Like this resin, which dries slowly, they do not provide quick fixes but deep understanding. They resist superficial pragmatism. They delve in, praying: "My soul is consumed with longing for your ordinances at all times" (Psalm 119:20). They are people through whom God honors his word: "I am the Lord your God, who teaches you for your own good, who leads you in the way you should go" (Isaiah 48:17).
> › *Venetian turpentine* represents people who keep a diverse community from becoming hard, brittle, and broken. Without them, fissures and splits spread via vanity and know-it-alls.
> › People who are like hard *copal* guard and strengthen faith and remain stable throughout crises, as well. Through them, God says: "Open the gates, so that the righteous nation that keeps faith may enter in. Those of steadfast mind you keep in peace— in peace because they trust in you" (Isaiah 26:2–3).
> › People like *benzoin* illuminate what was dim and dull through their words and listening. They have been given "the tongue of a teacher, that [they] may know how to sustain the weary with a word" (Isaiah 50:4). And so, just as with benzoin, a new radiance emerges.[11]

The River and the Water

Each substance in the violin's varnish has its own meaning. As it does not unfold in stubborn isolation but only in connection with others, violin varnish is a metaphor for the harmony of reconciled diversity. The only way to produce a good varnish recipe is by bringing diverse substances together at the right temperature into a good relationship.

Just as I, a master violinmaker, speak of varnish, so Raniero Cantalamessa talks about the realization of the church: "Diversity is neither a limitation upon nor a correction of unity, but the only way to realize it."[12]

The vulnerable fibers of the life entrusted to us should be primed with a holy recipe. Just as water comes from the rivers to give life to the lands, so the water of life finds its channel in outward structures. Even the Living Water of the Gospels had the humility to create the riverbed of the church. The church is called to be not only a structure but a carrier of water; not only an organization but also a Spirit-filled organism. A river may have a mighty riverbed, but that says little about how much water flows through it. The life of the church is found in her *strengths* and *gifts*, and not in impressive titles or buildings (see 1 Corinthians 12).

A riverbed is continually dug deeper by the water, yet the water gets its momentum from the riverbed; so are the living water of spiritual gifts and the riverbed of the holy sacraments entrusted to each other in mutual dependence. The riverbed guides the water, but if the formal elements (that is, sacraments and preaching) are officially established without the gifts being enabled, wanted, or permitted, then the river dries up. Without gifts of the Spirit, the river of the church does not fulfill its calling. Gifts and sacraments build a set of harmonious opposites through which we love and live.

~

The metaphor of the varnish makes one thing clear: neither the resin, nor the oil, nor the pigment is there for its own sake. Rather, they make up a good recipe in which everything comes together in the right proportions and at the right temperature. Warmth symbolizes love: we must *love the gifts of others into the foreground*. The "controlling spirit" that stifles life in the Spirit feeds on fear and power. We injure others not only by being know-it-alls, but even more by our fears. To love sometimes means overcoming fears and limiting one's own powers. Our gifts need encouragement and trust to overcome our fear and vulnerability. Therefore, I do not want to spend time on the alienating, self-centered question of what God wants to give me. For God may well reply: "It is up to you to recognize the gifts of your brother and sister; the calling that I long to fulfill in them will come to life through your love."

12

The Inner Fire

Living by the Holy Spirit

Let the light of your face shine on us.

—PSALM 4:6

*I*HAVE WRITTEN ABOUT the Holy Spirit in previous chapters. Now I would like to explore how we can receive the Holy Spirit in greater depth and grow from the Spirit in life. Many insightful books have been written about this kind of amazing experience.[1] There is no beginning and no end to be found here, so yet again I can do nothing else but look to the parables found in the evolving violin.

The Reward

The last step before putting the strings on the violin is polishing the varnish. In this most beautiful process, my thoughts are calm and I feel the shape of the violin that I made under my right hand. It is the reward for all the work. Here I find deep meaning due to three intertwining aspects that depict living in the Holy Spirit.

The varnish layers are made from many substances: the ground color, pore filler, pigments, oil varnish. I apply the varnish in at least fifteen distinct layers using brushes, cloths, and sometimes even my bare hands. The varnish has dried in the light, and now it can be polished. Polishing does not involve what a layman might expect. You are not simply wiping the surface; it is more like deeply massaging the layers. This is when the varnish first gets its inner "fire."

Preparation before beginning this process takes a few minutes. The precious tool is a simple linen cloth. It must be old in order to be soft, and it must have homogeneous threads. Coarse knots and strands must not be allowed to disturb its supple quality. It is folded in two to make a firm corner. Then I dip it in alcohol and add a drop of polishing oil. In order to distribute the dampness evenly throughout every fiber of the cloth, I roll it up like a little carpet on a clean, dust-free surface. Then I smooth it out and roll it up in a different direction. This process is repeated a few times, then it is spread out smooth to make the front folded edge. Now the cloth is ready.

All of this is important, because polishing the violin can be risky. If it is not done carefully, the new varnish can be ruined. But if it is successful, euphoria arises: the varnish shows its inner fire! The wood's surface suddenly becomes three-dimensional. The polishing process requires study. If you are too slow, if the cloth is too moist, or if the pressure is too firm, then the surface will be inevitably destroyed. That is why a precise hand position is required. The folded edge is held between the thumb and forefinger, and the back is secured between the middle and ring finger. Before touching the varnish, you wave your hand back and forth just over the surface to attain the right movement and speed. Only then can the cloth touch down. You must use circular, figure-eight-shaped motions matching the arching. These motions must not be interrupted as long as the cloth is still damp.

Good polishing is a secret art, for in it three elements must come together: the cloth's moisture, the intense contact between the cloth and varnish, and the speed of motion. If any one of these three elements is not right, then the varnish will be ruined. A cloth that is too moist will wipe off the varnish instead of massaging it. If the cloth is too dry, nothing will be accomplished and your efforts are in vain. If the motions are too slow, the cloth will stick to the varnish, but if the motion is too fast, the varnish will not be sufficiently massaged. Too much pressure is like moving too slowly; not enough pressure amounts to a surface wiping with no effect—the surface will shine a little, but the varnish will not glow deep within. At the start, when the cloth has more moisture, the pressure must be more careful. Only toward the end can the pressure be increased.

Then you can feel how to treat the varnish without damaging it. You feel its resistance. Everything must come together in the right order and measure.

The emergence of the violin's deep radiance is beautiful to behold. I find the varnish of the old Italian master, Domenico Montagnana (Venice, 1687-1750), especially enchanting. His instruments have a depth of colors that seems to change throughout the day with the lighting: at times honey-gold, then later deep red. In some places it looks like little orange lamps are glowing in the wood. The varnish shines out of its depths in great purity and beauty. You watch your own polishing cloth like a hawk. The more often it is used, the better it is. It must never be allowed to dry out if it is not used for a few days. That is why I store mine in an airtight, screw-top jar. There it remains soft.

A marvelous moment occurs toward the end of the polishing when the instrument's surface gets its inner fire. You get the feeling that you are looking through a filled water glass into the wood's depths. The surface ceases to be a surface. It is three-dimensional. You gaze into its depths; the upper tracheids of the spruce seem to be transparent. The light reflects off the bottom of the wood. The fine, microscopic pigments that took many weeks to produce and apply deflect and refract the light. An optical allure is created. But it only comes to fruition through the process of polishing. All the work and care are rewarded in that moment. Now the instrument becomes truly visible.

~

With the violin in my left hand and the polishing cloth in my right, my heart's prayer arises: "If you would only hold still in God's hand like this violin in the master's hand. If you would just feel this passion that you know all too well as you give this instrument its radiance and depth! And if you would just experience some of the Lord's joy when you get your inner fire through the Holy Spirit."

The polish gives the wood its depths and makes it glow, but, like life that comes about through God's touch, it does not cover the wood visually. In the three essential aspects of polishing:

> The moisture in the polishing cloth symbolizes the *purity of grace.*
> The proper contact between the cloth and the instrument stands for the *affirmation of faith.*
> The motion of the cloth symbolizes our *daily practice.*

These three reach their goal only when they are in balance with each other. So they must work together, all intertwined, in a spirit-filled life.

The Purity of Grace

In the light's refraction the violin takes on a new quality. It is as if a fire has been lit in the depths of the wood. Just so, God wants to give our lives an inner fire. This fire is the Holy Spirit.

As Jesus stood in the temple on the most important day of the Jewish Feast of Tabernacles, he called out: "Out of the believer's heart shall flow rivers of living water" (John 7:38). John adds this comment: "Now he said this about the Spirit, which believers in him were to receive" (7:39).

The Gospel of John says "Jesus said" or "Jesus spoke" over eighty times, but it says "Jesus called out" only *three* times. He is not just conveying information; in this moment he is literally calling something to life.

In Luke we hear Jesus say: "Is there anyone among you who, if your child asks for a fish, will give a snake instead of a fish? Or if the child asks for an egg, will give a scorpion? If you then, who are evil, know how to give good gifts to your children, how much more will the heavenly Father give the Holy Spirit to those who ask him!" (Luke 11:11-13).

Both of these Scripture passages give a startlingly clear answer to the question as to how we can receive the Holy Spirit: it is faith in Jesus combined with a request made to God. We will reflect on these two for a moment.

The Request

I have often asked myself why a request can be an appropriate kind of prayer. Shouldn't God know what I need? Or do I have to convince him first? Does God need that? Is asking not just a mindless chattering, lacking in the trust that God indeed knows what is good and what I need? Jesus said: "When you are praying, do not heap up empty phrases as the Gentiles do; for they think that they will be heard because of their many words. Do not be like them, for your Father knows what you need before you ask him" (Matthew 6:7-8).

But that is not all. Jesus taught us to present our requests to God with a trusting heart, because there is a spiritual power in asking. It is not *God*, but *we* who need the request! It is a radical form of openness. In asking, we can no longer shut ourselves off. He who asks shows that he himself is not enough and will not depend only upon his own capabilities. He faces his neediness and makes himself receptive. Therefore, our requests to God change us. It is completely foreign to the Bible to take on the spiritual attitude that "God will give me the Holy Spirit when he wants to." James says: "You do not have, because you do not ask" (James 4:2).

One man who considered himself to be humble and wise went to an old monk and said that it is not necessary to ask God for anything; one should be satisfied with what he has. The monk answered in mischievous irony: "I, too, in my great humility have asked God for nothing, and God, in his great goodness has heard my prayer—and has given me nothing!"

Faith in Jesus

God cannot be bought. When we ask God for the Holy Spirit, we should by no means cite our qualifications. We receive the Holy Spirit *purely by grace*. Grace is poured into us, not earned and not produced. It is a gift. It is the light that illuminates us.

What do we need to receive the Holy Spirit? The first disciples discovered they needed an inner purity that surpasses anything achieved by means of virtues, ceremonies, or moral striving. This crucial purity came through God's love alone. It is a love that, even when being tortured to death, uses its last bit of strength to say "Father, forgive them! They know not what they do."

Faith in this love's purity has been granted the right to prepare our hearts to receive the Holy Spirit. Anything else would be too weak. To be transformed into the state of love is to be reconciled. It makes things new and illuminates the depths of this world. An inner fire emerges with something new resulting. We no longer simply say: "God loves us," but "God's love has been poured into our hearts through the Holy Spirit that has been given to us" (Romans 5:5).

The early disciples knew that they did not receive the Holy Spirit by their own virtue. Why then did it happen? The book of Acts says: God "testified to them by giving them the Holy Spirit . . . and cleansing their hearts by faith" (15:8-9).

Purity of Heart

Jesus saw the human heart as an inner temple of God's presence. He said: "Blessed are the pure in heart, for they will see God" (Matthew 5:8). Every temple requires a purity suitable for God's dwelling place, but since the heart is not a temple of rituals, ritualistic purity cannot reach this place. It needs a different kind of purity. The Gospel of John gives us an image of how to get there.

> Jesus, knowing that the Father had given all things into his hands . . . got up from the table, took off his outer robe, and tied a towel around himself. Then he poured water into a basin and began to wash the disciples' feet and to wipe them with the towel that was tied around him. He came to Simon Peter, who said to him, "Lord, are you going to wash my feet?" Jesus answered, "You do not know now what I am doing, but later you will understand." Peter said to him, "You will never wash my feet." Jesus answered, "Unless I wash you, you have no share with me." (John 13:3-8)

In this act, Jesus made visible the essence of the Holy Spirit, for this was an act performed completely in the Holy Spirit. The only power that can transform us into something good is love. It is the power of God, humbly sanctifying everything that it touches. Nothing in us can be holy if we are not able to be recipients. *I receive, therefore I am.* This is what the washing of the feet stands for. The question then remains: Can you bear to be this kind of recipient before God?

The holiness that God requires cannot be earned; it must be granted to us. This is the purity that knows about our own behavior and questionable thoughts, yet still allows Jesus to come and be near in this fragility and intimacy. This brings existential healing: the healing of one's entire existence. I need quiet moments in which to close my eyes and take it in: "Jesus, I will let it happen!" There is a reason that he says: "Unless I wash you, you have no share with me."

Grace is poured out like water in the basin Jesus uses to wash the disciples' feet. It is not fortified by our magnificence. My feet have been washed, and I allowed it to happen. That is the whole of my riches. Sometimes it is actually harder to believe grace than to do good, because in good works, I am still looking at myself. Simply being loved creates a holy unselfconsciousness that is absent in works. Love that must be earned is not love but payment. Love can never be earned. It is the epitome of grace. It neither can nor needs to collect credits; it is purely a gift. If this is true for personal relationships, as we know, how much more is it true with God! Therefore, we must absorb this picture of the foot washing. There is a good reason for John's focus on this scene in his Gospel. We must spiritually sit in a row with the other disciples and know that our turn will come. Can we bear it? It is good to close our eyes and take in this picture until we see it before us.

～

I remember a church service that I attended while I was in training at Mittenwald. A young man with a mental disability stood next to me during communion. When it was his turn to receive the wafer, he looked at the pastor and asked: "How much does it cost?" The pastor answered off the cuff: "It's already been paid for!" He, himself, was later surprised by the twofold meaning of his answer.

We must recognize the existence of this wonderful gift, which is more important than anything we could earn by our morality. If our virtues were a prerequisite rather than the result of a holy life, then they would force people to be incessantly concerned with themselves. We can never say: "Now I am holy enough, mature enough, pure enough. Now my morals are good enough, I am consistent enough, social enough . . ." We are not and will never be all these things! Neither what we claim nor what we deny gets us any further. Our souls' most powerful bulwarks against God—self-righteousness and self-accusations—must be overcome in us by God's Spirit. Being filled with the Holy Spirit is not the result but the prerequisite for a holy life. We do not have to do good things to earn the Holy Spirit in us. It is the other way around: the Holy Spirit serves us, enabling good to come of our lives.

～

This chapter develops the idea of the necessary suffering of God's love, as set forth in Chapter 7, "The Closed Sound." The expression embodied by Jesus is *"for you."* In this Word (Logos) the world was created and has its permanent meaning. But now, a third idea arises: The promise of the Holy Spirit that we are to receive is revealed in this *"for you."* Jesus referred to this during his last conversation with his disciples shortly before his death: "I tell you the truth: it is to your advantage that I go away, for if I do not go away, the Advocate [Paraclete] will not come to you; but if I go, I will send him to you" (John 16:7). The word "Paraclete" (from the original Greek *paraklētos*) unites many concepts into one: Comforter, Teacher, Holy Helper, Inner Prophet. All of that is the *Paraclete*—the Holy Spirit (see also John 14:26).

Jesus says that the Holy Spirit gives himself for you, just as he did, because he "glorifies me" (John 16:14). The image of dedication becomes visible in the washing of feet: "If I do not do this, then you have no part in me." But this is followed with a command: "If I, your Lord and Teacher, have washed your feet, you also ought to wash one another's feet" (John 13:14). It is the command indicating that our neighbors should experience purification *through us as well!* If we respond faithfully to this commandment, then it becomes clear: We receive and grant life for others by the complete forgiveness of sins! To resist this is to oppose the grace that we have received and should give to others. That which we withhold from others, we withhold from God.

As in the Mishnah, the New Testament says that the Holy Spirit withdraws from sin, that through sins we "grieve" (Ephesians 4:30) and "quench" (1 Thessalonians 5:19) the Holy Spirit. This is not a contradiction of what has been said heretofore. If the fathers and mothers of our faith emphasized purity as an effective agent in receiving the Holy Spirit, then we cannot see this purity as a good work—as if it were some kind of currency that you can save in order to purchase God's Spirit. This is about a different kind of purity. It is the magic that opens our eyes of love so that we can see the beloved. It removes the heart's gloomy veil that makes us dull and indifferent, clueless and passionless regarding God's Spirit. That is why purity is important. It is a loathing for what is wicked; an attraction to what is helpful, purifying, true, upright, honest; a longing for God; a joy emanating from his essence of mercy, kindness, patience, friendliness, holiness, truth, and righteousness. We must not succumb to the misunderstanding that God will allow himself to be bought with purity if one can just produce enough of it. It is not *God* who needs our purity. *We* need it to live in his Spirit. Just as a person in love lives in an altered state, so it is with purity. It makes us sensitive and receptive to God. It opens our eyes. As Basil of Caesarea[2] said:

> Be cleansed of the filth with which sin has covered you, and find again your natural beauty, as you would restore an image to its original condition by cleaning it, and it becomes possible for you at last to come to the Paraclete. . . . The carnal man, whose mind is not trained to contemplation but is sunken rather in the muddy pit of carnal thoughts, cannot raise his eyes to the spiritual light

of the truth. This is why the world, that is, life enslaved to carnal passion,[3] does not receive the grace of the Spirit any more than an eye that is diseased can look on the light of the sun.[4]

Faith's "Yes"

Grace is the prerequisite permeating everything holy; indeed, "If anything is not reached by the Holy Spirit, it is not sanctified."[5] The second aspect in polishing the violin is touch. Grace permeates the cloth, it reaches every fiber, but then the cloth must touch the instrument. This is a role of faith. Faith always involves some sort of touch. Without faith, heaven and earth are separate worlds with nothing to offer each other. Abundant as heavenly grace may be, it is faith that brings it into the world!

Every decision of faith is preceded by grace, just as the polishing cloth must first be moistened. But without decisions of faith, grace comes to nothing. Unless the cloth touches the instrument, the moisture will evaporate without achieving anything. In this same way, the grace meant for a person's life can evaporate without having an effect. That is why the apostle Paul exclaimed: "We urge you also not to accept the grace of God in vain" (2 Corinthians 6:1), and: "Examine yourselves to see whether you are living in the faith. Test yourselves" (2 Corinthians 13:5). If our faith meant nothing to God, then he would just replace it with complacent heavenly actions. Faith is a vital connection to God. Indeed, we have to ask the question that challenges our authority: "Where is your faith?" (Luke 8:25). Faith gives grace to the human heart. It is still a gift, but faith unwraps it, coming alive in what it receives from God. In faith we receive life-giving truth. An inner fire is kindled in our lives, like the one given to the violin's varnish when the damp cloth touches the instrument.

～

Knowledge alone is not enough. Many people have a hollow relationship with God, because their faith has not claimed grace and its life-giving gifts! It is like a violinist who, having been given the most beautiful violin, immediately puts it on display in a glass cabinet. The idea of playing it does not occur to him. Just so, grace without faith remains silent. When it comes to faith, there is such a thing as the sin of not expecting enough.

Faith does not allow things to remain in an inert state of comfort. That would be like allowing the violin to gather dust in the display case; it loses its brilliance, and its fibers harden. I remember a customer who played an expensive, early eighteenth-century Stradivarius. The owner had purchased it merely as an investment, and so it had not been played in many years. Its sound was stubborn, brittle, and hard at first. The violinist to whom it was later given to play told me that it took him a solid nine months of tonal work before it found its dynamic range and velvety tone again.[6]

A violin that is not played for years loses its sound. You can bring it back to life, but you have to play it every day. In this, the violin can be a symbol for faith's new beginnings. To begin to live anew in faith—in stillness, prayer, adoration, love of work, community, the formative power of the Bible—may be difficult at first. Even then, if we do not immediately receive the gift of a free, beautiful sound, it is still our job to awaken the spirit. It is the daily interplay with faith.

Just as there are many styles of music, we must discover the diversity in grace. Spiritual mentoring is certainly one of faith's "etudes." Being close to a spiritual mentor to whom we can confess can awaken the power of thankfulness and repentance in us. It is important to see our lives from both of these points of view: without thankfulness, our negative lens makes the whole world bleak; without repentance, things look much too rosy. Thankfulness has a clarifying power—but what about repentance?

The apostle Paul writes that there is "a repentance that leads to salvation" (2 Corinthians 7:10). Because it comes from the knowledge of grace, it has nothing to do with playing the martyr. There is nothing destructive about the Spirit leading us to a place of inner knowledge. We will recognize when we have strayed or were too cowardly or lazy to believe the promise; we will recognize how we were deprived of the gift for days and years of our life by being blind to what we are commanded to do—but this regret can release the power to awaken the instrument of our lives to new life!

This new life is like the picture that Basil of Caesarea spoke of regaining its beauty after the dirt had been cleaned off; like the violin regaining its sound; this is the renewed sound of faith.

The Talmud says: "Where those who confess stand, those perfect in righteousness have no place!"[7] The holiest space a human can ever enter is the place of insight and repentance. It is the space of grace. Along these lines Paul says: "Do you not realize that God's kindness is meant to lead you to repentance?" (Romans 2:4). When my remorse reaches God's heart, it finds that his grace has already been waiting there for a long time. It is the only place you can bear to face up to things. Grace is not the place of good feelings, but of clear decisions. To ignore this would be to rob the Bible of its prophetic power: "Wash yourselves; make yourselves clean; remove the evil of your doings from before my eyes; cease to do evil, learn to do good; seek justice, rescue the oppressed, defend the orphan, plead for the widow. Come now, let us argue it out, says the Lord: though your sins are like scarlet, they shall be like snow; though they are red like crimson, they shall become like wool" (Isaiah 1:16-18).

In heaven, a single day of repentance can be like a thousand. There are moments of grace in a person's life that fill all of heaven with joy! (See Luke 15:7.) A brittle sound will be awakened to new life. I spoke with Rabbi Baruch about this, and he said: "Yes, that is why a change of heart can be viewed as the strongest force in the universe—it is subject to the human will."[8]

The deepest sin one can commit against oneself or God is to refuse forgiveness: the radical refusal to go through the open door of repentance and forgiveness and enter into God's love. In the most profound sense, forgiveness is God defending me from myself. In it, he overcomes that which destroys me and those around me. But my repentance must recognize what is destructive and call it by name. Everyone who starts the process of being honest with themselves will recognize an inner wound upon which God longs to place the finger of the Holy Spirit, full of gentleness and healing strength. It will be good. But our faith must allow it. It is faith's "yes" that God will hear.

Grace is a gift freely given, never forced. Only our faith can accept this gift, unwrap it, and put it into action.

Daily Practice

The third part of the process is movement. When we practice living in God's Spirit, it resembles the cloth's motion giving the varnish its fire. Neither moisture (grace) nor contact (faith) is sufficient to allow us to cross over from life in the Holy Spirit to "flesh and blood." As obvious as it may seem, in spite of grace, we still have a part to play in our own lives. We are challenged by things that will change us for the better: learning, practicing, doing things the right way. To think that life's issues will be solved in the blink of an eye when you receive the Holy Spirit would not be faith in grace, but faith in a magic trick. Grace does not mean that things happen on their own. Strength arises when we *practice* faith, hope, and love. It is easy to get emotional about grace and convince yourself that you are radical by taking large steps, but it is much more radical to change things in small, simple steps, moving unpretentiously. Large steps often get stuck in the planning stage, but little steps actually happen. Only such a faith has everyday power. The *stimulus and power* of the Holy Spirit find their resonance in our *actions and listening*. Grace does not replace the things of life but is active within them. It may appear as a promise that we trust; a rebuke that we take seriously; a memory that we hold close; a comfort that we receive; a new point of view that we adopt at the right time, creating clarity and orientation; truly practicing things that are still challenging for us. Only the person who takes something to heart and changes his life has shown that he is allowing himself to be touched.

Are we not taught by physics that a force can work in two different ways? It can *move* a body; but if it does not move it, then it will *bend* it. If we do not allow ourselves to be moved, God's power will pull away from us, because otherwise it would bend or break us. We can empower God's power only by allowing ourselves to be moved, to do what is known to us and *practice* what we have been commanded.

I am convinced that times of praise, silence, and prayer during a worship service are meaningful because they make our hearts malleable so that we can be moved. Praise does not abase the hardened heart, but the heart itself softens and makes itself workable in God's hands. Praise is like the hand of the potter kneading the clay to make it soft and malleable, so that a good vessel can be formed. A humble heart is like workable clay.

When God's love is poured out into our hearts, then we will be malleable and yet firm. We are too often as brittle as glass. We go our way and when a crisis hits, we break. At other times we are as soft as wax. We go our way, and when the heat of doubt and hostility comes, we dissolve. In a Spirit-led life we are shapeable, but not weak; we are firm, but not brittle. Being both malleable and firm is a contradiction that can find unity only in a holy heart. An impure heart, however, is full of hardness against others and is as soft as wax in the face of its own convictions.

Threefold Meaning

While polishing the violin, I first saw this marvelous fire and understood the three things that must interweave in a Spirit-filled life: *grace, faith,* and *practice.* It is only through them that an inner fire emerges in our life with God. The varnish itself contains a threefold purpose as well: it serves to *protect* the violin, and it benefits the violin's *sound* and *beauty.*

Protection

The varnish's resins protect the wood from mechanical wear and tear, sweat, and climatic influences.

The "balm" of the Holy Spirit is also like this, for the Bible describes him as a strength that sustains our life's hope when daily life wears on us. We should not succumb to resignation. The Holy Spirit encourages us with his voice. We can hear it. It straightens us up and gives us a spirit of comfort and encouragement when we are surrounded by troubles.

The Sound

The wood fibers are acoustically refined by the varnish. The primer, as it penetrates the wood, has a special meaning here. It influences the spread of the sound waves, affects the damping and cell density, and thereby refines the sound.

The "balm" of the Holy Spirit that the Bible describes is like this: the Spirit is a power that strengthens our calling. God's Spirit teaches and leads us along our path. He inspires every heart that is open to him. We should have the courage to ask him. Why do we not dare to put faith to the test? James encourages us: "If any of you is lacking in wisdom, ask God, who gives to all generously and ungrudgingly, and it will be given you" (James 1:5).

Beauty

The pigments illuminate the varnish with color. The interplay with the light's refraction index makes the instrument beautiful. The pigments have no other purpose than that of pure beauty. The fact that a good varnish has a delightful smell (especially after being polished) is icing on the cake. It is the sweet, spicy aroma of benzoin that maintains the varnish's brilliance. But that is also part of its beauty.

So it is with the "balm" of the Holy Spirit. The Bible says that he is a power effective for our inner beauty, because he leads us to grace and God's love. Love begins where usefulness ends. The violin varnish is a school of wisdom, because true beauty involves the paradox of what is useful by its uselessness. Fulbert Steffensky speaks of this allure when he says: "Beauty is not without results. It builds up our souls."[9] Beauty's meaning is fulfilled exactly because it is free from obvious utility. In this characteristic beauty is a constant metaphor for God's love.

~

I'd like to close with a wonderful Pentecost hymn from the liturgy of the medieval church, the twelfth-century English song "Veni Sancte Spiritus"–"Come, Holy Spirit."[10]

> Come, Holy Spirit,
> and send down from heaven
> the ray of your light.
> Come, father of the poor,
> Come, giver of gifts,
> Come, light of the hearts.
>
> Best consoler,
> Sweet host of the soul,
> Sweet refresher
> Rest in work,
> Cooling in heat,
> Comfort in crying.
>
> O most blessed light,
> Fill the innermost hearts
> Of your faithful.
> Without your power
> Nothing is in man,
> Nothing is innocent.
>
> Clean what is dirty,
> Water what is dry,
> Heal what is wounded.
> Bend what is rigid,
> Heat what is cold,
> Lead what has gone astray.

Grant to your faithful
who trust in you,
your sevenfold holy gift.
Grant us the reward of virtue,
Grant us final salvation,
Grant us eternal joy.

Amen. Hallelujah.

13

The Concert

From "Me" to "You"

Serve one another with whatever gift each
of you has received.

—1 PETER 4:10

*I*N THE PREVIOUS CHAPTER I described polishing the varnish: the last step in producing the violin. Now the sound post is placed, the bridge is cut, the strings can finally be put on, and the first tone sounds!

The All-Fulfilling Sound

When I had just graduated from Mittenwald at the age of twenty, I went on a retreat at a house of the Christustraeger Brotherhood. I didn't really know why; an elderly woman at church just told me that it would do me good, so I went. There must have been at least eighty people there searching for inner strength or some new spiritual direction. At first we felt strange around each other, for we came from various backgrounds, professions, and stages of life. But by the end we grew quite close.

The last evening was reserved for personal presentations. If anyone wanted to contribute, they were invited to do so. An architect displayed a charcoal sketch that he had made during the retreat that reflected a crisis that he was going through. An older lady recited a poem that she had written that afternoon. It went on like that. Many shared in their own way what they had experienced during their time at the retreat: moments of enlightenment or newfound hope. It was a profoundly courageous, authentic evening.

Finally, it was our turn. Jan and I had found piano music by J. S. Bach in the monastery's library that afternoon. We decided to play it, but not on the piano. We did what we could: Jan played guitar and

I played violin. Since Jan is a true jazz musician at heart, we noticed as we rehearsed that, after playing a couple of lines, we continually departed from the written music. The performance that evening, if all went well, would have to come from an inspirational source rather than a set template. But nevertheless, we kept returning to Bach's motifs.

I was nervous. I would have preferred to play from written music. When it was our turn, we started by playing the written part, but then the sound seemed to flow out of its own accord. I closed my eyes and played my melody into the guitar's fascinating harmonies—just as I heard it at that moment. I experienced something entirely new to me. It was as if I had already heard what Jan was about to play just before he played it. How he would guide the harmonies, and the rhythms and melodies that I would layer on them was crystal clear. There was complete unity between the instruments—sometimes quiet, sometimes more intense passages; everything welled up out of listening and the inspiration of being in the moment. We played on with no "safety net." After a while I began to forget that people were listening to us. It was no longer important. It was not a performance but a living occurrence, completely fulfilled in the communal sound. Absolute presence. In retrospect, what amazed me most was that, in the course of playing, I even forgot that I was playing the violin. It was as if the sounds emanated of their own accord. The instrument was part of my body. There was no longer a separation between the two. I was not actually occupied by playing the violin, even though that is exactly what I was doing; rather I was just listening to what was happening and letting it happen.

After a time (probably a long time!), it was like waking up. We played a bit more and then brought it to a close. I was almost startled as I wondered how long we had actually played, unsure as to how the others really felt about it. After a prolonged silence, loud applause followed. On the following day we received feedback from the gardener, a brother of the order, who was usually silent—or at most measured out moderate praise. It was, he said, impossible to put into words how we had made music the previous night. He had the impression that he was in heaven. Something had happened while he was listening. In the end, he implored us to keep making music that way.

Unfortunately, such moments cannot be reproduced on command. It was an extraordinarily insightful week and a special evening of fellowship and trust. We had experienced just how fulfilling making music together can be—especially when it is such an unfettered departure into inspired, communal playing. It is important for me to tell this story in order to differentiate between the "me" and the "you" in which we can live as we choose.

~

Some time ago, I heard an interview with an African jazz musician. I immediately understood her main point about making music. She said: "To improvise is to listen to what is happening right now. Improvisation is dedicating all that I am to the music. People are able to do this when they feel trust and openness. It also means to be quiet when necessary to enable others to enter with their part."

That is the main idea! It is the secret of our calling from "me" to "you": *listen to what is happening, dedicate all that I am.* It is too little to believe that God's Spirit would be satisfied if we discover our individuality *only for ourselves*! Anyone who has experienced fellowship knows that it involves more than just a gathering of individuals. That is, at best, just a group. Fellowship, on the other hand, remains sublime and unparalleled. Out of it comes a communal sound of self-confident service—and, above all, the joy of being excited for each other.

The Metaphor of Music

If we were to shut our eyes in a full concert hall before a concert begins, we would hear an acoustical metaphor. The multitude of human voices is a single subdued rustling. There is a certain fascination in how this set of simmering frequencies develops without any outline or composition. Then the orchestra comes out on stage.

After the entry applause, a short, expectant silence ensues—and then, the sound! Now the instruments' voices can be clearly heard in all their beauty. They join themselves together into a single, vast "you" in the composition. The sound is not a rustling; it is the unified tone of many in *one* work. Now the concept behind the composition can be heard! An orchestra is a powerful metaphor for the secret of the *Spirit-filled organism*, in which—as Paul says—each serves the whole in the measure of his gift, voice, and mission (see 1 Corinthians 12).

During my early years as a violinmaker, I often had the opportunity of experiencing the Munich Philharmonic's rehearsals with Maestro Sergiu Celibidache. Celibidache was one of the great maestros of the twentieth century, and he had built the Munich Philharmonic into a world-class orchestra. The acoustical institute of technology for which I was working at the time was responsible for making the sound adjustments in the Gasteig Cultural Center. It had a vast wide stage, so we mounted huge, transparent "sound clouds" overhead to help the various sections of the orchestra hear each other better. I was allowed to accompany the two acoustical technicians and experience firsthand the changes produced by different placements of the sound clouds. There I sat, witnessing this great maestro's work with the orchestra. He repeatedly interrupted the piece and interpreted the composition. He was mindful of how the musicians could hear each other. An orchestra is like an organism filled with spiritual gifts. Each section has its voice, pauses, and cues, so it is essential that they listen to each other attentively. Sergiu Celibidache knew that this is key to an orchestra's quality. That is why he requested the sound clouds, because the bassists in particular had complained that they could not hear the first violins.

The unity of a symphony depends on each person giving up the right to play whatever they want. If we do not give up this right, then we have no place in the orchestra, and no place in God's orchestra, known as the *Basileia* (kingdom of God), no matter how brilliantly we play. So it is in the symphony to which God calls us. If we do not give up this stubborn right to do or not do as we please, we lose our place in life's orchestra. This requires us to know the composition of God's Word, watch the baton of the Holy Spirit, and practice our part. No instrument plays itself. In these three spiritual truths of composition, baton, and voice we have a metaphor for the "Spirit-filled servant" living in God's will.

~

The concept of the symphony was introduced in the sixteenth century. It is an instrumental work containing multiple movements in which the entire orchestra sounds together. The term comes from the Greek *symphōnein*—"that which sounds together." The profound connection between music and human "interplay" is a familiar theme in the New Testament. Jesus spoke to his disciples using an expression borrowed from music when he said: "If two of you agree [the verb here is *symphonein*, to sound together][1] on earth about anything you ask, it will be done for you by my Father in heaven" (Matthew 18:19). Therefore, a "symphony" is, in biblical terms, the epitome of *becoming one*.

True, some reasons for unity are neither righteous nor good. Yet we have been told: Where there is unity, astonishing things will become possible (see Genesis 11:6)! Jesus prayed for the fellowship of his disciples. He did not pray that they would all be the *same*, rather that they would all be *one* (John 17:21). Being alike does not have much to do with the *symphōnēsis*, the harmony, of which Jesus speaks. The contrabasses are not like the violins, but in the communal work they become one. We should understand God's kingdom as a concert in which we sound together with other people and communities. As in a symphony, each person has his own voice, but the composition becomes audible only through the unity of the instruments. When we become one, the result is a lovely concert. Everyone does not play the same, but they all play together. This represents what is special about a Spirit-filled community: we must listen to each other's callings and our own as they span across the spectrum and the world. Otherwise it is all nothing more than a rustling, seething frequency without any shape.

~

The "you" of the Bible does not always refers to an *individual*. More often it refers to the "you" of the community, the "you" of a life shaped and lived with one another. It is like the resonances in the instruments in an orchestra, where we should each find our space, tone, melody, tone color, and contribution. *The community's "you" is God's true counterpart.* Scripture paints powerful pictures clarifying this basic concept. From a heavenly point of view, communities are living organisms; they are a "you." The letter to the Ephesians, focusing on community more than any other New Testament passage, says: "But speaking the truth in love, we must grow up in every way into him who is the head, into Christ, from whom the whole body, joined and knit together by every ligament with which it is equipped, as each part is working properly, promotes the body's growth in building itself up in love" (Ephesians 4:15–16).

The Resonance Profile

The violin helps us understand these thoughts from Ephesians more deeply. Just as God gives his kingdom its unique sound in every epoch, so my acoustical gift as a luthier consists of adjusting the resonances in the right way to create the instrument's sound. If the Helmholtz resonance is too strong, the violin will boom, but if it is too weak, it will lack breath. If the body's resonance is too strong, the violin will sound brash, but if it is too weak, the tone will be flat. If the resonances in the nasal region are too strong, the tone color will be harsh, but if they are too weak, the tone will be closed and lack courage. If the brilliant resonances are too strong, the tone will be sharp and shrill, but if they are too weak, it will be dull and lack intensity. In short, the resonances must maintain just the right measure and good relationships.

Nothing can be done with one resonance alone. A lovely, extraordinary resonance creates, on its own, an ordinary, one-dimensional sound. Harmony can emerge only when the resonances are ordered and serve each other in the right way. Each person's identity is like

a strong resonance, and just as each resonance bears three characteristics—its frequency, oscillation, and damping—so each individual
forms a triad of *charisma*, *character*, and *competence*.[2] Just as a resonance can give its offering only *in relationship to other* resonances, the
"me" of the individual can only fulfill its calling in the "you" of the
community. For the sake of the community I will work on my *character*, I will master *competence*, and I will ask God for *charisma*. Out
of this triad, I should serve others: "To each is given the manifestation
of the Spirit for the common good" (1 Corinthians 12:7).

Each individual is preeminently needy, so we must respect and
care for one another. To seek this mutual respect is to seek God; to
live in this respect is to find God. There are powerful prophecies
that talk about the "you," such as when God spoke through Jeremiah: "I have loved you with an everlasting love; therefore I have
continued my faithfulness to you" (31:3).[3] We read these words
somewhat individualistically and like to apply them to ourselves,
but the "you" in this passage refers to the community, not to any
loud, individual "me."

Just before this verse, we read: "The people . . . found grace in
the wilderness when Israel sought for rest" (31:2). A community can
rest only when it is living in its calling. There can be neither peace
nor power in avoiding it. Only in our communal life can we overcome and deal with the crises of this needy life. Our calling finds its
basis in our need to become loving people who respect each other
and are there for one another. The individual's crisis is always the
community's calling (see 1 Corinthians 12:26). In this we either prove
ourselves or utterly fail as God's counterpart—as the "you" that we
form together before God.

If we are not ready to truly live in the community and serve it,
then how will we win over a heart to know God? For God shows us
who is in need right now and says: Now the time has come to know
me—not through what you believe, but through what you are doing. At times the prophets confront us with a very uncomfortable
kind of knowledge of the Holy One. The most provocative passage of
the Bible for me is the message that the prophet Jeremiah defiantly
hurled at the unrighteous king: "'He [your father] defended the cause
of the poor and needy, and so all went well. Is that not what it means

to know me?' declares the Lord" (22:16 NIV). Our actions must show us (and God) what we truly believe.

If our faith is, above all, a "me" faith, it should not be surprising when it is shaken. It is faith sent out on thin ice, and it will break when our self-respect disintegrates or when we confront negative circumstances or experiences. We will wonder: "Is God really good? Look how miserable my life is!"

People whose existence revolves only around themselves are not only immature but extraordinarily unsound. If the measure of my trust depends on how well I am doing, then faith must experience crisis. In this immaturity I inform God: "If I am OK, then God is good. I am blessed. If things are bad for me, then God is not there—or he is not blessing me." But if our crises are incorporated into the community, then an individual crisis becomes a test for the *community*! Now the community shows its true self.

We can experience life in God only to the extent to which we live out our calling. Faithfulness to our calling and experiencing truth are inseparable. We will not answer before God merely as many separate individuals, but as the "you" of the community that we form together. It will be a communal fruit! Does it not require an overflowing and shaken down measure of naiveté and stubbornness to understand our lives as something purely individual and all our own? How many good things that I can do or accomplish are only possible due to the blessings and gifts that others have given me? What do I have that I did not receive? To whom does it then belong—to me or to those around me? That is what this metaphor means: making music is a *communal* sound! We are closely intertwined with one another in life's beautiful and mysterious nature, in the good and in the bad. It is the fabric made of the colorful threads of the visible world woven across the invisible threads of grace that support and preserve all things.

The Transcendental "You"

A foreshadowing of our *communal* "you" before God can be found in the letters to the seven churches in the book of Revelation (chapters 2–3). In each letter, Christ depicts himself differently, and each congregation is characterized differently as well. Each hears a different admonition, a different reassurance, and, in the end, a different promise. Interestingly, all these communities are addressed as a singular "you." The letters do not begin: "Write to the people in the congregation at Ephesus . . ." or "Write to the people in Smyrna. . . ." Instead they say: "To the *angel* of the church in Smyrna write . . . ," then "To the *angel* of the church in Pergamum," in Thyatira, in Sardis, in Philadelphia, and finally in Laodicea.

This unusual salutation of "angel" conveys *the transcendental "you"* that every congregation is before God—how it is known, called, and protected. A congregation is not just a sum of individuals; it consists much more of a spiritual attitude, character, and essence before God. It is possible for individuals to have a humble heart for themselves, and yet they build up a congregational "you" that is collectively vain and proud, looking down on others. Thus, the letters to the churches do not criticize and praise the life and faith of the individual, but the reigning spirit in the "you" of the community, its collective sound. Yet this does not remove individual responsibility: on the contrary, it accentuates it! Because now you are not only responsible for yourself before God, but for the community in which you live and interweave with others!

Someday we will see what kind of pattern we created as communities before God; we will see to what extent we experienced grace. The loyalty that we held true, the truth through which we loved, the love that we lived, the difficulties that we overcame—these are the colors of the community.

If we see our faith as only the cultivation of our "private" relationship to God, then it takes on a poor, sickly quality. Every community is a transcendental "you." Partnership, friendship, marriage, a business, a society, a country—all the communities in which I live are a "you" before God. As a violinmaker creates the instrument's tonal color by bringing the resonances (the individuals) into harmonious relations with each other, so must each person and community be brought together to form the joyful creation of "you." Outside the "you" of the community, the self-confident individual will still have a strong resonance, but it will not create a good sound.

It also follows that if one race or nation deems itself to be a loud "me" above all the others, "taking the place of honor" creates a vulgar sound. Various cultures are like resonances in a mighty concert of humanity. The unmistakable tone color of each era arises from the instruments playing together. Amongst the peoples there may be "trombones" and "flutes," "violins" and "timpani." But it is one concert to which humanity of each and every era is called. If an orchestra were large but made up of all the same instrument, the sound would be powerful but terribly poor. We should not think that the aesthetic sound of humanity consists of one homogenous culture. We are called as instruments, not to uniformity, but to unity; we should not all be the same, but we should all be one.

In a certain respect, heaven's signature sound is already audible when a partner, family, friends, community, society, or nation is in concert with others. In the end, "conversion" is always the same: a turning away from a purely individualistic existence. The "me" gets its contour only in the "you." It is not about one loud, solitary voice, but about a communal, unified voice that finds its resonance in the "you." Many individuals acting alone produce nothing but noise. We are called, instead, to be part of one composition. That is the meaning of the *symphonia*. The humility and genius of the kingdom of God and its righteousness consist of every era and every culture contributing its own sound. How does this planet of life sound in our age?

Breathing Praise

The praise of the congregation is the expression of the communal "you" cast in music. The deepest fellowship in church often comes during the time of praise. Your own desire steps aside. The focus is not on preaching or sharing experiences or consulting about tasks. It is purely and simply about praising God together. Now the faith community is audible. We stand together before God in songs of praise, in silence, in listening. It is like a communal breath.

A violinist from the Berlin Philharmonic expressed this in surprisingly similar terms when she described what her career meant to her. "I love the precise moment when the entire orchestra begins to breathe along with the music."[4] This is a musical metaphor for this faith experience. When God's Spirit fills a congregation with praise, it is like breathing together with God.

14

The Sculpture (II)

The Meaning of Beauty

I am the Lord your God,
who teaches you what is best for you,
who directs you in the way you should go.

—ISAIAH 48:17 (NIV)

*H*UMAN HISTORY SHOWS THAT all cultures have developed life rules that go beyond natural instincts. As mindful people we should likewise formulate a sort of rule for our lives—something that states what is essential, what is worth striving for, and what is unconditionally true. You do not have to force yourself to invent a brand-new rule, but whatever you adopt, make it *completely yours*, as if you composed it yourself. Take it to heart daily and know this: if we have forgotten or broken the rule, then we have stolen some beauty away from life; we have damaged something that is lovely and makes life worth living.

Beauty is not random; it, too, follows certain rules. The extent to which these are predetermined by our individual culture or express our innate nature is hotly disputed, but there is no such thing as beauty that does not follow certain rules. I have already described some of these rules with regard to the sound and beauty of the violin. These structural rules have been given to us so that we may learn something deeper. We share responsibility for the beauty of our lives and should therefore ponder the rule of life.

In the sixteenth century Martin Luther said: "Everyone is a theologian."[1] In the twentieth century Joseph Beuys said: "Everyone is an artist."[2] The difference in terms is determined by their context, but the meaning is the same: everyone has the task of interpreting and shaping his or her life. We should all use our spiritual strength to be theologians and artists of our own existence. Thereby a work is drafted. A culture's "Gesamtkunstwerk" depends on how we choose to live together. The phenomenon of being human is shown in this: all cultures have developed life rules that go beyond natural instincts.

347

The Second Nature

The contemporary sculptor Tony Cragg says: "Most of the time I admit I do not know who is leading, me or the sculpture."[3] In his exhibit *Second Nature*[4] we see that a person's culture reveals his second nature. Who has the say? On the one side, culture has the power of forming and interpreting. On the other, nature is powerful with its instincts and needs. These powers work inside of us in an uncertain but captivating struggle. Who has the say in the spiritual world? Is it I, or the sculpture? I do not want to meekly surrender to my own nature, for that would mean to degenerate. It would obliterate my calling to be a theologian and an artist of my own existence.

Concerning the dignity of this calling, Giovanni Pico della Mirandola (1463–1494) wrote:

> The Supreme Maker [said], ". . . I have placed you at the very center of the world, so that from that vantage point you may with greater ease glance round about you on all that the world contains. We have made you a creature neither of heaven nor of earth, neither mortal nor immortal, in order that you may, as the free and proud shaper of your own being, fashion yourself in the form you may prefer. It will be in your power to descend to the lower, brutish forms of life; you will be able, through your own decision, to rise again to the superior orders whose life is divine."[5]

Our nature has been given to us; we cannot do anything about that. But we form ourselves through our culture, and in this there is much that we can do. It leads us to ask: what are the inner laws that our lives should obey? What do we choose? What do we listen to? The one who follows only his nature has made no choices. What do we shape and fashion into the form we have chosen? In the spirit of Luther and Beuys: How do we interpret and form?

A rule of life is neither universally applicable nor final. It is neither an authoritarian claim nor an objective law of nature. It is a witness. Such a witness does not merely list off rules but tells what we will experience with the rule. As a result, all great and holy writings contain not only laws but also stories. The Talmud has two basic, distinct layers: the halakah and the haggadah. In the first we find religious law; in the second we find narratives, examples, legends, and wise sayings that illustrate the laws.

The Gospels are similar. We find many good rules for life in them, but more often we come across life stories. In them we sense the inner struggle between a person's nature and their culture. We can make life's rules our own only if we feel this struggle in our own existence. It must be deeply understood and lived out in one's life. When we not only have knowledge of life's holy rules but also make them a part of our own story, then we allow the door to be unlocked and enter the secrets of the kingdom of heaven (see Matthew 23:13).

Alexandria

Some time ago I wrote a rule of life. I was on my way from Alexandria back to Cairo. I had just had a profound encounter with the nature of beauty. The director of the Bibliotheca Alexandrina, Ismail Serageldin, had invited me to give lectures in the Arts Center about sound and instrument making. The Bibliotheca Alexandrina, with its overwhelming architecture, is certainly one of the most important and most modern Arab cultural centers. Over two thousand people are employed there, not only because it is the most comprehensive, worldwide establishment of Arab culture but also because seven museum districts and eight research institutes are affiliated with it. One of these is the Arts Center, where the topic of the day covered the history, aesthetics, and visions of musical instrument making.

Ismail Serageldin, who holds an impressive twenty-one honorary doctorates, had invited numerous Egyptian composers, musicians, and musicologists to a symposium on questions of beauty and sound. I was on edge but also felt overwhelmingly inspired. After I had spoken about tone modulations one morning, at lunch a musicologist began showing me pictures depicting the concept of the koni. The koni is a traditional Vietnamese string instrument that uses the human mouth as its resonance body in order to physically modulate certain tone colors. Yet again, I had stumbled across something that opened doors to new sound spaces. The koni combines the human body with an instrument's tone. We also started discussing various tonal systems of the Arabian and the Western world, and we continued this passionate musical conversation later at a round table under the warm-hearted and winning leadership of Serageldin. Then our conversation was interrupted temporarily while we toured the museums.

The tour of the Bibliotheca Alexandrina was a class in and of itself. We visited outside of normal operating hours, so these rooms full of the most ancient human manuscripts, holy scriptures, and prehistoric images offered up their very own tranquility and grandeur. It was like diving deep into humanity's culture, spirit, and history.

During that evening's concert, it became clear to me just how art, dance, compositions, music—yes, basically all cultural beauty—are capable of dispelling harmful religious fanaticism. A key element of our humanity suddenly becomes clear in spite of all our differences and painful questioning. It is the shared love for these forms of expressing what is beautiful and highly treasured.

After the concert, we experienced a rehearsal with the newly founded Alexandria Chamber Orchestra and Choir. The voices of the opera kept ringing in my head hours later, deep into the night. The Arabian soloist, who was perhaps fifteen years old, debuted a newly composed piece for choir and orchestra with luminous power. She had a breathtaking voice. The composer had taken part in the symposium that afternoon, but now I could witness him as a conductor. The musicians spontaneously tried out instruments. I had brought along my most recent violin, which had "come into the world" only four days earlier. As the concertmaster tried it out, I became acquainted with the captivating Arab tonal system including micro-tones.

It might sound trite, but I will say it anyway: our technical interests brought us together, but we left this conference as friends—all of us hoping to keep in contact with each other and share what we were working on in the future.

~

During the days we had some free time, and I visited a workshop where papyrus was produced in the traditional manner. The unique rustling, murmuring sound of the papyrus sheets between my fingers took me by surprise. The unusual fiber grain seemed suited to the research I was conducting on resonance plates. During the past few years, I had already tried to bring out musically attractive, almost inaudible nonlinear elements via delicate inner patches of linen, carbon fiber, and parchment. The result was some concert instruments that are still played today by fine musicians in case of "emergency solos." There, in the Alexandrian workshop, future trials using papyrus inserts started developing in my mind's eye. I would work them into some individual vibration antinodes in the front of the violin. I had not planned this, of course, but the sound and feel of the papyrus between my fingers was impossible to ignore. What could I do? I purchased a few large sheets, because the encounter with the rustling papyrus felt like unexpected but very promising guidance for my ongoing experiments with producing new sounds from the violin.

Vibrato

Normally, when we talk about "vibrato," we mean the partial tones produced by the periodic movements of a violinist's left hand, something that string players have used for as long as we can remember. Now, however, I am talking about resonances that "vibrate" in their resonance frequencies depending on the amplitude of excitation. This is not a frequency modulation of the tone's individual components (partial tones), but a frequency modulation of *the resonances themselves* that give weight to the partial tones. This is quite unusual for a violin; only the human voice can do this. To this day, no acoustic instrument in which an oscillator (such as a vibrating string) plays with a resonator (such as the violin's body) can produce a resonant vibrato without the musician activating it with the left hand.

An instrument that could surpass that limit would have a marvelous sound. It would create a strong, controllable partial-tone am-plitude modulation, and thereby a palpable liveliness, even when the musician chooses not to vibrate the note being played! As a result, resonance vibrato would create a modulation of the excitation pat-tern of the inner ear. It would originate from the dynamic of the bow stroke itself, because the violin's body would react completely differently to fortissimo than to pianissimo. My speculation is that, to a large extent, the true liveliness lacking in new, terribly linear, flawless instruments is hiding here. The micro-flaws present in old instruments create a lively-sounding, reactive body that depends upon amplitudes. This effect is called "non-linear damping."

But the maturity that comes with age is not enough. I seek to combine the strength and resilience of young instruments with the adaptable, smooth vibrating resonance peaks found in older instruments. This is the basis of my experimentation for the past few years: to create nonlinear effects out of fibers like flax, hemp, carbon, parchment, and now perhaps papyrus as well. Perfection is linear, but it bores you to death. It lacks the defects that come from nonlinearity and that are indispensable for producing resonance vibrato. The musician should vibrato the string with confidence, but as a violinmaker, I must create a body whose *resonances* vibrate! This would be something new and would have a new quality, a new beauty: the sound of the human voice in the hands of, and joined with the virtuosity of, the violinist!

Life's Rules

Excited and inspired by all these meetings and positive experiences, I wrote down my own "rules of life" on the way to Cairo from Alex-andria. They emerged from the first simple sentence: "*Allow yourself to be led.*" I heard this sentence internally, almost audibly. It was born as if out of nowhere, and the other sentences followed of their own accord. I simply had to write them down, one after another. It was like a brief dictation, and then it was over. Every person may have their rules to clarify their life. These ten points set out the essentials for my own life.

> Allow yourself to be led.
> Make sure that your life remains in adoration.
> Let go of what you want to attain by force. Only selfish things can be compelled; what is essential should be received.
> Do not be slow to do what has been revealed to you.
> Do not think that you are clever; rather, allow God's wisdom to surprise you.
> Be ready to give an answer before God concerning your ways, and do not say that you are morally weak, for you are supposed to live from the forgiveness of sins granted to you and other people.
> Only the pure of heart will see God. Therefore, avoid all bitterness. Be surprised, but don't get worked up. Keep your soul calm through constant prayer.
> Maintain reverence before the mystery and nearness of God and be compassionate to your neighbor and his weaknesses.
> Turn your troubles into prayer requests and let them come to rest before God.
> Mind your tongue so as not to hurt others through gossip, lies, spitefulness, and severity. Do not repeat the bad things you hear. Instead, entrust them to God.

What does it mean to write a rule? "Everyone is a theologian" (Luther). "Everyone is an artist" (Beuys). But what does this mean? It is the courage not to act arbitrarily in the moment according to your own sensitivities. A rule is not objective, but it is not random, either. It is personal, but not individualistic. It must prove itself in life together with others. I feel my life's rule in the "you." There it chafes, it is criticized and confirmed, strengthened, complemented, or tossed aside. But where is objective truth in all this?

Truth

I believe in the sovereignty of truth. It reveals itself, and the willingness to hear these revelations is truthfulness. More important than the question that Pontius Pilate posed to Jesus—"What is truth?"—is a question whose scope fits us better: Am I ready to live out what I know is true? Am I willing to repent when I have strayed from the truth? Or would I rather declare my mistakes and negligence to be "authentic"? The question is: What kind of person am I? The one who is interested in truthfulness will always have to deal with a truth that is *over against him*—against his own questionable actions and inaction. This is a truth that takes a stand against us! If it does not do this, then what is it worth? We need opposition to ourselves! The rule of life offers the opposition that we flawed, weak human beings need when our actions contradict the truth. In this moment, the authentic person repents rather than turning to self-appeasement. A person can show what he truly believes only through repentance. The one who *wants* to do the right thing will recognize if he is following God's will or his own (see John 7:17). God is truth. We do not have command over him. Truth respects our truthfulness and does not ignore it. This is truth's humility. It is precisely in the midst of opposition that I will sense when I need to repent—how I must scrutinize and change my behavior and therefore mature along my path. The fact that truth does not reveal itself as something objective demonstrates its respect for the subject—that is, each person who should be its counterpart as artist and theologian. Truth does not want to abandon the searcher, the one who loves.

The next morning—still strongly under the influence of my positive experiences in Alexandria—it became clear to me that the first rule (*"Allow yourself to be led"*) could be elaborated by the nine points that followed it.

If a person is not awed by the mystery of life, then rules of life will serve neither for internal nor for external things. Without reverence we will not submit ourselves to any truth—or if we do, only to avoid pain. Perhaps pain is the last power able to show us any boundaries. For in a pinch, when our culture fails, our nature will protect life against us. We have contact with the secret fruit of knowledge through our culture's rules and beauty, but the rules and pains of our *nature* forbid that we stretch out our hand and pluck the fruit from the Tree of Life. This inexorable boundary will offer resistance against us like a flaming, flashing sword when our culture fails us.

Life rules are given to cultures like sound-rich instruments that should be played. It is important to decide which rules to adopt—not because they will rule over us, but because they are instruments that we serve as free, unfettered musicians. Their intonation, colorful tones, dynamics, and resilience should be respected for the sake of the beauty of the sound. A musician shows her true greatness by being ready and able to understand and interpret a composition with the gifts entrusted to her. To me, the beauty and fullness of a successful life is the epitome of truth. But this beauty and fullness do not come on their own. Rules are given to us so that we can *practice* in truth.

To disregard the intonation required of us is not proof of freedom or authenticity but of neglect and stupidity. A sign of true self-confidence is being strict with oneself when the rules have been forgotten or forsaken. This strictness is not unmerciful. It is called *repentance*, and it is a holy power. It is strength for our calling. This power eludes the person who is driven by nothing other than himself.

~

And so there I sat, in the café of the Egyptian Museum in Cairo, after this fulfilling conference, contemplating all these good experiences in Alexandria, the rich interactions with others, the shared forms of expression found in music. These encounters had been warm and full of appreciation and mutual inspiration. I believe that, during my presentations, I imparted a deeper understanding of acoustical research and the experiences that inspire me; I passed on strength, and yet I received much strength as well. We found common ground not in the question of truth but in the much more delicate question of beauty.

It is difficult if not impossible to find agreement on questions of religious and ideological truth. These questions are often hard and loud, and we go on the offensive under the power of our grand convictions. We hurt each other in our vulnerability; we try to dominate or desperately assert ourselves. On the surface the issue might seem to be about truth, but in fact it is much more frequently about power. In such a state I do not hear the question that God (through

355

others!) is asking me; rather I reinforce my own position in dogmatic self-evocations. The fight is about superiority, and the weapons are arguments with which opponents humiliate each other.

But perhaps truth and beauty, correctly understood, are much closer together than we think. To see this, we must develop a deeper spiritual understanding of truth in faith. Faith is not about the *right proof* but about the *truthful witness*. Just as science demands *stringent evidence*, spiritual truth demands a *trustworthy witness*. The very person—and not merely his thinking—will be made a witness of spiritual truth. Accuracy is about "experiments and research." It pertains to "deliberating and proving." But truths are much more about what Philip said to Nathanael: "Come and see!" (John 1:46). The Psalms' way of speaking about the experience of God is applicable here: "Taste and see" (Psalm 34:8). I do not live from the bread of knowledge alone, but I also experience assurances that carry me. For the Scriptures, love is the mightiest witness of truth. It eludes all proof, and yet it is the certainty that carries the beloved.

Therefore, it is essential to take two things to heart and live from both of them: accuracy and truth, proof and witness, knowledge and assurance. What we recognize most in spiritual truth is that it *changes* us. In other words, God does not *prove* himself; he *witnesses* for himself. The truth of God seeps sparsely into the intellectual knowledge of human thought, but it is incarnate in human life. The witness to spiritual truth is the changed person! This is summarized in the Gospel of John: "The Word became flesh" (1:14).

When I first became a serious and passionate believer as a thirteen-year-old, my parents were initially dead-set against it. Some time later, my mother said: "There must be something to this faith, because it is obvious how much you are working on yourself. You've changed a lot." My experience was different; I did not find it troublesome—it was not like work—I simply lived out of joy and fellowship with Jesus.

Truth is more deeply layered than is implied by the reasonable and yet superficial question: What is truth? Truth reveals itself through the person—through the *justice, wisdom,* and *beauty* of one's life. The successful, fulfilled life is made manifest in these three aspects, as in the exhilarating communal searching and questioning on my visit to Egypt. We can serve one another in *justice*, inspire each other with the question of *wisdom*, and help each other plumb the deepest human values by exploring the question of *beauty*. Art has this purpose: that we give one another insight into creative power, share passions and forms of expression, and surprise each other and expand the horizons of the beloved. In the end, this is how we witness to that which bears us and, correspondingly, how we suffer when it is painfully lacking in our lives.

My encounters in Egypt were valuable to me because we met each other authentically and passionately in the questions of beauty and calling. But is it like that with religious people? Isn't the question of beauty suspect in religion? Does it not rightly pose the question of truth? The thought of only being able to *witness to* truth and not to *prove* it lies very near to something I mentioned above: the more important I consider a truth to be (and I should consider truth to be important!), the mightier should and must be the power that it arrays *against me*. For this alone will make me compassionate, open, soft, and approachable to others. Only in this state can we be an invitation and enter life's most holy space together—the space in which God testifies to *himself*. How much humility and malleability must be present in a person so that this can happen in the precious moments of grace! For me, to be convincing is to be a witness of truth. But for this, truth must overcome my own falsehood. Otherwise everything is just an assertion, and it will become a spiritual condemnation of those who do not share my truth.

~

After writing down these thoughts and allowing the experiences to resound inside of me, I drank the last of my cappuccino and went into the adjoining Egyptian Museum. What I had just written down resonated there unexpectedly and powerfully. What an entrance hall! The essence of truth stood out in the enormous sculpture of the royal couple, Amenhotep III and Queen Tiye from the Eighteenth Dynasty: *warm, calm*, and *powerful*. The statue's individual idiosyncrasies were overshadowed by the charm of the traditional pose. For one thing, the queen is the same size as the king! For another, the queen's right arm is placed gently behind the king on his lower back, supporting him from behind.[6] Both of these aspects are common for sculptures of Egyptian ruling couples. The queen supports and strengthens the king!

It spontaneously reminded me of the Hebrew concept of the Holy Spirit (*ruach ha-qodesh*, literally holy wind, breath, spirit). In the Gospel of John, Jesus spoke of God's Spirit with feminine attributes when he said that the Spirit of truth is a Comforter (*paraklētos*). There is something supportive and strengthening about this Spirit.

We should learn to be truthful with our own feelings. Maturity means being aware of one's feelings but not being driven about by them. Therefore, truth should touch these feelings because they are a potent power and source of life. It is *here* that truth should support, strengthen, and teach us! Our reasoning should learn to feel, and our feelings should learn to listen; they should learn to listen to truth. Then I will not believe what I feel; instead I will feel what I believe.

After I had intently contemplated the enormous sculpture of the king and queen for quite some time, an Egyptian visitor asked me if I liked it. I awoke from my trance and walked on. Upon entering the hall of miniatures (Hall 19, Vitrine 256) a quiet cry escaped my lips: "For goodness' sake—what beauty!" Made by a kindred spirit thousands of years ago, these figures still speak! Here too I encountered humanity's truth through beauty: sought after, protected, and created metaphorically in art and love. These little figures are like our life's rules: small, and yet possessing great beauty when we decide to live by them.

～

When I returned home from Egypt, I found that Nahla, a composer from Cairo, had already written me with a link to her latest compositions. She asked me to tell her what I thought about the work acoustically, and she agreed to write a composition to be played on my new instruments when they were finished. A few days later I received a letter from Ismail Serageldin thanking me for my visit. But who truly should have been expressing thanks? I had learned, seen, and received so much!

The Beauty of the Encounter

My visit showed me quite clearly that the most important part of beauty is found in our encounters with others. When I ask myself what stood out or what the people of Egypt are like, my first response is to say: They are like me! So similar! Very much so. They are people with the same needs, the same passions, the same troubles and fears, the same hunger and love. My second response is that they have a strong awareness of dignity and respect. Anywhere this offering of honor and respect is felt, the doors of friendship and neighborliness naturally open up. It is important to see how good and instructive this culture is. For me, it was obvious: I had much to learn there, and now I can understand it in a new way. As a foreigner you can shed new light on things that the locals have long since ceased to notice because it is too familiar to them. You notice the inspiring nature of the foreign culture. The papyrus workshop is a metaphor for this. I had known only my own wood, but there I experienced a new, acoustically rich sound. When alert interest is lacking, if you do not come as a listener and a learner, then a plug of arrogance or fear is stuck in your ear; you cannot hear the new sound. And yet there is the beauty of the encounter. It comes from mutual appreciation.

15

Conclusion

A New Beginning

O sing to the Lord a new song;
  sing to the Lord, all the earth.

—PSALM 96:1

*I*N TELLING ABOUT MY WORK as a violinmaker in these pages, I have tried to heed Hundertwasser's advice to which I referred in the preface: "create metaphors for life." A metaphor is dialogue between what is visible and what is invisible. Everything creative is a metaphor if we learn to truly listen and truly see. In the words of the first letter of John, it is "what we have heard, what we have seen with our eyes, what we have looked at and touched with our hands, concerning the word of life" (1 John 1:1).

A "common man" once came to a great Jewish scholar and asked him to teach him the entire Torah while he stood on one leg. He perched on one leg and waited. Then the rabbi referred to Leviticus 19:18, "Love your neighbor as yourself." "That is the whole Torah. The rest is explanation. Now go and learn." Hillel, the rabbi in question, was born in Babylonia in the first century BC. In his youth, he was taken to Palestine where he lived in abject poverty, surviving the early years by means of hard labor. He earned one *tropaïkon* (Latin *victoriatus*, a coin worth half a denarius) each day, half of which he used to support his family while the other half went to pay an entrance fee to the school of Shemaiah and Abtalion.[1] The following story is told of him:

> Hillel wanted to learn but did not always have enough money for entry into the house of teaching. So when he did not have enough money, he climbed onto the roof in order to hear the discussions from there. One winter day, he did not have the entrance money. And so he climbed onto the roof. It began to snow. But he was so deeply engrossed in listening that he did not notice. The next

morning, someone noticed that it was particularly dark in the schoolroom. Then they saw that a half-frozen man was covering the skylight. They brought him down and warmed him up, and from that time on he was allowed to take part in the discussions free of charge. It is also of interest that this happened on the Sabbath, and the scholars said that water could be warmed (although that is forbidden on the Sabbath) in order to wash him and bring him back to life.[2]

Hillel's generous heart and patience became proverbial. He is credited with founding a school for interpreting Scripture that is still of foremost importance today, especially in the field of ethics.

Have we not been accorded a wonderful respect in that we may know what is required of our lives? We experience the beauty of our lives only when we act accordingly. Hillel said: "Go and learn!" Does that sound moral? I hope so! For not just at the end of a fairy tale but at the end of each life, one should ask: "What was the moral of the story?"

In my life, has God's truth drawn out my calling? Was my faith willing to comply and my love able to overcome myself when bidden? And when the strings fall silent, will the tones have wings so that my life will sound anew in God? I will finally see the face of the One who laid lifelong blessings upon me. And he will say: "I saw you living in Christ and now I see you coming through him. Be warmed, for the night was cold. You did not notice, because your passion bore it. Let me bring you to life again. I know you are poor. The entire entry fee has been paid for you. Come in and experience the sacred Sabbath rest. You could have had reason enough to lose your faith and love. How much you did not understand! And yet you persisted. You put yourself to the test and kept the faith. You sustained my love. My Spirit, who rested on you, was startled by your unbelief, but never by your doubt; he was repelled by your hopelessness, but never by your tears; your lack of love pushed him away, but never your weakness. For in him your weakness, despair, and doubts were transformed into pleading that no god could resist. I have heard the sound of your life. So come and rest yourself. Then listen and learn, for tomorrow your calling will dive into a new day."

Acknowledgments

First of all I would like to thank my wife, Claudia, who (humorously, but sometimes with justified annoyance as well!) put up with my mental absence when, in the middle of everyday life, the work on the book swept me away once again.

Special thanks to my friend Ulrich Eggers (Weggemeinschaft Dünenhof Cuxhaven), who has urged me over the years to trade in my chisel for a notebook and pencil every once in a while. Without his encouragement I could never have kept believing that this violinmaker could carve a book. Special thanks to Donata Wenders as well for understanding my work and transforming it lovingly into pictures! Thanks to the publisher Winfried Nonhoff (Kösel-Verlag) for his faith in my first book and his helpful support.

The English version of the book would not have come into being without the epic devotion of Janet Gesme. Her determination to understand how a devastating personal crisis could become an opportunity and a calling made an English translation possible in the first place. After her surprising initial contact, numerous phone calls, and extended email discussions, I finally met this wonderful person face to face when she visited my wife and me in my workshop in southern Germany. My sincere gratitude to Ulla Mundil and David Jacobsen for making this book possible, and to all those who volunteered their time and passion to help Janet in the fine sanding and polishing of this translation, above all William Paul Young.

Notes

Preface

1. WhiteBox, Kultfabrik, Munich. Exhibition from October 16, 2004, to January 23, 2005.
2. Translated freely from Bonaventure, *Collationes in Hexaemeron* 13.12.

Chapter 1

1. Isaiah says, "Seek the Lord while he may be found, call upon him while he is near" (55:6). Amos: "For thus says the Lord to the house of Israel: Seek me and live" (5:4). Jeremiah: "You will seek me and find me; when you seek me with all your heart, I will be found by you, says the Lord" (29:13-14a RSV).
2. Chuang-tzu, *Reden und Gleichnisse des Tschuang-Tse*, ed. Martin Buber (Zürich: Manesse Verlag, 1951), 151.

Chapter 2

1. Medullary rays, also called vascular or pith rays, are cell structures found in certain species of wood that conduct substances between the inner and outer layers of the tree.
2. Herman Hesse, *Bäume*, ed. Volker Michels (Frankfurt am Main, 1984), 9-10.
3. Fulbert Steffensky, *Feier des Lebens* (Stuttgart, 2003), 31, 32, 37.
4. The great hymn *Veni Creator Spiritus* calls this to mind by speaking to the Holy Spirit with the words: "Kindle a light in our senses." The hymn is describing the work of the Holy Spirit in an individual's life. It enlightens the spirit (see Hebrews 6:4 and 2 Corinthians 4:6). On Pentecost, according to Orthodox Christianity, the whole world received the baptism of light. See Raniero Can-

talamessa, *Come, Creator Spirit: Meditations on the Veni Creator* (Collegeville: Liturgical Press, 2003), 5, 41–42.

Chapter 3

1. Umberto Eco, *History of Beauty*, trans. Alastair McEwen (New York: Rizzole, 2004), 72.

2. Born January 27, 1687, in Eger; died August 19, 1753, in Würzburg. Some of his structures include the Basilica of the Fourteen Holy Helpers, the Residence, and the Pilgrimage Church in Würzburg, and the Münsterschwarzach Abbey. (Balthasar Neumann's portrait appeared on the 50 Mark bill.)

3. For more information see Juan G. Roederer, *The Physics and Psychophysics of Music*, 4th ed. (New York: Springer Science + Business Media, 2008), 11–13.

4. Without mastering this ability, a violinist's playing would never be "clean." Intonation demands that the musician have the ability to hear the note that he is about to play ahead of time.

5. Herein lies an essential difference to electric violins. The tone of an electric instrument speaks significantly faster, because it is not impaired by an acoustic resonating body. But the fact that this "impairment" is missing is exactly what makes the tone flat and ordinary.

6. These stories can be found in Genesis 28 and Exodus 3 and 20.

7. Raniero Cantalamessa, *Come, Creator Spirit* (Collegeville: Liturgical Press, 2003), 278.

8. During the trial sentencing Jesus to death he answered the Roman judge: "My kingdom is not from this world. If my kingdom were from this world, my followers would be fighting" (John 18:36).

9. For the question as to what extent Jesus brought a new morality or wisdom to the Judaism of his day, see David Flusser, *Jesus* (Jerusalem: Magnes, 2001).

10. Nicolás Gómez Dávila, *Escolios a un Texto Implícito* (Bogotá, Colombia: Villegas Editores, 2001), 171.

11. The Septuagint (the Greek translation of the Old Testament) and the original Greek New Testament texts use the Greek word *psychē* for the word "soul." This term appears more frequently in the original manuscripts than many current translations imply. In other passages it is translated as *life*, as in Luke 17:33 and John 10:17.

12. Martin Buber, *I and Thou* (New York: Charles Scribner's Sons, 1958), 3–4.

13. According to Merriam Webster, legalism is "strict, literal, or excessive conformity to a religious or moral code—the institutionalized *legalism* that restricts free choice."

14. Chuang-tzu, *Reden und Gleichnisse des Tschuang-Tse*, 142.

Chapter 4

1. This spiritual tension has been recognized from the beginning. Leo Baeck writes: "That which God the creator gave and that which the Commanding One commands, constitute the life of man. Man experiences both love and justice as the revelation of God. As expressed in his two ancient biblical names, God is simultaneously the eternal Being, *Yaveh*, and the eternal Goal, *Elohim*. The Rabbis interpreted the first to mean eternal love and the second to mean eternal justice, which are the source and path of life. It is the one and only God who manifests himself in both aspects. To concentrate on the one aspect and neglect the other would mean to deprive the revelation of God and our faith in him of their unity." Leo Baeck, *The Essence of Judaism* (New York: Schocken Books, 1948), 140.

2. Max Frisch, *I'm Not Stiller*, trans. Michael Bullock (Orlando: Harvest, 1994), 215.

3. Baeck, *The Essence of Judaism*, 52.

4. *Confessions* appeared around AD 400. It describes a sort of self-observation phase in the spiritual development of Augustine, who lived and worked in Africa in what is now Algeria.

5. Brother Roger of Taizé, *The Sources of Taizé—No Greater Love* (Chicago: Ateliers et Presses de Taizé, 2000), 37.

6. Paraphrased from Geri Keller, *Father: A Look into the Heart of God* (Morning Star Publications, 2004), 39–40.

7. See Thorleif Boman, *Hebrew Thought Compared with Greek* (London: SCM, 1960), 192: "That God was in the person Jesus Christ and revealed his essence through him is conceived in a Greek way; that he sent his Son and through him actualized his will is conceived in an Israelite way." Boman considers the scandal of Christian understanding to be that these two ways of thinking are found together in the New Testament.

Chapter 5

1. The term "eigenvibration" (also called "mode of vibration") is used when studying complex vibrating systems to identify and analyze individual, unique vibrations produced by a set of factors. Metaphorically, the entirety of eigenvibrations of a certain violin could be called its "acoustical fingerprint." Eigenvibrations are standing waves that result from the unique material properties (like stiffness and density of the wood) and the geometrical properties (like plate thickness, size, and arching) of the instrument's body. Eigenvibrations can be made visible by means of sophisticated laboratory methods like modal analysis.

2. "Eigentones" (or "tap-tones") are the sounds produced by eigenvibrations when tapping the structure.

3. For more information about acoustical details, see Martin Schleske,

"Speed of Sound and Dampening of Spruce in Relation to the Direction of Grain and Rays," *Catgut Acoustical Society Journal* 1, no. 6, series 2 (November 1990).

4. This is well represented in the book of Proverbs (chapter 8), the book of Job (chapter 28), and the book of Wisdom from the Apocrypha (chapter 7).

5. The line comes from Hundertwasser's famous manifesto, "Dein Fensterrecht–deine Baumpflicht" (Your Window Right–Your Tree Duty) of 1972, which ends with the declaration: "The human-tree relationship must take on religious dimensions. Then you will finally understand the sentence: 'The straight line is godless.'"

6. Hermann Cremer, *Biblico-Theological Lexicon of New Testament Greek*, 4th English ed. (Edinburgh: T. & T. Clark, 1962), 190–91.

7. Baeck, *The Essence of Judaism*, 224.

8. Sanhedrin 65a. See also Irun R. Cohen, *Rain and Resurrection: How the Talmud and Science Read the World* (Austin: Lands Bioscience, 2010), 37.

9. The prophecies against unrighteousness in Scripture burn with this conviction: "I know that the Lord maintains the cause of the needy, and executes justice for the poor!" (Psalm 140:12). The Psalms and the prophets are on fire because "the Lord is a stronghold for the oppressed" (Psalm 9:9) and he does not "forget the oppressed" (Psalm 10:12). Yes, the question "Who is our master?" (Psalm 12:4) is nailed down by the Lord's answer: "'I will now rise up,' says the Lord; 'I will place them in the safety for which they long'" (12:5). The words "rise up" imply crisis and judgment. Therefore, the effects of prophecy are neither polite nor harmless: "Hear this word, you cows of Bashan who are on Mount Samaria, who oppress the poor, who crush the needy!" (Amos 4:1). "The spoil of the poor is in your houses" (Isaiah 3:14). Prophetic speech rarely speaks of "poverty and riches" but, in contrast, of "the impoverished (oppressed) and enrichment (grabbing wealth)!" The prophets recognize and criticize unrighteous structures. It is not enough for them to occupy us with the question of what we should give the poor, but they ask when we will stop plundering them through our systems: "Ah, you who join house to house, who add field to field, until there is room for no one but you, and you are left to live alone in the midst of the land!" (Isaiah 5:8).

10. A cycloid is formed when a circle rolls in a straight line and the path of a single point on that circle is traced. If the point is on the inside of the circle, then a cycloid with "channeling" develops. The great Italian masters of the seventeenth and eighteenth centuries (most notably A. Stradivarius, J. B. Guadagnini, G. Guarneri del Gesù, and D. Montagnana) oriented themselves using the cycloid to develop the cross-arching of their violins. Although cycloid curves were already used in ancient times (as in Greek architecture), a successful mathematical formula representing this type of curve was first developed in the seventeenth century. In 1658, Blaise Pascal challenged the mathematicians of Europe in a wager to come up with an equation to describe it, and so almost all of the important mathematicians of the seventeenth century, including Descartes, Leibniz, and Newton, worked on it.

11. Compare with John 7:17 and John 14:21, 23.

12. Cyril of Jerusalem (fourth century AD), *Catecheses* 16.16. Quote from Cantalamessa, *Come, Creator Spirit*, 282.

13. Cantalamessa, *Come, Creator Spirit*, 264.

14. In the original texts, there are different terms for the concept of sin. One of the main Old Testament words for sin (Hebrew: *hata'*) means *miss the mark* or *do wrong*. Another term (Hebrew: *pasha'*) means *break away from* or *pull back*, and by extension *sin against*.

15. Augustine, Sermon 80, 7.

16. The Book of Wisdom is a noncanonical book of the Scriptures that was written in Greek in 50 BC by Jews in the Egyptian diaspora. A clear echo of this text is tangible in the apostle Paul's discourse on "The Gift of Love" (1 Corinthians 13, circa AD 55).

17. See Zechariah 4:6; Isaiah 30:1–7; Matthew 11:28–30.

18. Martin Luther and almost all German translations use the word *Gesetz* (law) where the original Hebrew text has *Torah*. Other Jewish translations are different: Leopold Zunz translates *Torah* as *Lehre* (teaching); see *Die vierundzwanzig Bücher der Heiligen Schrift* (Basel, 1995). Martin Buber and Franz Rosenzweig translate it as *Weisung* (instruction); see *Die Schrift*, first edition (1925–1929).

19. Chapter 8 of this book addresses this topic thoroughly ("Reworking the Violin: The Pain and Crisis of Faith").

20. Mark 2:27 has this tone as well: Jesus said, "The sabbath was made for humankind, and not humankind for the sabbath." In alluding to this saying, David Flusser says that Jesus's words were definitely not outside of Judaism. Learned Jewish rabbis had said: "The Sabbath has been handed over to you, not you to the Sabbath." *Mekhilta* on Exodus 31:14 (103b). See David Flusser, *Jesus*, 62.

21. Augustine, *Tractates on the First Letter of John* 7.8.

22. Babylonian Talmud, Pirqe Avot 1:3.

23. See Isaiah 22:13 and 1 Corinthians 15:32.

24. In the parable of the laborers in the vineyard (Matthew 20:1–16), Jesus provoked the protest of an immature faith fixed on retaliation and rewards in a similar manner.

25. With this I am not evaluating a question of truth, but merely saying that rewards and punishments must be discussed only with those who are immature!

Chapter 6

1. Spiegel Online, September 11, 2005. Interview by Jürgen Kesting for the *Frankfurter Allgemeine Sonntagszeitung*, http://www.spiegel.de/kultur/musik/interview-mit-anne-sophie-mutter-ist-ihre-geige-erkaeltet-a-374114.html.

2. Chuang-tzu, *Reden und Gleichnisse des Tschuang-Tse*, 223.

3. *The I Ching, or the Book of Changes*, Bollingen Series 19, trans. Richard Wilhelm and Cary F. Baynes (Princeton: Princeton University Press, 1967), 136. *The Book of Changes* (*I Ching*) is the oldest Chinese book and is undisputedly one of the most important books of world literature, containing mature wisdom from many centuries. Both branches of Chinese philosophy, Confucianism and Taoism, have their common roots in it. As C. G. Jung put it in his foreword to the volume, it is a book of wisdom used "throughout the millennia of Chinese civilization."

4. Babylonian Talmud, Avodah Zara 3a.

5. Friedrich Schiller, *Letters upon the Aesthetic Education of Man*, letter 15, http://public-library.uk/ebooks/55/76.pdf.

6. This idea is central to the biblical concept of God's relationship to the world. God is not only facing the world, but also not simply *in the world*. He is much more *through the world*. As the apostle says: "one God and Father of all, who is above all and *through all* and in all" (Ephesians 4:6). This means that we are present through him, but it says the other as well, that God is present through us.

7. Buber, *I and Thou*, 136–37.

8. Colin McGinn, *Wie kommt der Geist in die Materie?* (Munich, 2005).

9. Chuang-tzu, *The Complete Works of Chuang Tzu* (New York: Columbia University Press, 1968), 201.

10. Pierre Itshak Lurçat, *Rabbinische Weisheiten* (Munich, 2003), 15.

11. Fulbert Steffensky, *Schwarzbrotspiritualität* (Black Bread Spirituality) (Stuttgart, 2005), 17.

12. For more information, see http://www.jesuiten.org/jesuitenmission.ch /pdf/JHS2007_3.pdf.

13. Amazing photos of these children can be seen at https://geigenkinder .wordpress.com/.

14. See http://www.eugen-papst-schule.de/.

15. Interview with Helmut Mauró, *Süddeutsche Zeitung* 258 (November 9, 2007): 16.

16. Brother Roger of Taizé, *The Sources of Taizé*, 9.

Chapter 7

1. For example, three of the 81 passages of the *Tao Te Ching* are about the human heart. In the original Greek version of the New Testament, the word "heart" (*kardia*) appears in 148 places; in the Old Testament it appears 273 times, 55 in the Torah alone and 88 times in the prophets (Isaiah to Malachi).

2. Chuang-tzu, *Reden und Gleichnisse des Tschuang-Tse*, 86.

3. The Hebrew word for Satan is like "accuser." He is, as we see in the books of Job and Zechariah, the accuser in the heavenly courts, testing the religious

integrity of humans and charging people with sins. See also Revelation 12:10 and Mark 8:33.

4. Biblical Scriptures (especially Isaiah) show the ambiguity in the servant of God. On the one side, the servant of God is the One called by God; on the other it is the called community, God's people. There is one thing they always have in common: there is no space "free of suffering," in which the calling of God's servant can be lived out, because it is in this dark world that God's servant will become perfectly unified with God's righteousness. See Isaiah 41:8-10; 42:1-9; 44:1-5; 49:1-6; 50:4-11; 52:13-53:12. The New Testament quotes this last passage from the Old Testament (directly or indirectly) more often than any other. It refers directly to Jesus.

5. Thoughts about God limiting and relinquishing himself, making the creation of the world possible, are not new. Rabbi Baruch ben Mordechai Kogan introduced me to the ideas of the famous sixteenth-century Rabbi Yitzchak Luria about suffering as an act of creation. His student Chaim Vital wrote down his teachings.

6. Origen was a Greek scholar and Christian theologian born in AD 185 in Alexandria. He died in 254 from the effects of torture that he had suffered during the Christian persecution under Emperor Decius.

7. Quoted in Raniero Cantalamessa, *Life in Christ: A Spiritual Commentary on the Letter to the Romans* (Collegeville: Liturgical Press, 1990), 91.

8. The common distinction between "active" and "passive" is unsatisfactory here. If someone can prevent something but does not do so, he is an active participant in the event by virtue of his negligence. This parable asks instead: what *restrains* God from doing what he *can* do?

9. Klaus Berger, *Wozu ist Jesus am Kreuz gestorben?* (Gutersloh, 2005), 36.

10. Lao Tzu, *Tao Te Ching* (New York: Vintage Books, 1972), section 81.

11. Chuang-tzu, *Reden und Gleichnisse des Tschuang-Tse*, 12.

12. God's proper name as taught by Hebrew thought is based on Moses's encounter with God in the burning bush in the wilderness of Sinai. God commanded Moses to return to Egypt to free the Israelites from slavery. This is a metaphor for the slavery of the human existence to the power of sin. Moses balked and asked God: "When the people ask me, 'What is his name?' what shall I say to them?" God answered: "I AM Who I AM. Thus you shall say to the Israelites, 'I AM has sent me to you'" (Exodus 3:14-15).

13. Hans Jonas, *Der Gottesbegriff nach Auschwitz. Eine jüdische Stimme* (The Concept of God after Auschwitz: A Jewish Voice) (Suhrkamp, 1987), 33ff.

14. There are two distinct terms for time in the Bible. *Chronos* is chronological time—one could say it is the ticking clock. *Kairos* is fulfilled time. In the concept of *kairos*, time is not *quantitative* but *qualitative*. It is the meeting of God and man. The crucial quality in *kairos* is not *how long* life is but *what is fulfilled in it*. The question of lived faith will always be one of how much space and privilege we give these very different concepts of time in our daily lives. In the Greek

translation of the Old Testament (the Septuagint), *kairos* appears three times as often as *chronos* (about 300 instances). In the New Testament we find *kairos* in about 100 passages as opposed to 60 that have the word *chronos*.

15. Klaus Berger, *Wer war Jesus wirklich?* (Gütersloh, 1999), 73.

16. Luther translates *elachistos* as *der Geringste* (1 Corinthians 15:9), which has the meaning of "the least," "the unimportant," or the "quite small, very unimportant" (see Matthew 5:19). It can also be translated as "downright worthless" or "very least" (Ephesians 3:8).

17. An echo of this thought can be found in Paul's statement that Christ has been active in a hidden way from the beginning of the appearance of the human form (see 1 Corinthians 10:4, 9). Augustine said as well in *Retractions* chapter 12: "For what is now called Christian religion existed even among the ancients and was not lacking from the beginning of the human race until Christ came in the flesh." Augustine, *Retractions* (Washington, DC: Catholic University of America Press, 1968), 52.

18. As much as this new counter-meaning explodes Hebrew thought, it can yet be seen in the Torah: "Anyone hung on a tree is under God's curse" (Deuteronomy 21:23).

19. Plato, *The Republic*, trans. Desmond Lee (New York: Penguin, 1974), 44.

20. Plato, *The Republic*, 45.

21. Plato, *The Republic*, 44.

22. Plato, *The Republic*, 45.

23. Section 78. This translation of the *Tao Te Ching* is a compilation of translations done by Robert Eno, Lin Yutang, R. B. Blakney, Jane English, Gia-Fu Feng, and Richard Wilhelm with special help from Meiru Jia and Lin Hong.

24. Martin Luther, *Book of Concord*, article 11.

25. Jonas, *Der Gottesbegriff nach Auschwitz*, 9.

26. This is what the famous passage in 1 John says: "Whoever does not love does not know God, for God is love" (4:8), and "God is love, and those who abide in love abide in God, and God abides in them" (4:16).

27. Buber, *I and Thou*, 135.

Chapter 8

1. The Holy Spirit is feminine in Hebrew (*ruach ha-qodesh*: literally, "holy breath"). Count Zinzendorf (1700-1760) spoke of the "Holy Spirit's role as Mother." It is not a question of whether God is "masculine" or "feminine," for God is neither. It is about the principal parable of faith, that God is completely father and completely mother. There are situations and events that shape our faith in which God must be more of a Mother than a Father to us. The image of Motherhood arises not only because, as children of God, we are "born of God" (John 1:13; 1 John 3:9). The

prophets reveal these characteristics as well: "as a mother comforts her child, so I will comfort you" (Isaiah 66:13; see also 42:14).

2. Hans Küng, *What I Believe*, trans. John Bowden (New York: Continuum, 2010), 153.

Chapter 9

1. Gerrit Pithan, "Brief an die Mitglieder der Künstlergruppe," *Das Rad*, August 2008, Editorial.

2. Baeck, *The Essence of Judaism*, 36.

3. Television program (3SAT) from August 10, 2005, about the Dalai Lama's seventieth birthday.

4. Such as in Galatians 3:11; Romans 1:17; Hebrews 10:38. The superior importance of faith is also expressed by Jesus when he tells his disciples: "I tell you, [God] will quickly grant justice to them. And yet, when the Son of Man comes, will he find faith on earth?" (Luke 18:8).

5. See Hebrews 5:8.

6. Matthew 8:10; Mark 6:6; compare with Matthew 15:24-28; Luke 9:31; John 8:28.

7. http://thecatholicreader.blogspot.com/2013/06/st-vincent-de-paul -quotes.html.

8. http://www.vatican.va/spirit/documents/spirit_20010821_vincenzo-paoli _en.html.

9. J. P. Vijn, *Carlyle and Jean Paul: Their Spiritual Optics* (Philadelphia: John Benjamins, 1982), 232.

10. A note to classify such experiences may be necessary: of course, for the thinking person, the question arises as to whether such experiences are normal and healthy. Due to neurobiology and psychiatry, we are familiar with diseases that include hearing voices. This kind of "auditory hallucinations" can result in slavery to the disease for the one afflicted, and it can result in serious danger for those around him or her. When a person is no longer able to *differentiate* between visions and reality, this question becomes deadly serious. Inspirational Christian experiences are very different from this lack of ability to differentiate. It would be a frightening and cynical God who would take away our ability to recognize the difference between "visions" and "reality." External hearing is not the same thing as spiritual listening. One is quite clearly different from the other, even if both can create a very clear experience. It is a gift of God to be able to perceive events and situations through inner images and to listen with the ears of the heart. This gift is not an escape from reality, but quite the opposite: it is a deepening awareness of our life's calling in the here and now.

11. The Midrash interprets religious texts in rabbinic Judaism. The word *midrash* stems from the Hebrew verb *darash* (to seek, to ask). It is meant to delve

deeply into the Holy Scriptures, as well as into the results of this research: hence literary works including Bible interpretations. The majority of the written documents in the Midrash stem from rabbinic Judaism starting in AD 70. These consist of independent collections of texts that developed along with the Midrash and the Talmud. Palestine is the predominant place of origin for the Midrash. G. Sternberger, *Einleitung in Talmud und Midrasch* (Munich, 1992).

12. In G. Sternberger, *Einleitung in Talmud und Midrasch*, 127, paragraph 9.

13. Heidi Zimmermann, *Thora und Shira—Untersuchungen zur Musikauffassung des rabbinischen Judentums* (Bern: Peter Lang, 2000), 340.

14. A quote from my wife: "Finally your world is spinning around me!"

15. Fulbert Steffensky, *Wo der Glaube wohnen kann* (Stuttgart, 2008), 27.

Chapter 10

1. Most of Antonio Stradivarius's violins have acquired their names over the course of centuries, often from a musician who once played it. The "Schreiber" Stradivarius from 1712 belonged to someone of that name who lived in St. Petersburg during the nineteenth century. It was also played in the Russian Court by the famous composer Henry Wieniawski. There are superb recordings of this violin from the 1970s in which Pinchas Zuckerman plays it along with Jacqueline du Pré on cello and Daniel Barenboim on piano.

2. J. S. Bach, Partita No. 2, BWV 1004, fifth movement.

3. Helga Thoene, "Ciaccona—Tanz oder Tombeau," *Cöthener Bach-Hefte* 6 (1994) and "Der verschlüsselte Lobgesang. Sonata 1 in G Minor," *Cöthener Bach-Hefte* 7 (1998). Christoph Poppen and the Hilliard Ensemble performed Helga Thoene's analysis on February 12, 2005, for the first time in concert. The chorale quotation was written into the violin voice and performed by the Hilliard Ensemble in lovely, vibrato-less purity and great clarity over which the violin sings out. The CD appeared in 2001 (*Morimur*, J. S. Bach, Christoph Poppen, violinist, Hilliard Ensemble, EMC Records GmbH, New Series 1765, 461 895-2).

4. Proverb of Rabbi Yisroel Salanter. Pierre Itshak Lurçat, *Rabbinische Weisheiten*, 15.

5. The verb "to tolerate" comes from the Latin word *tolerare*, to bear, to endure, to sustain.

6. This was also the case with the most precious thing that the Israelites received—the Torah. It was given on the "outside." That is why it is said in rabbinic Judaism: "How can we gather that even a foreigner who occupies himself with the Torah is like the High Priest? It is said: 'You should preserve my sayings and my laws that the person should practice and live in them.' It has not been said: Priests, Levites, or Israelites, but the person. From this you can learn that even a foreigner that learns the Torah is like the High Priest. God wants to reach not only Israel, but all of humanity with the message of his will: 'They camped in

the wilderness, the Torah was given in the open air for all to see on a location that belonged to no one.' If it had been given in the land of Israel, then it would have said to the nations that they do not have any part in it; therefore it was given out in the open, for all to see, in a location that belonged to no one. And whoever will accept it, come and accept it" (Midrash Mekilta R. Yishmael on Exodus 19:2 and 20:2).

7. Chuang-tzu, *Reden und Gleichnisse des Tschuang-Tse*, 235. Martin Buber treats the encounter between Confucius and Lao-Tse as a historical event.

8. *Tao Te Ching*, section 28.

9. Martin Buber, *The Way of Man according to the Teaching of Hasidism* (New York: Citadel Press, 1994), 10.

10. Rainer Maria Rilke, *Letters to a Young Poet* (New York: W. W. Norton, 1954), 27.

11. For more information, you can read his fascinating autobiography: Gabriel Weinreich, *Confessions of a Jewish Priest* (Cleveland: Pilgrim Press, 2005).

12. Gabriel Weinreich, "Musical Acoustics in the Twentieth Century," *The Journal of the Acoustical Society of America* 106, no. 4 (1999): 2143.

13. The negation that God declares against sin is a characteristic of grace because this "no" is grounded in God's desire *to create space for life*. The Bible calls this negation "the wrath of God." (See also note 14 from chapter 5 for more on the biblical concept of sin.)

Chapter 11

1. Mastic gets its name from this characteristic: *mastichan* = to gnash the teeth (Greek). It is known as Arabic chewing gum.

2. The German word for amber is *Bernstein*, from the medieval word *bernen* meaning "to burn." In old varnish recipes it is also called *Angststein* (fear stone).

3. Jakob August Otto, *Über den Bau der Bogeninstrumente, und über die Arbeiten der vorzüglichsten Instrumentenmacher* (Jena, 1828).

4. Jean Felix Watin, *Der Staffirmaler oder die Kunst anzustreichen, zu vergolden und zu lackieren* (Leipzig, 1774), 192.

5. Compare with Eszter Fontana, Friedemann Hellwig, and Klaus Martius, *Historische Lacke und Beizen* (Nuremberg: The German National Museum, 1992), 12.

6. The dissolving of spruce resin and mastic in naphtha is described in the Marciana manuscript (1550).

7. Watin described dissolving sandarac in alcohol in 1722.

8. Le R. P. Bonanni, *Traité des vernis* (1713).

9. Stewart Pollens, *The Manual of Musical Instrument Conservation* (Cambridge: Cambridge University Press, 2015), 330.

10. These measurements give information about vibration characteristics and therefore of sound causation. See Martin Schleske, "On the Acoustical

Properties of Violin Varnish," *Catgut Acoustical Society Journal* 3, no. 6, series 2 (November 1998).

11. There are easily dozens of varnish resins and oils that could be listed, each of "its own kind." The Scriptures also include countless descriptions of gifts. My account is not meant to be an exhaustive kind of typology but to clarify the beauty and diversity of the gifts promised to our spiritual communities.

12. Raniero Cantalamessa, *Die Kirche lieben: Meditationen zum Epheserbrief* (Freiburg, 2005), 38.

Chapter 12

1. One of the most beautiful and profound works about the Holy Spirit that I know is the book by Raniero Cantalamessa, *Come, Creator Spirit: Meditations on the Veni Creator* (Collegeville: Liturgical Press, 2003).

2. One of the prominent church fathers from the fourth century.

3. Flesh (*sarx*) is not the same as the body (*soma*). The differentiation in the New Testament is important, because otherwise one can wrongly interpret many passages encouraging life that is at enmity with the physical body. The "fleshly" or "carnal" life speaks of a whole person (including body, spirit, and soul) who has set himself at enmity with God. "The mind that is set on the flesh is hostile to God" (Romans 8:7).

4. Quoted in Cantalamessa, *Come, Creator Spirit*, 5, 249.

5. Cantalamessa, *Come, Creator Spirit*, 249.

6. Many violinists confirm that you need a good half hour every day with a well-played instrument before it "wakes up" to the playing and the sound opens up to the fullness it had on the previous day.

7. Babylonian Talmud, Berakhot 5:155, 34b.

8. Rabbi Baruch ben Mordechi Kogan, personal conversation, November 2009.

9. Steffensky, *Wo der Glaube wohnen kann*, 36.

10. Attributed to the Archbishop of Canterbury, Stephen Langton (1150–1228).

Chapter 13

1. The root of this word is also used in the New Testament in the sense of *agreement* (2 Corinthians 6:15) or *match* (Luke 5:36). Pavlos Hatzopoulos, a friend of mine from Greece who is a concert pianist, confirmed this linguistic root of the verb *symphōnein* and added: "It is used in the sense of 'identifying completely' with another; as 'sounding a tone'; 'contribute to musical harmonies.' The noun *symphōnein* means harmony with oneself and others in thoughts, words, and deeds."

2. This triad harkens back to my spiritual mentor, Helmut Nicklas, who had a significant impact on my life.

3. Another way to translate this verse is this: "Therefore I pull you through with kindness."

4. Kotowa Machida, first violin, Berlin Philharmonic. Concert program of the Venus Ensemble, Gauting, September 21, 2007.

Chapter 14

1. "Omnes dicimur Theologi." WA 41, 11,9-13 (from a sermon on Psalm 5, January 17, 1535).

2. Joseph Beuys, *Jeder Mensch ein Künstler* (Frankfurt am Main, 1975).

3. Roderick Conway Morris, "Inventing a 'New Visual Language,'" *New York Times*, October 13, 2010.

4. *Second Nature* exhibit, Staatliche Kunsthalle (State Art Gallery) in Karlsruhe, Germany, 2009.

5. Giovanni Pico della Mirandola, *Oration on the Dignity of Man*, trans. A. Robert Caponigri (Chicago: Regnery, 1956).

6. The area of the body where the queen's hand is placed is referred to in the Bible as the "reins," which *Easton's Bible Dictionary* defines as: "the kidneys, the supposed seat of the desires and affections; used metaphorically for 'heart.'" The "reins" and the "heart" are often mentioned together, as denoting the whole moral constitution of the human being. In Paul's description of the "armor of God," this area of the body, the center of emotions, should be protected with "the belt of truth" (Ephesians 6:14).

Chapter 15

1. Zadoq ben Ahron, *Talmud Lexikon* (Neu Isenburg, 2006), 314.

2. As told by Chaim Eisenberg in a lecture given in Vienna in 1985.

Index of Names and Places

copyeditor   James Bratt
proofreader   Tim Baker
interior designer   Leah Luyk
project editor   Jennifer Hoffman

text set in Edita, designed by Pilar Cano